THE
MURDER
OF LORD
SHAFTESBURY

**THE TRUE STORY OF THE PASSIONATE LOVE AFFAIR THAT
ENDED IN HIGH SOCIETY'S MOST SHOCKING MURDER**

MICHAEL LITCHFIELD

JOHN BLAKE

Published in Great Britain by
John Blake Publishing Limited
3 Bramber Court, 2 Bramber Road
London W14 9PB

www.johnblakebooks.com

www.facebook.com/johnblakebooks 🄵
twitter.com/jblakebooks 🅃

First published in paperback in 2016

ISBN: 978-1-78418-991-4

British Library Cataloguing-in-Publication Data:

A catalogue record for this book is available from the British Library.

Design by www.envydesign.co.uk

Printed in Great Britain by CPI Group (UK) Ltd

1 3 5 7 9 10 8 6 4 2

Papers used by John Blake Publishing are natural, recyclable products made
from wood grown in sustainable forests. The manufacturing processes
conform to the environmental regulations of the country of origin.

Every attempt has been made to contact the relevant copyright-holders,
but some were unobtainable. We would be grateful if the
appropriate people could contact us.

ACKNOWLEDGEMENTS

Firstly, I must thank the 12th Earl of Shaftesbury and his management team for their hospitality, inviting me to St Giles House, and help in putting me straight on numerous important issues. It was all the more generous of the Earl considering the traumatic upheaval in his life over more than a decade. Noteworthy was his consistent loyalty to his father's name and reputation, and his single-minded focus on perpetuating the Shaftesbury traditions of charity and championing reform.

I owe a deep debt of gratitude to the late Jacques Reichert and Lucille, who does have a surname, for their frank input, freely given and with no eye on clock or purse. I am especially grateful for the fact that their English was so much better than my French.

Finally, but far from last, I thank Toby Buchan, Executive

Editor of Blake Publishing, for his diligence, amazing eye for detail, encouragement, unmatched professionalism and constructive collaboration throughout the entire writing process. It was a joy to work with such an icon of publishing.

MICHAEL LITCHFIELD

CONTENTS

PROLOGUE

ROGUES' GALLERY

Throughout history, the English aristocracy has been liberally peppered with rakes and rogues, hellraisers of every persuasion of ribaldry. Collectively, they have had a bad press, the venerable tainted by the depraved and hedonistic among their haughty fraternity.

Lord Lambton, for example, who died in 2006, had been photographed in bed with prostitute Norma Levy. Bedding prostitutes was not his only anti-social habit. Popping illegal recreational drugs, while consuming vintage champagne in bed with avaricious call girls – often more than one at a time – was another of his ungentlemanly proclivities. In addition to being a swaggering toff-about-town and a louche denizen of clubland, he was also a Member of Parliament, the Under-Secretary of State for Defence (for the RAF), no less, with his own castle in County Durham, though he preferred to reside ostentatiously in London's affluent Mayfair, near a number of expensive escort agencies and sumptuous brothels. Such were the ramifications of his scandalous lifestyle that Britain's secret service initiated an undercover operation to determine if national security had been compromised. Clearly, Lambton was exposed to blackmail, especially as he was privy to the country's most sensitive defence initiatives.

The Lambton vice scandal was also to prove the downfall of another contemporary Tory political aristocrat – Earl Jellicoe, the Lord Privy Seal and Leader of the House of Lords. Not only was he leading a double life, keeping a mistress and a devout Roman Catholic wife, he was also bed-hopping with hookers leased from Norma Levy's stable of attractive young women. Levy's services had come highly recommended by Lambton. Networking is nothing new: the cross-pollination of vice in high society has been rife and well documented for centuries.

Jellicoe died in 2007, a year after Lambton.

In the 1970s, the original Eve Club in London's West End listed seventy aristocrats among its members. The Eve, a 120-capacity basement suite of rooms in Regent Street, staged nightly floorshows, featuring scantily clad high-kicking dancers, and employed hostesses who would keep customers company for a fat fee and sleep with them for a considerably fatter remuneration. Jellicoe was a habitué and would share secret government documents with giggling prostitutes while they sat on his knee at his reserved table, where, most nights from Monday to Friday, he consumed vast quantities of champagne, though always by the half-bottle, another quirk – or fetish – of his.

The club – now defunct – was owned by Helen and Jimmy O'Brien. Unbeknown to the staff and clubbers, Helen was a spy for MI5, the intelligence agency, reporting on all the sexual liaisons between the aristocratic fraternity and the call girls. After the demise of this iconic London landmark in 1994, Helen and Jimmy O'Brien retired to Nice in the south of France. In 2004, Helen, then aged seventy-eight, was living as a widow, still on the French Riviera; Jimmy had died from a heart condition within six months of their uprooting. Helen believed that the British aristocracy was a lost world for her, but fate had other ideas, as will become apparent in this labyrinthine narrative.

Lord Lucan was another who certainly did nothing to bolster the reputation of the indolent and self-indulgent aristocracy. Although no libertine, he was undoubtedly a murderer, bludgeoning to death the nanny of his three children, Sandra Rivett, on 7 November 1974. An inveterate gambler, he lost a fortune in the gaming clubs of London's Mayfair, especially at the fashionable and exclusive Clermont Club in Berkeley Square. His passions were chemin-de-fer and backgammon; one year, he was the backgammon champion of the west coast of America. But his heavy losses – frequently thousands of pounds in a night – were at the poker tables, at which he was reckless because he was consistently drunk on champagne.

The separation in 1972 from his wife Veronica, a former model, was the catalyst for murder. He became obsessed with gaining custody of his three children, leading to a messy and vindictive legal battle, which he lost. Although he was a gracious loser at cards – probably because he had so much experience of it – he was no gentleman when the judicial decision ruled against him. From that point, his drinking and gambling escalated out of control, and his chain-smoking did not help his health.

On 7 November 1974, Richard John Bingham, the 7th Earl of Lucan, aged thirty-nine, forced an entry into the basement of his estranged wife's smart residence at 46 Lower Belgrave Street, Belgravia, where he lay in wait in the darkness, presumably for Veronica. When, finally, a woman descended the stone steps into the basement, he attacked her with an improvised deadly weapon, a length of lead piping. The hapless victim was the nanny. When his wife eventually appeared on the bloody scene to investigate the commotion, she, too, was assaulted, but managed to escape with her life, although injured.

After phoning his mother, asking her to collect the children, the Old Etonian and former Coldstream Guards officer drove in a borrowed car to a friend's house in Uckfield, East Sussex. The following day, the car was found abandoned on the south coast at Newhaven. There were bloodstains on the upholstery and in the boot, plus a bandaged lead pipe, identical to the one used to batter to death Sandra Rivett. But there was no sign of Lucan; like a phantom, he had vanished into the ether, never to be positively sighted again and now officially presumed dead.

At the subsequent inquest into the death of Sandra Rivett, in his absence, Lucan was named by the coroner as the murderer.

What a different denouement there might have been to this story if Lucan — tall, handsome and in the image of Roger Moore — had accepted an invitation from movie producer Albert 'Cubby' Broccoli to undertake a screen test for the role of James Bond. Not a role in life for a *gentleman,* he told his snooty chums!

Through the centuries, debauchery has been pivotal to the profligate lives of so many *noblemen.* The Prince of Wales, who was to become King Edward VII, was a connoisseur of Continental brothels, especially those of Paris, something that was to resonate with the protagonist of this book. The Prince's favourite bordello was the Chabanais, where he had his own suite of rooms and his name and heraldic crest engraved on the bedroom door. This palatial establishment, where the dining and décor rivalled the finest hotels and restaurants in the whole of France, was so exclusive that admittance was reserved only for international royalty, the aristocracy and visiting heads of state. The heir to the throne was provided with a butler, a manservant and a private secretary to enable him to keep up with his official correspondence and, more importantly to him, juggle his amours in London while dallying in Paris. Beside his bed in the brothel would always be a photograph of his mother, Queen Victoria, although she despaired of him, having accepted that he was a confirmed lecher. The Prince had been brought up to say his prayers every night at bedtime and he continued this practice in the brothel, usually with at least a couple of whores joining him on their knees, before they all got down to the business of *le noir.*

Going back to the eighteenth century, the Duke of Wharton was friend and protector of many of the most notorious bawds in London. William Douglas, the 4th Duke of Queensberry, would be seen every night in a West End brothel run by Sarah Dubery. Frederick Calvert, 6th Baron Baltimore, converted his London mansion into an Arabian-style harem, similar to those he had sampled in Constantinople and Cairo. Although there was a steady turnover of *inmates,* the combination never changed – five white women and one black. Mistress of the harem was his wife, who had been born Lady Diana Egerton, a daughter of the 1st Duke of Bridgewater. Three brothels in St James's Street were patronised regularly by at least six Lords: Cornwallis, Buckingham, Loudoun, Falkland, Bolingbroke and Hamilton.

However, throughout the ages, the lineage of one aristocratic dynasty had remained unblemished – the Shaftesburys. The 1st Earl of Shaftesbury was a swashbuckling hero of the English Civil War and an adviser to Cromwell. He formed a cabal to restore Charles II to the throne, rose to the exalted rank of Lord Chancellor and became the founding father of the Whig (Liberal) Party.

But the template for this humanitarian family was established indelibly by the 7th Earl, an energetic political reformer, credited with the abolition in 1875 of child chimney sweeps, little boys who were often forced to climb 30 feet up the inside of soot-blackened chimneys to clean parts that couldn't be reached by brushes. Often the children became trapped and many died, just left to rot and perish from smoke inhalation when fires were lit in the hearth beneath them. He was also responsible for the law prohibiting women and children from working down mines and established the maximum ten-hour working day for factory employees, a truly radical industrial reform for the heartless times.

Despite always being in the top ten richest families in the country, philanthropy was the mantra of the Shaftesburys and, not surprisingly, they were at the forefront of the movement to bring about the abolition of slavery. Social responsibility and an unerring duty to society's underbelly underpinned their altruistic credo. Although they owned a stately home set in 9,000 rolling acres of picturesque Dorset landscape, an art collection worth millions, property scattered all over the globe, and even the largest freshwater lake in the UK, providing drinking water for 40 per cent of the entire population of Northern Ireland, by tradition each Earl and his family lived soberly, modestly and with reserved dignity.

After becoming the 10th Earl of Shaftesbury in 1961, at the age of twenty-two, Anthony Ashley-Cooper seemed the epitome of his illustrious and reputable ancestors. He was a dedicated conservationist, a patron of the arts, a lover of wild life (the countryside sort!), and a champion of underprivileged children. Villagers knew him as 'The Squire', a kindly, paternalistic member of the landed gentry, a father figure, and as at home chatting with a farm labourer as with the Queen. He was a shy, rather introverted and introspective nobleman who seemed rather embarrassed by the privileged status thrust upon him purely because of the womb from which he had emerged, without any input from himself: not the meritocracy in which, apparently, he believed.

Then, quite suddenly, at the age of sixty-one, the scandalous Mr Hyde, who had *seemed* to be lurking dormant in his character for so long, mischievously usurped the sober Dr Jekyll with calamitous consequences. An irresponsible, roistering, ruttish, boozing, cocaine-sniffing and womanising rebel was born, sending shock waves through the House of Lords and royal circles, plus the villagers of deepest Dorset, where so many locals depended on the Shaftesbury estate for their livelihood.

The catastrophic, almost unprecedented descent into darkness and violent murderous oblivion in such noble circles had, it seemed, begun.

1

MUMMY'S
BOY

Death changes everything, especially for the living; it certainly did for Anthony Ashley-Cooper, 10th Earl of Shaftesbury, when his mother died of cancer in 1999. Despite his deceptive air of authority and insouciance, remoteness at times, he was very much a mummy's boy, even in his sixties, something recognised only within the family and by a few outside female intimates. His upbringing and background had shaped him emotionally and irrevocably. He was born in London on 22 May 1938, just over a year before the outbreak of World War II. An ancient tradition of the family was that the heir to the title in each generation should assume the name Anthony Ashley-Cooper.

The Earl's mother, Françoise Soulier, was French and very proud of her heritage. She was attractive and gregarious, the life and soul of any party, but was sniffy about London's high-society balls and lavish dinner parties, which bored her. After a few glasses of bubbly, she was more ready to try her legs at the cancan – equivalent to a knees-up down the Old Kent Road – than a stately galliard.

Right from a small boy, young Anthony was mesmerised, but also overpowered, by his mother's dynamic personality. Because she was so cosmopolitan and a city girl at heart, Françoise was never really at home in the backwaters of rural Dorset. In any backwater, in fact.

The family stately home, St Giles House, very Napoleonic in style, dominated the rolling landscape at the southern edge of Cranborne Chase, a long way from vibrant civilisation in the urban mindset of Francoise, who was never really comfortable there. An entire village, Wimborne St Giles, was built on the estate, so every Earl has also been a Lord of the Manor, tantamount to a godfather figure, to the villagers. The village has a pub, The Bull, a magnificent church and a school.

It was the 9th Earl who decreed that no English village could be considered replete until it boasted a proper village green – for cricket and picnics – a school and, most importantly, a thriving pub and a church with a loyal congregation. And it was he who set about ensuring that those provisions were established. Also, the great house was reroofed, the plumbing modernised, and electricity installed. Paintings and tapestries were restored. Trees were planted and grand gardens were landscaped. Following a fire in 1908, the church was virtually rebuilt under the watchful eye of renowned architect Ninian Comper, who was also responsible for the construction of a small chapel in the house's south-west wing. This was to appease the High Anglicanism of the Countess of Shaftesbury at the time, who was a devotee of fire and brimstone sermons. She was determined that the Devil should never be allowed to set foot in Wimborne St Giles. How she must have turned in her grave a century later!

As one would expect, there is a vivid history to the epicentre of the Shaftesbury dynasty. The lineage really begins with a Robert Ashley, who, with his wife, Egidia, moved from Wiltshire to Wimborne St Giles in neighbouring Dorset. The second Sir Anthony became Secretary-at-War to Queen Elizabeth I. Possibly less noteworthy is that he is reputed to have introduced the first cabbage into England from Holland. The solid brick alms-houses adjoining Wimborne St Giles Church also date back to this era. This Sir Anthony died in 1628 and at the foot of his canopied tomb, inside the church, is the kneeling figure of his only daughter, Anne, who married Sir John Cooper of Rockbourne and was the mother of the Sir Anthony Ashley-Cooper who was destined to become the first Earl of Shaftesbury.

The 1st Earl was only ten when his father died and a vast amount of his inheritance was squandered or plundered due to the incompetence and corruption of the trustees. Distinguished contemporaries described him in archaic language as 'sagacious, bold and turbulent of wit'. He learned fast from the treachery of others, especially those who had been paid to protect him, and he matured into one of the most influential statesmen of the late seventeenth century. In the Civil War, he began as a Royalist in addition to being

Governor of Weymouth and Portland, but changed sides to lead the Parliamentary attack on the walled river town of Wareham, followed by a ferocious assault on the fortified garrison of Sir John Strangways, at Abbotsbury, near the coastal town of Weymouth. Later, he was to admit that he had endeavoured to burn to death every man in the garrison; it was hardly an exhibition of the charitable and compassionate nature that was later to emerge as the Shaftesbury ensign.

Ten years later, he changed sides again, resigning from Cromwell's Council of State in protest at its bigotry. Four years afterwards, as a key player in the restoration of King Charles II to the throne, he was rewarded by being made Baron Ashley and appointed Chancellor of the Exchequer. Then, in 1672, he was promoted to Lord Chancellor and created Earl of Shaftesbury.

The turbulence in his political life returned when he aligned himself with the Duke of Monmouth against the succession of the Catholic Duke of York. He was never one for a quiet life, because this latest act of defiance led to his twice being incarcerated in the Tower of London, facing two charges of high treason, the punishment for which, if convicted, was beheading. After desperate, nail-biting months in the Tower – equivalent to being on Death Row – the charges against him were finally dropped. However, still feeling that influential courtiers were after his head – literally – he fled to the Netherlands, where he died two years later of natural causes, something of an anti-climax for a man who had diced with death for so much of his life.

Historians have branded the 1st Earl as not only

unscrupulous, but someone who bore grudges, content to make more enemies than allies. However, it is generally conceded that, as the founder of the Whig Party, he was probably the first truly modern politician, with a gift for Parliamentary debate, who would have been in his element in the cut-and-thrust of today's politics, especially at Prime Minister's weekly Question Time and in TV verbal fisticuffs with aggressive interviewers. He was anti-monopolies, pro-immigration, fervently in favour of religious tolerance and the supremacy of Parliament. Of the monarchy, he was unequivocal: 'The power of the king does not extend further than the laws Parliament determine.' Not surprisingly, in view of his status and the mores of the period, he had the tastes of a country gentleman, dabbled in alchemy and horoscopes, and indulged himself in three marriages. He is said to have loved his wives 'equally', finding 'full satisfaction from all three'.

The 3rd Earl of Shaftesbury was born in 1671 in his grandfather's London house. His father, the 2nd Earl, was reported to be 'of feeble constitution and understanding'; in other words, he was somewhat simple, more village idiot than squire. The 1st Earl was so frustrated and fearful of the fate of the Shaftesbury future and bloodline that he made himself responsible for the upbringing of his grandson, entrusting the boy's education to the philosopher John Locke.

As a fledgling physician, Locke had successfully operated on the 1st Earl, and in time became his most trusted adviser and closest friend. However, despite his relentless tutelage, it would be hard to imagine two more different men in temperament than the sabre-rattling 1st Earl and his introspective, cautious and philosophical grandson.

Although the subdued and studious 3rd Earl won a seat in Parliament for the Whigs, representing the port town of Poole in Dorset, ill health soon compelled him to retire prematurely from politics. London's choking fogs had worsened his asthma, so he turned to literature and philosophy, rarely venturing outdoors. He once wrote, 'The role of philosophy is to learn what is just in society and beautiful in Nature [sic] and the order of the world; to have a sense of right and wrong. Thus virtue is the good and vice the ill of everyone. Taste should be expressed in human conduct, no less than in architecture and painting.'

Despite the fact that the daredevil 1st Earl despaired of him, here we see the seedling of what was to flower into the much-admired ethics of the subsequent Shaftesbury clan. His collection of essays was published in 1771 as *Characteristics of Men, Manners, Opinions and Times*, not a title to set alight today's publishing world.

However, the 3rd Earl breathed oxygen into the family's philanthropy. His letters from London to his steward and housekeeper at St Giles House demanded that 'hospitality' should be afforded to strangers in need of a roof over their heads. He also wanted reported to him 'all cases of need' and that they should find out which children living on the estate justified further education, which he would finance in total, as if their guardian. Some folk actually referred to him as their 'guardian angel'.

He was almost forty before he eventually married.

Earlier, he'd been 'heartbroken' when denied marriage to a young woman with whom he was deliriously besotted. His prospective father-in-law rejected him as a suitable suitor for his desirable daughter on the grounds that, due to health problems, the Earl was not 'manly enough' to sire an heir. The spirit of the Suffragettes had not yet surfaced and women in families of substance rarely rebelled against their parental 'masters'. Crushed by the humiliation, the Earl sank further into seclusion and depression.

Unknown to him, a bunch of his male friends were scouting for a woman for him and persuaded a Miss Jane Ewer, described as 'of good breeding and considerable intelligence', to volunteer her services for a reward that might be beyond her wildest dreams. Much to his astonishment, the friends went ahead and arranged a blind date. Even more outlandish was the fact that the blind date was to take place at the Earl's own wedding! Bride and groom met for the first time at the altar. When the bride raised her veil, the Earl was speechless and entranced by the most beautiful woman he had ever seen. And she, virtually in the blink of an eye, had become a countess, a story that surely upstages *Cinderella*. His friends had certainly gone to a lot of trouble, drawing-up a shortlist, holding interviews, and finally making a democratic choice in a free vote among themselves – never mind the Earl! What surprised his friends most of all was that the Earl went along with it. Afterwards, he was to say humbly that, 'after all the trouble' they'd gone to on his behalf, it would have been churlish to let them down, and rude to the brave lady who 'had no idea what she was taking on'. He was only too aware of the distress of rejection. He did admit, however, that he had feared his friends might have picked the 'ugliest wench they could find in the whole of the kingdom'.

Among the aristocracy it was unheard of for a society wedding without a prior long engagement and respectable courtship. Naturally, the Earl's bizarre behaviour dominated conversation at upper-class dinner parties for weeks, with one waggish master of his household commenting, 'If I'd known any wench was up for grabs, I'd have willingly donated our unwed and pregnant scullery maid! Now I'll just have to give her notice.'

Incredibly, the marriage was a blissful success, with the Earl declaring himself 'as happy a man as ever'. Jane gave birth to a son and heir, further pleasing both of them, but poor health continued to plague the Earl and he was advised by his physician to leave his native land for a country where the air was 'purer and kinder on the lungs'.

Jane was adamant that they should take the medical advice seriously, so they decamped to Holland, where the Earl admired the Dutch 'tolerance and free-thinking way of life'. Still, the winters were too cold, 'more hostile than in England,' he lamented to his friends, so they uprooted yet again, this time for southern Italy, where the Earl eventually died in Naples. The Countess wrote to her family about her husband, saying, 'He died with perfect cheerfulness and the same sweetness of temper he always enjoyed when in the most perfect health.'

The 4th Earl was devoted to his father and cherished everything he had stood for. He was determined to perpetuate that credo. He promptly set about modernising St Giles House, incorporating in the great state rooms all the ornate brilliance and decorative craftsmanship of the period. The dining room was the work of Stephen Wright, a protégé of the Earl of Newcastle. The Tapestry Room depicted the Triumph of the Gods; the tapestries were imported from Brussels. Two new west wings were built and gradually the house was filled with fine furniture and paintings that would grow in value to become worth a fortune. The Earl's first wife was the power behind the man and architect of the adventurous, pioneering way ahead. She was an early disciple of Chippendale and a friend of Handel, who was a frequent guest at St Giles House, composing special music for his visits, much to the delight of the infatuated countess.

The surrounding parkland was landscaped by the 4th Earl as a symbolic tribute to his father's belief in a 'natural' pattern to life. A visiting celebrated landscape designer described the park as 'beautifully laid out, in a serpentine river, pieces of water and lawns, and very gracefully adorned with wood'. He added, 'One first comes to an island on which there is a castle. Then, near the water is a gateway with a tower on each side, and passing between two waters there is a fine cascade from one side to the other, a thatched house, a round pavilion on a mount, Shakespeare's house, in which a small statue of him and his literary works reside in a glass case. There is a pavilion between the waters and both a Chinese and a stone bridge between them.'

The 5th Earl was educated at Winchester College and rose to Deputy Lieutenant of Dorset. When he died in 1811, he was succeeded by his younger brother, who went on to represent Dorchester in Parliament and was a member of the Privy Council. Later, he was elevated to Speaker of the House of Lords.

However, it was the 7th Earl who ensured that the Shaftesbury name would be enshrined in history for its connections to radical social reform. Every student of history in the UK – at all levels – will have been familiar with the crusades for the underprivileged by this robust, campaigning giant.

He was born in 1801, his mother, Anne, the daughter of the 3rd Duke of Marlborough. By the age of twenty-five, he was already an MP, but there was no fire in his belly at this stage. In fact, he wrote of himself as 'neither wise, nor good, nor useful', feeling inadequate and rudderless. The turning point for this wealthy young landowner came two years after winning a seat in Parliament when the report was published of an inquiry into mental asylums. The 7th Earl was incensed by the catalogue of wanton cruelty and the inhuman conditions in which inmates were entombed. Now his conscience was set alight. Suddenly there was a raison d'etre to his life. He experienced a compulsion to act for the helpless and hapless in society. Indeed, he became so angry his sleep-pattern was interrupted to such an extent that he slept only two or three hours a night. He was overcome by a sense of guilt for his own advantaged life, cushioned by enormous wealth and luxury when there were so many 'fellow countrymen living in such squalor and misery through no fault of their own', simply the lottery of birth. From that moment, he was a man driven with the zealousness and tunnel vision of a messianic missionary.

No longer was the Earl prepared to recline in the sumptuous setting of Parliament, reading reports of social privation and inequality. It was time for action, so he spurred himself to abandon his comforts and conduct a first-hand series of investigations. He travelled north to the mills and factories, brushing aside protests from the outraged, heartless industrial despots. What he encountered further horrified him: children beaten for falling asleep at machines during eighteen-hour shifts; men paid so meanly by the fat-cat bosses that their wives and infants had to work in order that they would have bread on the table; workers losing limbs, even their lives, because there were no factory safety regulations. Children as young as five were shackled to heavy coal trucks down mines, while their mothers hacked away at the coalface, which all took place in claustrophobic darkness. For up to eighteen hours a day the children, under the foreman's whip, had to drag coal along the dangerous, leaky shafts, where escaping gasses were common and pit collapses far from a rarity.

MPs were genuinely shocked by Shaftesbury's revelations. Few of them had ever seen inside a factory. Not wanting to dirty their hands, they relied entirely on anecdotal evidence for information. And *information* in the main had come from the pit bosses and factory owners. Now there was a groundswell of opinion for reforms on the issues highlighted by Shaftesbury, despite vociferous opposition from the West Midlands and Northern industrial barons.

Quickly an Act was passed prohibiting anyone under the age of thirteen from working underground. In 1847, the first of the Factory Acts became law, limiting the working day to a maximum ten hours. This was only the beginning of Shaftesbury's combative crusading. He was on the warpath, battling simultaneously on several fronts. Next on his charter of sins to be exorcised was the disgrace of thousands of children living like vagabonds on the street, so many in London and typified by Fagin and his urchins in *Oliver Twist*.

For forty years, Shaftesbury chaired the union of the Ragged School movement, which gave 300,000 children a basic education. Boy chimney sweeps were outlawed, but this was only a small part of his tireless effort to improve the lot of the downtrodden. He oversaw a building programme for new, sanitised housing in the inner cities, established children's sanctuaries (on the lines of today's women's refuges), promoted the work of the Church Missionary Society, fought for hospital sanitisation and the crucial hygiene improvements advocated by Florence Nightingale, exposed the evils of the Chinese opium trade and was a firebrand opponent of slavery.

Despite his passion, the Earl was no soapbox orator. He relied on rational bullet-point facts rather than jazzy rhetoric. In fact, all his life he was rather quietly spoken, almost diffident, but he was tall and handsome with a commanding presence that compensated for any shortcomings. He was undoubtedly a male version of the female head-turner. Aged fifty when he succeeded to the earldom in 1851, in old age, he was tormented by severe gout and deafness, which infuriated him. He died at the age of eighty-four, one of the truly great Victorians and a monument to munificence. He was one of the few statesmen and social transformers to whom historians of every persuasion could be nothing but kind.

The accolades and public recognition have been many, including the Freedom of the City of London. The national memorial to the legacy of this legend is Alfred Gilbert's fountain of 'The Angel of Christian Charity', more popularly known as Eros, which dominates the Shaftesbury Avenue end of Piccadilly Circus, in the heart of London's Theatreland and at the hub of tourism. Of the millions who photograph Eros every year, I wonder how many realise that its arrow is deliberately pointing in the direction of Wimborne St Giles, at least 150 miles away to the west.

But one donation that the 7th Earl cherished more than any other was a donkey from the capital's costermongers (street sellers of fruit and vegetables from barrows). The donkey saw out its days on the Shaftesbury estate in Dorset, fondly pampered by the ageing Earl, who treated it like a domestic pet. To him and his family, the mule had almost biblical status, reminiscent of the Saviour riding into Jerusalem on an ass, mobbed by his followers, represented in this case by the cockney costermongers who owed him so much.

The 8th Earl was a captain in the Navy, but held his earldom title for less than a year. His successor was only sixteen when he inherited the title in 1886 and was to occupy St Giles House until he was ninety-three. He married into wealth, through his bride Lady Constance Grosvenor, in 1899.

When the Prince and Princess of Wales (later King

George V and Queen Mary) stayed at St Giles House in 1907, the 9th Earl boasted that more than 1,200 partridges were shot in one weekend, an apparent contradiction with the family's conservation trademark (and no animal rights' protesters in those days to shame them!). In summer, the estate's cricket team played a match once a week on the Green. Later in the year, the Portman Hunt assembled at the stately house, where sherry and port were served by the downstairs' staff before the riders set off chasing foxes with baying hounds. And the Hunt Ball, a major feature in the winter social calendar, was staged in the staterooms, presided over by the Earl and his Countess.

Like so many similar households, it could have been the blueprint for the TV series *Downton Abbey*, especially as the latter's creator, Julian Fellowes (now Lord Fellowes of West Stafford), lived just a few miles away in Dorset. It was not long before the Countess gave birth to a son and heir, Lord Ashley. Three daughters followed and finally another son, John Ashley-Cooper, who made his name as an acclaimed salmon fisherman; he was the author of a collection of well-received books on angling.

Everything changed dramatically on the estate with the outbreak of World War I. Labourers left to join regiments. Part of the house was converted into a hospital for the war-wounded, creating an influx of doctors and nurses. Most of the twenty-plus horses stabled at the house were commandeered for military duty.

Between 1916 and 1952, the Earl was also Lord-Lieutenant of Dorset. However, during World War II, he enlisted as a humble private in the local Home Guard, junior to his head gamekeeper, a Captain Carter. The platoon's sergeant and drill instructor was his lordship's butler, a Mr Curry. Whenever a senior officer was due to conduct an inspection, the Earl always allowed the expansive terrace to be used as a parade ground.

During the Great War, the Earl and Countess moved into a flat in the house while the remainder of the rooms were taken over by around sixty girls of Miss Faunt's Academy, a Parent National Education School, evacuated from London. In addition to the girls, there were teachers and matrons, who were really the girls' governesses and nannies. From all accounts, while the school was at St Giles House, it resembled *St Trinian's*. One of the boarders was the daughter of Lord Mountbatten. It is reputed that the Earl would never venture from the flat until the Countess had checked that 'the coast was clear', because the girls had played so many pranks on him, such as setting up tripwires and firing pebbles at his buttocks with catapults. And one time when the couple left the flat, forgetting to lock the door, a dead rabbit was planted in their bed, resulting in terrified shrieks from the Countess and a blasphemous outburst from the Earl that night. Pillow fights were a nightly event and the younger girls were always sliding down the banisters of the great staircase, exposing their regulation dark-blue knickers to anyone passing.

After the war, the 9th Earl wrote mournfully in a notebook, 'Domestic servants are practically unobtainable. Girls nowadays will not have anything to say to domestic service, and footmen no longer exist, with the result that these large houses are no longer a practical proposition.'

Although the Shaftesburys have always been seen as the saints among Britain's aristocratic sinners, there was, however, a blip in the bloodline at this time that could have hinted at a more serious scandal on the horizon, though never to the extent that was to make worldwide headlines between 2002 and 2007. The 9th Earl's heir, Lord Ashley, and father of the protagonist of this saga, had already shocked London's high society by marrying a chorus girl, Sylvia Hawkes. She was a leggy, bottom-thrusting beauty who the peer had dated at nightclubs and, at first, paid for her intimate services. Payment for sex no longer became an issue when Sylvia saw the chance of marrying into the aristocracy and having a stake in everything that went with it, especially the fortune, of course. To hell with the notability! The marriage appalled Lord Ashley's parents and they both warned their son that it would not last; in fact, they prayed – literally – that they would be proved right, and both stated categorically that they would not have 'that trollop' in the house. The Earl even went as far as threatening to disinherit his son, who was an army Major. Such a drastic step was unnecessary, however, because the disastrous marriage was short-lived, as predicted.

Sylvia had been born in unfashionable Paddington on 1 April 1904 – and was to make a fool of many men. From her time in the far-from-salubrious Soho clubs, she managed to be accepted as one of the glamorous Cochran Dancers, the

British version of the Ziegfeld Follies, before appearing in the chorus line of a number of West End musicals.

In 1925, two years before marrying Lord Ashley, she auditioned in front of the distinguished theatre producer George Grossmith for a part in the musical *Primrose,* but she was unhappy about having to sing, protesting that she was just a dancer.

'Must I sing, Mr Grossmith?' she pleaded sulkily.

'Yes, Sylvia, you must,' he replied firmly. 'All of you must sing if you want jobs as showgirls in *Primrose.* The Gershwin score demands it.'

'Oh, very well!' she said huffily, sashaying to the pianist and whispering in his ear. The pianist looked rather sheepish, from all accounts, as he hit the first chord and Sylvia broke gustily into 'God save our gracious king', whereupon Grossmith jumped to his feet and stood rigidly to attention, copied by his minions. Sylvia proceeded to sing every verse of the national anthem as solemnly as if performing to royalty.

When Sylvia finally finished, Grossmith applauded rapturously and she got the job. Grossmith was a traditional monarchist, something Sylvia had been tipped off about. The national anthem had been assiduously rehearsed and was no off-the-cuff improvisation, demonstrating just how astute and exploitative she was.

There is no doubt that Sylvia Hawkes was not only a stunner, but also very adept at serial seduction, always aiming high and going for the bull's eye when gunning for marriage. After Lord Ashley, she secured a second wedding ring from another English peer, the 6th Baron Sheffield, before dumping him and sailing the Atlantic for Hollywood and marriage to matinee heart-throb Douglas Fairbanks Snr. After her third marriage was dissolved, she climbed even higher, betrothing herself to box-office superstar Clark Gable, who features prominently later in relation to the doomed 10th Earl.

Virtually self-educated, the social-scaling Hawkes had bedded her way to untold riches and a Los Angeles mansion with all the trimmings of Tinseltown in its rip-roaring, brash heyday. Of course she had cheated on all her husbands before Gable – and after.

It was a way of life, her currency, the economy and trading she understood. She had seduced Fairbanks while she was still wed to an English peer and was an outcast among aristocratic women, much to her amusement. She delighted in antagonising countesses, saying to one at a Mayfair cocktail party, 'Do you know, I hardly recognised your husband with his clothes on!' Nevertheless, she had come a long way from her days touting for tips in Soho's clubs. She had to be thick-skinned to survive in the rarefied air of flunky banquets and snooty masquerade balls, glittering gatherings with smug Old Etonians and posturing nubile *ladies* fresh from Swiss finishing schools. But she more than held her own during the rapier-thrust banter, with so many after her blood, and they usually ended up the wounded ones, making her all the more appealing to the blue-blooded rakes who enjoyed a waspish scrap among their tiara-bedecked escorts.

Clark Gable was not the end of her marriage mountain ascent. She reached the summit in 1954, when her marriage to Duke Dimitri Djordjadze made her a princess: from the back streets of Paddington to Princess Sylvia! This marriage lasted until her death in 1977, from cancer, when she was buried in the Hollywood Forever Cemetery. Her grave is 680 feet north of where Douglas Fairbanks Snr was buried.

To be fair, in her early days in LA there was more to her life than partying and husband hunting. She gave up a lot of time to packaging and despatching food for the refugees of war and other unfortunate displaced people all over the world.

During World War II, the 9th Earl served as a British Intelligence officer with the Auxiliary Units, covert Resistance groups trained to engage and counteract the anticipated invasion of the UK by Nazi Germany. These soldiers were stationed all over the British Isles in underground bunkers. While the Earl was being trained at Coleshill House, near Highworth in Wiltshire, for his forthcoming counter-espionage duties, he was also in command of the overall defence of Dorset and Somerset. Although the details of his assignments and secret operations remain classified, even now, it is known that he was responsible for ferreting out spies in the south-west and recruiting men and women whom he judged would be ideal for espionage work on the ravaged Continent. He liaised by radio with French Resistance groups and supervised the training of saboteurs in England, who would be parachuted into France to support the overstretched underground guerrilla fighters already disrupting life for the occupying Nazis.

Just two years after the end of World War II, Lord Ashley, the 9th Earl's son, died suddenly in London of a heart attack, leaving his nine-year-old boy as the new Lord Ashley and heir to the earldom. The boy, Anthony Ashley-Cooper, continued to live in London with his French-born mother, who had been his father's second wife, and his sister, Lady Frances Mary Elizabeth Ashley-Cooper, who was two years younger than her brother. However, after just a few weeks, Françoise decided to return to France with her two young children, re-joining her parents in Caudebec-en-Caux, twenty-seven miles north-west of Rouen on the River Seine in Normandy. Her father, Georges Soulier, was prominent in the local community and worked tirelessly throughout the war with the Resistance, helping to finance the purchase of equipment and weaponry.

It is hard to see Françoise as an archetypal grieving widow. Her husband, Lord Ashley, had died in March and within five months she had married again: her new husband was Frenchman Colonel François Goussault. Rumours had been rampant in the UK that Lord Ashley's marriage was on the rocks when he died. Right from the outset, the marriage had been built on quicksand. Lord Ashley had bounced blindly into the marriage on the rebound from his calamitous and embarrassing earlier marriage to an ex-chorus girl. Much of the dirt of that affair had been brushed under the carpet. But gradually, bit by grubby bit, Françoise had learned from the soiree gossips about Lord Ashley's previous roistering and uninhibited lifestyle. The more malicious gossip-pedlars spread poison to the effect that he had slipped into his old 'degenerate' ways; in other words, he was sleeping around with 'hostesses' picked up in the nightclubs.

However, the scandalmongering was double-edged. While society women were blackening Lord Ashley's reputation yet again, the men on the champagne circuit were more than hinting that Lady Françoise had also been playing away from home. Colonel Goussault had been a regular visitor to London and they had been spotted together at Covent Garden Opera House and classical music concerts. It is fair to speculate that an affair had developed before Lord Ashley's death and would explain why the period of mourning – if it existed at all – was so brief. Certainly there was much hostility and resentment in Wimborne St Giles when news of Francoise's re-marriage reached the estate and village.

As for nine-year-old Anthony Ashley-Cooper, he rubbed along famously with his new father and they were very soon devoted to one another. The heir to the earldom already spoke fluent French, having been tutored by his mother since he was a toddler.

Continuing the tradition of all the Shaftesbury heirs, he went to Eton, while his sister was sent to private Heathfield School in Ascot. They would shuttle the Channel by ferry together to and from their respective boarding schools. Holidays were spent either in France with their mother and stepfather or with their grandparents on the estate in Wimborne St Giles.

While at Eton, the 10th Earl-in-waiting became an accomplished mountain climber, a skill finely tuned by trips south to the Alps in his holidays. In winter, he enjoyed skiing in the French Alps with his family, coached by his mother who was adept on the slopes. His love of music, something also encouraged by his mother, was to lead later in life to his being appointed chairman of the London Philharmonic Orchestra, between 1966 and 1980.

His mother's influence was again evident when, in the Eton College magazine, he rubbished English girls, especially debutantes, who he derided as 'round-shouldered, unsophisticated garglers of pink champagne'. In fact, he never had an English girlfriend. During his time at Christ Church College, Oxford – later the setting for the dining scenes in the Harry Potter movies – he dated as much as anyone, but only Continental students, favouring those whose natural tongue was French.

When in 1961 he became the 10th Earl of Shaftesbury, aged just twenty-two, on the death of his grandfather, it was with much trepidation – and most certainly not without justification. Mind you, it would be quite a few years before the devil in his destiny took its deadly grip on him.

2

ANOTHER
WALTER MITTY

The 10th Earl owed a lot to the canny prudence of his grandfather, who had invested wisely and shrewdly, organising his financial affairs so that his heir avoided death duties. This allowed the new Earl to inherit the vast fortune more or less intact, free from an invasion from the Inland Revenue. The stately home, the sprawling estate, the loughs, antiques, a priceless art collection, jewels, and residences in London, Hove, Versailles, Paris and Nice on the French Riviera were all his, making him one of the ten richest people in the UK and certainly the youngest.

However, he considered himself more French than British and always had done. Although of British country stock, he had been raised as a city-dweller, firstly in London, then in the French provinces and Paris. During the summer, he mixed easily and freely with the carefree cosmopolitan joyriders of the French Riviera, including the Hollywood glitterati. It was a rich and heady mix, a relaxed, over-indulging, mercurial community that included relatively few Brits, another reason why it was so attractive to him.

Consequently, the truth is that he had not a clue how to run a normal middle-class household, let alone a mansion with endless acres of land embracing a village, its trades and inhabitants, and many commercial interests and ventures. It is no exaggeration to say that he was terrified of the challenges and intimidated by the responsibilities, so he did what he had always done from boyhood – he turned to his mother, his rock and oracle. She was to become the grand matriarch, the stiff backbone her son would rely on: the ruling countess without the title.

And she was more than up to the demands. There was an element of bile in her soul, a sort of opportunist spur for retribution; embedded in her was a belief that she had been denied an official stake in this grand estate and aristocratic heritage by the dissolute lifestyle of her first husband, Lord Ashley, and his premature death. Now she intended making up for lost time, fully aware that her son would be incapable of managing without her intuitive guidance. She was the ultimate backseat driver, though her steering and directions were very welcome. In the immediate future, she would be the architect and navigator, leading her son through the numerous commercial minefields. Her role was crucial in the lead-up to the Earl's ultimate meltdown, and his date with the violent hands of destiny.

Looking back for a moment, to the last years of the 9th

Earl... he had vacated the estate with his countess when in his eighties, he was tired and defeated by all the demands of basically being a chief executive of a global company but with too few staff to juggle all the balls without dropping a few. Nevertheless, after the death of his wife in 1957, he returned to his seat of power, determined to see out his days at the helm. Despite his failing health, he soldiered on, staging the occasional concert and opening his stately home to the public during the summer months. When he eventually died in 1961, he was one of the last survivors of a generation born within a few years of the Charge of the Light Brigade, having lived through two world wars, witnessed the invention of the car and, even more to his horror and amazement, metal machinery that could fly and carry passengers. He really believed that with his death a whole way of British life would also be dying.

The year 1961 was to prove pivotal to this narrative, with the birth in Lens, Pas-de-Calais, France of Jamila M'Barek. Although there were twenty-three years difference in age between the new Earl and the newborn Jamila, one day they would find themselves locked into a destructive and lethal collision course.

Lens is a communal settlement in the far north of France; its people are called Lensois. By the 1960s, Lens and Douai had formed a metropolitan area with a population of well over 550,000. From the end of the nineteenth century, it became a coal-mining centre and a magnet to men, especially immigrants, seeking heavy-labour work. It later became known as a rather unattractive industrial region, the landscape scarred with the evidence of intensive coal mining, in particular slag heaps.

Jamila was one of seven siblings. Her mother was born in Tunisia, while her father came from Morocco. The parents, then unmarried, had entered France via Marseille, a city with a large North African Arabic community. Through much of the twentieth century, Marseille had the dubious reputation of being France's cut-throat city, with many no-go neighbourhoods after dark, mainly the narrow, cobbled, dimly-lit alleys where shady characters with criminal intent lurked in many of the Moorish doorways. Drugs were smuggled in daily from Tangier and territorial battles took place nightly among the dealers competing for black-market business, mostly in the bars and illegal brothels near the port. Although situated on the romantic Mediterranean coast, Marseille was a world apart from the cities of Nice and Cannes further to the east along the same south coast, playgrounds that were to figure so prominently in the future turbulent lives of both the Earl and Jamila.

Jamila's father, now deceased, had difficulty finding regular employment. However, he never seemed to be short of money for drink, which led to considerable domestic conflict.

Mr M'Barek described himself as an odd-job man, available for virtually any assignment, 'within reason', which had a very liberal interpretation. However, his persistent drinking made him unreliable. Even so, he was a flash dresser and was always bragging that he was on the brink of a breakthrough to the big time, like a risible Walter Mitty. Few people took any notice of him, apart from some of the women who frequented the tawdry bars and who were attracted to his swarthy looks and muscular build. When off the cheap wine, he could also be very attentive and amusing. Unfortunately, he did not do sober very often.

Mr M'Barek married soon after emigrating to France and babies started arriving with a regularity that put the family under further economic stress. The firstborn died in infancy in mysterious circumstances, but no one was ever charged with a crime. Then came Jamila, followed by a further five. It was after the death of the firstborn that Mr M'Barek decided he must find a permanent job.

Around that time, there were frequent reports of workers being sought in Lens, right at the top end of the country, almost as far as it was feasible to travel without crossing the border into Belgium. So he packed a bag and set off alone by train, telling his wife he would sleep cheaply at a pension and send for her as soon as he had found regular work and secured a decent place for them to live as a family.

Mr M'Barek soon secured employment in a coal mine and rented a small home, equivalent to a property on a British social-housing estate. As soon as his wife received this news, she set off to join him in Lens, where Jamila was born. Despite being employed in a large pit and earning a substantial wage, Mr M'Barek had not curbed his drinking habit. Paid weekly in cash, he would promptly squander a large portion of his earnings on drink and women, but not his wife. There were constant heated rows when his wife asked for housekeeping money, witnessed by the children and causing them much distress. There can be no disputing that Jamila and the other siblings had a very harsh upbringing in their early life and this experience was the architect of so much that followed.

Finally, the marriage reached breaking-point. Mrs M'Barek, on the verge of a breakdown, could take no more, but she was scared of her husband, so her plan to abandon him had to be kept secret. On a Monday, after he had left for work at the coalmine, she packed as many possessions as she could carry, dressed her six children, and departed for the railway station, dragging two cases; she did not have enough spare money to pay for a taxi. At the railway station, she bought tickets for Marseille, via Paris, where they had to cross the city to catch their connection. Jamila was six years old.

The train from Paris to Marseille was an overnight express. Of course they could not afford a sleeper compartment, so they huddled together on ordinary seats to keep warm, sleeping in snatches, the children tired and tetchy. From Marseille, they boarded a ferry to Tunisia, Mrs M'Barek's homeland, and headed straight for Nabeul, the place of her roots, where she and the children immediately relaxed. In this historic trading port, she had relatives and old friends who remembered her. Their welcome was as warm as the weather, so different from the damp and relatively cold Lens, France's Barnsley.

Nowadays, Nabeul is a seaside resort on Tunisia's north-east coast, near the Cap Bon peninsula, with a population of more than 70,000. Tourism had brought a thriving economy to the town, with new luxury hotels springing up year-on-year. It was the main centre of the country's pottery industry;

Stoke-on-Trent by the sea, if you like, except that it was making money instead of being moribund, like the UK's potteries. There is a huge beach, a bustling medina, and the ruins of Kerkuane. The medina sold everything from leatherwear to spices, carpets, drinks and souvenir bling for the foreign tourists. Archaeologists dated the Carthaginian ruins to the fifth century and lauded them as remarkable examples of Phoenician (mainly associated with ancient Syria) town planning.

Soon Mrs M'Barek had an outlet in the medina. She and her children, who were well fed and clothed in Arabic style, lived comfortably. Jamila learned quickly at school. She was bright, alert and frisky, and loved the climate that was so similar to that of the French Riviera. She was also very precocious. By the age of twelve, she was very conscious of her already prematurely shapely body. Boys, a few years older than her, were always hanging around her home and flirting with Jamila whenever the opportunity presented itself. All this flirtatious attention fed her vanity; she became a mirror-watcher, grooming herself for hours. She could not pass a shop or car window without being drawn to her reflection and would stop to preen herself. Men told her that she was vivacious enough to become a model, even an actress, though not in Tunisia. The Western world beckoned. France would have to be the gateway to the fulfilment of her fanciful dreams.

When you have lived in rags and penury, as Jamila and her family had done in Lens, then money and security become all-important. Jamila quickly outgrew the boys of her generation and by the age of sixteen she was already experienced at servicing a number of wealthy, married Arabs in order to finance her future. All she needed, she knew, was enough money to buy a collection of sexy Western clothes, including fancy lingerie, and to be able to survive at least a couple of weeks on the French Riviera, and then the rest of her life would be a walk in the park.

Jamila had the way ahead all mapped out and never doubted for one moment that once she was back on French soil, in the glamorous, rich zone this time, the money would flow in. Her body would be her passport to a fortune and she was ripe and ready to go to work in her dream factory. So in 1978 she waved goodbye to Nabeul, quickly forgetting her mother's tears and her plea, 'Whatever else, be good. Never sell your principles.' Mother was apparently unaware that it was already far too late for that entreaty.

3

AN EVIL
SPIRIT

Meanwhile, much had been happening in Wimborne St Giles, though on a much more mundane scale.

The 10th Earl took his onerous responsibilities seriously as the landlord and caretaker of the monumental ancestral estate and commercial empire, but he always turned to his mother for inspiration. He hoped to go down in history as the 'Good Earl', but acknowledged that he had none of the political fire in his belly that had made the Shaftesbury name so great and revered, especially among scholars. Politics did not interest him, despite urgings from his mother to find himself a controversial cause that he could champion. His desultory nature and conscious avoidance of the spotlight frustrated his mother because she was ambitious for her son to rival the 7th Earl as a radical world changer.

This Earl was genuinely concerned about conservation,

the impact of the modern environment on wildlife, and the necessity for the opulent to be active in trying to improve the lot of the impoverished, but because of his inherent reticence, he was not attracted to the soapbox. He preferred to spread his message quietly, without fuss, and through deed rather than flamboyant oratory.

His disdain for politics was exemplified by his rare appearances in the House of Lords and the fact it was thirty years before he made his maiden speech! And when he did, there was an almost tangible buzz around the Palace of Westminster. When a Shaftesbury spoke one could always expect pyrotechnics, so there was an electric air of anticipation when the Earl rose to address his fellow peers for the first time in the sumptuous chamber of the House of Lords. That was on the evening of 10 November 1999, just three months after his mother's death. And with what did he enthral his fellow peers and the press? An eight-minute drone about such issues as marrows and courgettes, albeit metaphorically!

Here it is, as recorded by *Hansard*. 'My Lords, I apologise to noble Lords for this dramatic last-minute, but not opportunist maiden speech.' The Earl of Clancarty had asked how Her Majesty's Government believed that arts and sport related to social exclusion.

The Earl continued:

Although I inherited my title thirty years ago and have attended spasmodically, particularly during the early 1970s when we rigorously debated the Industrial Relations Bill and the European Community Bill of Accession, both in Committee and on Report until extremely late at night, my heart has not entirely been in the thrust and cut of politics, unlike my more distinguished ancestors.

In fact, building a society the Shaftesbury way is not a matter of imprisoning a presumed evil spirit of mankind. It is a matter of beauty and truth. Both Goethe and Voltaire were influenced by the 3rd Lord Shaftesbury. The former particularly reminded us that we must cultivate our garden. We all know about large prize-winning marrows, but are not succulent baby courgettes more perfect? Small is beautiful, too.

One of the best sermons I have ever been privileged to hear was by the late Bishop of Winchester. Social exclusion? He said virtually that if one sheep from a flock of a hundred goes missing, the good shepherd worries frantically about that single sheep until it is safely found. There are too many sheep, men, women and children being marginalised. John the Baptist had the answer; why do we not? I remain concerned in these turbulent times, but thank you for your patience. It has been my privilege to be able to speak in your Lordships' House.

The speech was greeted with paralysed bemusement. The microphones picked up one peer saying to another, 'What was that all about?'

'I didn't understand a word of it,' said the other. 'I think he must have been drinking.'

'I'd like to know what. It must have been strong stuff!'

'Certainly stronger than marrow juice!'

Encouraged by his mother in his early years as Earl, he had set about the restoration and upkeep of the land. He supervised the planting of more than a million trees, became the joint winner of the Royal Forestry Society's National Duke of Cornwall Award for Forestry and Conservation, presented by Charles, Prince of Wales. He also served as president of the Hawk and Owl Trust and as vice-president of Sir David Attenborough's British Butterfly Conservation Society. In addition, he was also fanatical about bats.

Philip Rymer, who had been appointed manager of the Shaftesbury Estates organisation, was witness to the limitless time and energy the Earl expended on trying to save one particular endangered species of bat. Nature and its preservation were pivotal to his existence. He cared for animals as much as he did for people, always stressing how one depended upon the other.

Ownership of Lough Neagh in Northern Ireland, the largest freshwater lake in the UK, could have yielded millions of pounds annually for the estate. But the Earl would not countenance charging the people of Northern Ireland for its extraction to be used as drinking water. His generosity was truly unfettered. While his philanthropy was applauded by numerous like-minded people connected to the estate, the accountants were disturbed by his obvious indifference to the profit-making aspect of private enterprise. He seemed oblivious to the economics of basic housekeeping and husbandry. In order to preserve, expand and also improve on the scale he envisioned, sufficient money had to be coming in to underpin the necessary outgoings. In truth, he was no entrepreneur. He was accomplished at spending money but not at generating it or at thrift.

If the Earl is beginning to come across as something of an eccentric recluse, then this is portraying a false image. He could be very gregarious. And his coyness, carefree youthful charm (even in middle-age) and classical good looks combined to create a chemistry that appealed to many women. And because of his mother-bond, he was always more at ease in the company of women than men.

While on a skiing holiday, he met Bianca de Paolis, an Italian, who was considerably more mature. They hit it off right from the outset. She was the daughter of Gino de Paolis, a prominent banker in Rome. Bianca was twelve years older than the Earl and had previously been married to American movie producer Jack Le Vien. She and the Earl had fun together, enjoying wining and dining each evening. They also had much in common, particularly a love of music, especially opera. The title of English Earl embraced enough charisma to compensate for the actual Earl's intrinsic lack of it.

Bianca was acceptable to the Earl because, first and foremost, she was a Continental and not British, which meant she did not have round shoulders, nor did she gargle with pink champagne!

After a whirlwind romance, they married in July 1966 at Westminster Register Office with only a handful of friends present and not a single relative of either the bride or groom. The Earl was twenty-eight, his bride forty. Françoise, the Earl's mother and very much still the matriarch, had not given her approval. While not having anything against Bianca personally, it is reputed that she was not happy about the age difference. She was sufficiently discerning to appreciate that her son had married a mother figure rather than a wife. She also suspected that her own influence over her son would diminish: Bianca would now be the chatelaine and have the Earl's ear, as well as the more intimate areas of his body. Françoise could now be overruled, especially as Bianca was a typical fiery, Latin-blooded Italian with a temperament completely opposite to that of her husband. There were quite a few bust-ups because the Earl sidestepped arguments. When there was a disagreement, he would remain passive and stoic, while Bianca blew her top. This male passivity merely enraged Bianca all the more. She would probably have been happier with plates flying across the dining room.

The marriage did not produce a child, quite possibly because of Bianca's age. As the Earl's mother had feared, and indeed prophesied, the marriage was soon floundering and showing signs of coming apart at the seams. What was always kept a closely guarded secret was that, even in those early days of his earldom, there was a dark side to the 10th Earl and he was vulnerable to flattery; he had a number of affairs even before the third anniversary of their marriage. Inevitably, all the women were foreign, but the secret was even darker than that. On his visits to London, which became increasingly frequent, instead of taking his seat in the House of Lords he would trawl Soho and Shepherd Market in Mayfair, where a small colony of French prostitutes had their 'workshops'.

By midnight, he could be seen at the Eve Club, at ease

in the dimly lit atmosphere among other aristocrats who were there for the champagne, the chorus girls and hostesses. One of the high-kickers in the line-up appeared to him as obviously Continental. He wrote a little note on his napkin, giving his table number, and asked the head waiter to hand it to the girl he fancied at the earliest opportunity.

The head waiter knew the identity of the Earl, as did the joint owners of the club, and probably told the chorus girl who had caught Shaftesbury's roving eye that one of the country's richest men wished her company at his table. Still in her scanty costume, the young woman, who happened to be French, was more than happy to join him. She explained that she had another show before she was finished for the night and that was why she had not changed. As soon as he discovered that she had been born and reared in Paris and had performed at the Moulin Rouge before being headhunted by Eve Club owner Helen O'Brien, they spent the rest of the night conversing in French. For several years during his first marriage, whenever he was out on the town in London, he always ended his red-light crawl at the Eve, tippling champagne with his Parisian kindred spirit and escorting her to his flat around 4 a.m. As soon as he had bubbly on the brain, he was no longer a withdrawn, solitary soul, an image that was to fool most people of his acquaintance right into old age. In reality, he was already a closet rake and roué.

One night he arrived at the Eve to discover that his Parisian soulmate was missing. When asked where she was, the head waiter just shrugged. So the Earl asked Helen, who told him that she had gone home to Paris to marry her long-time boyfriend. Seeing his sadness, Helen told him not to despair because a French replacement, who had also been poached from the Moulin Rouge, spoke several languages fluently and was highly recommended by other aristocrat members of the club, was on hand. Another relationship was embarked upon and the Earl was content again. Some people gorge when they are stressed. The Earl turned to risky sex; *risky* because it was fraught with danger should his double life be unmasked. Divorce might be the least of his problems. Alcohol was yet another salve for him; though it was not yet out of hand, the inherent flaws to his character were no longer dormant – like cancer cells, they were beginning to spread.

His marriage lasted exactly ten years, though in real time it had been over long before then. The Earl admitted adultery with one unnamed woman, although a hundred or so, if whores had been included, could probably have been cited.

The divorce was fast-tracked so that in 1976 he could marry Christina Eva Montan, who was two years younger than the Earl. Christina was the daughter of Nils Montan, a former Swedish ambassador to Germany. True to character, the Earl had fallen for another Continental bride, one of the numerous women who could have been named in the divorce petition, though dignity and anonymity prevailed. Later events, however, never before aired, would throw up a name, who, if she had been identified at the time of the divorce would have resulted in an international scandal and the talk of Hollywood.

This time the Earl's mother approved of his son's choice.

The new Countess of Shaftesbury, who spoke French – a strong point in her favour with the matriarch and also, of course, with the Earl – was also a divorcee and had two children from her first marriage: Frederic Casella, who became a TV producer and director in the UK, and his sister, Cecilia, who later qualified as an attorney in New York.

The new Countess was very popular among the Shaftesbury family and also with the local community. Employees believed that Christina was an asset for the estate. Unlike the Earl, she possessed an astute business brain and did not crack under pressure, thriving on the challenges, while her husband seemed to wilt. They lived in a comparatively modest property on the estate because St Giles House required so much renovation.

On 24 July 1977, the Countess gave birth to a son and heir, named Anthony Nils Christian Ashley-Cooper. In the summer two years later, another son was born – Nicholas Edmund Anthony Ashley-Cooper – and the future looked more promising for the Shaftesbury clan than it had for several decades.

An example of how appearances could deceive so cruelly!

4

SWINGING
IN PARADISE

From Tunisia, Jamila M'Barek headed straight for Saint Tropez; this was 1978, the year following the birth of the Earl's first son. The Swinging Sixties were over, but Brigitte Bardot still lived in Saint-Tropez and it was a honeypot for the beautiful flower people, those who wanted to make love, not war, and every summer thousands of them flocked to the Côte d'Azur and the surrounding region, including Provence. More importantly for Jamila, who was by now calling herself Sarah, Saint-Tropez was also a millionaires' playground. Spectacular yachts and gigantic cabin cruisers (known enviously as 'gin palaces') were moored close to the beach. Their owners and 'shipmates' would dive from the decks into the tepid, azure sea for a refreshing dip, skins as smooth as those of dolphins and just as graceful in the water, too. The bliss of it all! But it was not to last.

For Jamila, after the first grotty seventeen years of her life, this was paradise. She recalled to friends how within minutes of appearing on the silky sand in a scanty bikini, she was surrounded by pushy photographers, the fledgling paparazzi who were hunting glamour for a living, shooting with their rapid-fire cameras. Of course their main prey was Bardot and other celebrities, especially any who were cheating on their partners, but budding beauties, models or starlets of the future could also be a prize catch. And the French Riviera was where they gathered in summer in shoals.

Most teenagers ambushed by that amount of attention would have been flattered and easily cajoled into posing, but not Jamila. Already her brain was a mechanical cash register. How much were they prepared to pay? No money, no posing. With Jamila, everything was already strictly business. She had seen and experienced how the poor were exploited and had vowed that it would never happen to her. She did not have wealth or property, but she had been endowed with one stunning asset – her body. Her brain was not as beautiful as her body, but it was just as well developed. Even so, there was a gnawing seam of insecurity running through her and was the reason for changing her name from Jamila to Sarah.

Whenever she looked in a mirror, which was often, there was no mistaking her Arabic features. Despite being French by birth, she had been shaped by her parents' DNA. She was troubled by this because of the undercurrents of racism so prevalent in much of French society, particularly in the upper echelons. Embedded in her head was the staunch belief that her parentage would be an impediment to her progress. So, within her, there was an abundance of confidence, tempered by conflicting uncertainty, a sort of soul-searching tug-of-war.

The amateurs among the snappers shrugged, snatched a few shots of her, and moved on, but a couple of professionals agreed to pay her if she would pose topless in teasing, provocative positions. Jamila had no objection whatsoever. After all, most of the women on the beach, even the oldies, were sunbathing topless. But having already made money as a prostitute, she had no intention of giving any service free. So, as in the bedroom with punters, it was a case of money upfront before any action took place. She did not pitch for a grand payday because, as the photographers pointed out in all fairness, they were speculating and there was no guarantee of making a sale. Jamila, though greedy by nature, accepted the logic and readily went with them into a wooded area, where, with her bikini-top dangling from one hand, she hugged a tree, as if it was a hunky male. After that, she posed stretched across the bonnet of a flashy red sports car.

Jamila was so obviously eager to please that the two snappers became more emboldened. Their proposition was that she should straddle a motorbike completely naked. 'Non,' she said emphatically, arguing that they had not bargained or paid for anything like that. So they decided to see if the carrot of more money might persuade her to cooperate, to which she replied, something like, 'How much more?' A fee in the region of the equivalent of £25 was proposed, but Jamila did not readily bite. She had one more question: was that £25 from each of them, making a total of £50? It transpired that they were hoping to get away with just one flat £25 payment, but after more haggling, they agreed to Jamila's new demands.

After the motorbike shoot, the snap-happy camera boys had one more idea; photographers always want 'just one more'. Now they wanted her to lie on her back, arms splayed over her head, nibbling a blade of grass, one leg bent at the knee, and a dog licking her naked breasts.

Jamila was not in the least shocked. The proposition was not obscene to her. But her response this time was, '*Non! Non!*' It was twice as emphatic as previously, but the reason was the same as before: a financial consideration. Like so many of the specialists in nude and erotic photography, they were upping the ante with each request and from their reaction, apparently, it appeared that aspiring young photo models rarely balked, but Jamila was a one-off.

Where was the dog and what breed was it, she wanted to know. They did not know, because the idea had only just come to them. They would borrow a friendly one, they promised, sensing correctly that she was relenting. Then it was down to some more hard-nosed brokering. How much more were they prepared to stump up? The same again, they proposed. Not enough, said Jamila, who was then accused of avarice and overselling herself. OK, no deal, she told them, starting to put back on her bra, whereupon they appealed to her not to be so hasty. After some more haggling – just like in a medina, where Jamila was at home – the snappers finally succumbed to handing over a further £50 each. One of them stayed with her to ensure she did not run off with their money without performing for it, while the other went in search of a suitable dog.

What followed was something like a scene from a *Carry On* film. The dog was a giant black poodle with a pink decorative bobble on its head and tail. The owner, a woman in her thirties, would not release it in the sole care of the photographer and insisted she be present, not out of any concern for Jamila but because she wanted to ensure that her pet was not abused or stolen.

The dog owner found the whole charade a hoot, especially as the poodle pranced around Jamila, licking every part of her *except* the breasts. The snappers tried everything to entice the poodle towards Jamila's nipples, but the pooch had different ideas. Finally, the owner suggested that if they were able to pour some milk on Jamila's bust, her pet would almost certainly be tempted.

By then, however, Jamila had had enough. She was not prepared to wait for them to go off to milk a cow! But as she was fastening her bikini top, so the dog cocked its leg on her, as if she was a convenient lamppost. The snappers rocked with laughter and captured the moment on film, but the hilarity was short-lived when Jamila made it clear she would not be returning the £100 advance because she had fulfilled her part of the bargain. The photographers accepted her resolve with good grace and asked for her name. 'Just call me Sarah,' she said.

'Sarah *what*?' one of them pressed.

'Sarah to be Remembered,' she replied, with a giggle. And she would be.

Before they all parted, each photographer gave Jamila a business card and the owner of the poodle invited her to a champagne dinner that evening on the yacht where she was a guest. The reason for the invitation was that they were one woman short for equal numbers of the sexes.

It had been an excellent first day's work for Jamila on the French Riviera.

The owner of the yacht was a middle-aged multi-millionaire, who flaunted his wealth. He greeted Jamila with a full-on kiss, which she found disconcerting, as the woman she presumed was his wife had an arm around his paunch. He was wearing shorts, a short-sleeved, garish silk shirt, and sandals. His belly was almost popping the buttons. Only later did Jamila learn that the *wife* was, in fact, a call girl hired from a Cannes escort agency. Despite that, she wore a thick wedding ring and another ring with a diamond rock as the sparkling centrepiece – a gift from a previous client, she was to tell Jamila while chatting casually.

During a lobster dinner on deck, the boat owner mono-polised the conversation. In passable French, he bragged about his personal fortune and as the champagne flowed, so, too, did the anecdotes. Regaled as a boast, he claimed that his father had been seduced by Jackie Kennedy, who had been married to JFK, the former US President assassinated in Dallas, Texas. His yarn included Jackie telling his father how she hated Americans, because they were all philistines and that she was a Euro-aristo, nurtured on classical literature and music, and belonged intrinsically to the Old World.

Most of the time Jamila was drowning in the heady

conversation, out of her depth, but she was content to swig the champagne and feast on the rich food because she had not eaten a proper meal for several days. The wine was poured by a girl no older than Jamila, who wore nothing more than a skimpy bikini. The girl, hired from a local restaurant, also served the food, which was prepared below in the galley by the owner's permanent chef, cooking for him at home on land as well as at sea.

For dinner, they all sat at a round table. Although nothing had been formalised, it soon became apparent to Jamila that she was there to be paired with the owner's son, who wore a wedding ring, like most of the people at the table. His French was impeccable, although it was not his native language.

Eyeing the wedding ring, Jamila asked him if he was indeed married. 'But of course,' he is said to have replied.

'So where is your wife?'

'At home.'

'How long will you be at sea?'

The father interrupted, saying, 'Until the weather turns. Probably all summer.' This was normal for him. He would be at sea, cruising the Mediterranean from April until the end of September or October, putting into ports on a whim, overseeing his business on the phone. Saint-Tropez, Cannes, Nice and Monaco were his hot spots, a cue for him to relate how he'd lost the equivalent of a million pounds sterling in one night at the casino in Monte Carlo playing roulette. His credit was so good that he was allowed to keep cashing cheques, however, frittering away the million or so as if it was Mickey Mouse money.

The dessert, in addition to huge bowls of a variety of ice creams, was cocaine. This was Jamila's introduction to 'playboy snuff'. From that first dizzy sniff, she was hooked, never before having felt so exhilarated and high. Nothing seemed beyond her capacity; she could even fly if she so chose, she believed. Her dull, drab past was well and truly dumped. Never had she felt so alive. This was the life for her, she decided there and then.

Very quickly all inhibitions were blown away into the balmy night. The music started and they all began dancing. Jamila was wearing a thin, short yellow cotton dress, no straps or bra, so plenty of décolletage on show. Her high heels had been kicked off. The dancing was close up, the men groping. Around midnight, nude bathing began. There was frolicking in the sea. Many couples from other yachts were threshing around in the water; some were clearly coupling.

By 2 a.m., they were all beginning to crash out. The drinking and sniffing had continued from dinner, only pausing while they gambolled in the Med. Jamila was still not certain how the night was supposed to climax. She had booked into a pension favoured by ex-hippies who no longer found it romantic sleeping rough beneath the stars or under moth-eaten canvas.

Only the yacht owner went below deck, with his escort-agency whore. But when Jamila's partner for the night began to make his play, she demurred. It would have been churlish of her to overtly ask for payment. Even after so much champagne and coke-sniffing, she was sufficiently self-possessed and in control of her faculties to connive a situation in which *he* had to make the proposition. And sure enough, eager to round-off the night in the way he had foreseen, Jamila was offered money, at which she initially balked, as if offended, protesting that she was no cheap tramp. (Cheap she was never to be!) Fearing that he had screwed-up, the spoilt rich kid apologised profusely, saying that he had been gauche and did not mean to offend. The offer of money was as a genuine gift, a gesture of gratitude for such a lovely night together and maybe of more to come.

The posturing was over. Jamila took the money, about £500 in French francs. Her first day and night on the French Riviera had got better by the minute. Now she had a template for the future, which was to prove the downfall of one very rich, unsuspecting British toff, at that time blissfully unaware, a thousand miles away.

5

THE VANISHING EARL

When pressure built up for the Earl, he would often just 'take off' for a few days. This behaviour, at the outset, was known, semi-humorously, as his 'vanishing trick'. It was accepted as his way of coping with the stress when management hiccups and tensions interrupted the smooth running of the estate. This gradually became such a regular element of his modus operandi that no one took much notice for quite a while, although it was soon no joke any more. His wife, Christina, was au fait with the demands of the various business facets and automatically took charge seamlessly during her husband's periodic absences; so, too, did his sister, Lady Frances, and his mother, Françoise, who was always ready to offer constructive advice, even from Paris. They were a team, a harmonious team but, sadly, not a winning one. Results were on a downward curve. The captain was enthusiastic but did not have staying power. He was not endowed with the marathon temperament of his younger son, Nicholas, who was destined to become the 12th Earl.

Most people who met the 10th Earl in a semi-social capacity eulogised about him as a 'lovely man'. True, but he was not a man of steel. Storm clouds metaphorically sent him running for cover. The wind of change had swept through the landed gentry as much as in every section of society and industry. The good life was no longer guaranteed when once, in certain quarters, it had been a birthright. Now everything had to be earned and new tricks had to be learned. Owning a stately home and thousands of acres of land could be a millstone rather than a money harvester. Trying to live up to the greatness of his iconic ancestors was always a burden that weighed the Earl down; in that respect, it would be true to say that he had an inferiority complex. Even in the House of Lords, he felt the necessity to apologise for his shortcomings. He ascended the throne, so to speak, when the task facing him cried out for a hard-nosed, swashbuckling entrepreneur who was capable of creating a citadel from ashes, and the Earl was the very opposite. It was not his fault. He had not applied for the job; it was thrust upon him. And therein lay the problem, and why so many of the grand estates and rural empires were crumbling. Lineage was producing too many losers. Some people thrive on pressure: the 10th Earl was not one of them. Darkling clouds darkened his mood and spirits.

In the 'engine room' of his team were three strong women who could be relied upon to competently manage the day-to-day challenges, however testing, but the final say and sanction would rest with him. When it came to his pursuit of women, he would be headstrong, but in business he tended to vacillate, which frustrated those around him who were eager to forge ahead.

Throughout his life, the Earl had not only trusted women – he had relied upon them implicitly. It is not an exaggeration to say that he worshipped women, a trait that was to lead him to his own Lady Macbeth. In particular, his fondness for foreign women would eventually be tantamount to his drinking from the poisoned chalice or his kiss of death.

It had always been assumed that when he went AWOL, without warning, he had flown to Paris to spend a few days with his mother or was staying with old friends from his boyhood. Everyone close to him knew full well that Paris was in his blood and was, in fact, an integral component of his personality. He always said that every month or two he needed to be in Paris, where his batteries would be recharged. Paris restored his energy, like a tonic, inflated his oxygen levels and rekindled his vision. The City of Light also liberated his libido. To the 10th Earl, Paris would always be the City of Romance.

But Paris was not always his destination. Frequently, he visited London, also Brighton, on the British south coast, staying at his property in adjoining Hove, and Nice on the French Riviera, where he had a holiday home.

Nice, of course, is just a few miles along the coast from the pint-sized principality of Monaco, best known for its casino until the arrival of Princess Grace, the erstwhile Hollywood ice maiden Grace Kelly. According to Jacques Reichert, a resident of Cannes and frequent drinking companion of the 10th Earl, the introverted (only when sober) British aristocrat had been incorrigibly infatuated with the former movie legend, a favourite of Alfred Hitchcock.

As an upper-crust aristo from one of the truly great historic families, the Earl was always welcome at the palace in Monaco, as a guest of Grace's husband Prince Rainier III, the little country's autocratic ruler. 'But really he was there to cosy up to Grace,' Reichert explained to me, when we met in Cannes. Although still internationally revered and embraced as movie star Grace Kelly, her official title was Her Serene Highness the Princess of Monaco.

This infatuation seems to have begun in the 1970s, when Grace would have been in her early forties and married for at least fifteen years. Moviegoers the world over in the 1950s probably respected Grace Kelly more than any other actress. She was prim and proper, a statuesque blonde with porcelain skin. Born in Philadelphia, she spoke with a perfect English-Roedean accent. Grace was serene and graceful, her public persona groomed by her name. She epitomised the ultimate in feminine purity and gave the impression of being beyond reach, a tantalising challenge for a raffish young blue blood who, unbeknown to most, was adept at these high-profile conquests.

Most people in British public life saw the 10th Earl as one-dimensional: very staid, colourless and introverted. His family saw him very differently. But neither his family nor the rest of the British aristocracy would have recognised the 10th Earl who was known to the racy swingers on the Continent. The truth is that he was an enigma with a wardrobe of personas that could be worn like masks. His changes of character were no doubt subconscious; he was certainly no deceitful rogue. Neither was he by nature a sexual predator. His inborn reticence and habit of understatement proved to be traits that appealed to many women, certainly those who had been exposed to flashy, self-opinionated braggarts. The Earl was a refreshing change, a breath of fresh air, for women bored by self-promotional males.

However, the hoodwinking undertaken by Princess Grace was in a different league altogether. Her past and present were manufactured, carefully crafted to deceive. Rainier still believed that Grace was a virgin when they married, thanks to the duplicitous Hollywood publicity propagandists. But the Earl was privy to all the scandals, which had been in circulation for years and were even corroborated to a large extent by Grace, but only after she had made her catch. From insiders it would appear that the attraction of Princess Grace to the Earl was commensurate with her burgeoning scandalous reputation.

Feared Hollywood gossip columnist Hedda Hopper branded Grace in print a 'nymphomaniac'. Marilyn Monroe complained of having to sleep with producers in order to be offered meaty movie roles, but Grace Kelly could not get enough sex, from all accounts. She did not sleep her way to the top because she rarely used bed for slumber; it was by all accounts purely for action. Bryan Mawr, a screenwriter who collaborated on Hitchcock's *Dial M for Murder,* said of Grace,

'She fucked everyone, even little Freddie.' Frederick Knott was another screenwriter.

'These things titillated Tony [the 10th Earl],' Reichert stated. 'He couldn't get over the fact that Grace Kelly appeared so pure and angelic, and was worshipped as such by the public all over the world, yet she was a man-eater. His ideal woman was someone beautiful, stylish, well spoken, well mannered, confident, seductive in a subtle way and shameless. He couldn't get Grace Kelly out of his head. She was as iconic to him as his mother, well, nearly. Grace was the only reason he ever went to Monaco. Looking up Rainier to exchange pleasantries was just an excuse.'

Reichert continued, 'Tony carried pictures of her and he also had books about Grace's Hollywood career.' He recalled the night the Earl said that 'Marilyn Monroe did nothing for him whatsoever and she "didn't hold a candle to Grace". I can see Tony sitting with me. We were worlds apart, but he was no snob. He never looked down on anybody. He admired people who had made good from humble beginnings, even when they did things a little naughty, like me. He understood. He knew about people having to survive and then keep going.'

One day Reichert asked the Earl outright, 'Have you fucked her [Princess Grace]? In the Palace?' Reichert said that the Earl 'just grinned' and answered with a question of his own: 'What do *you* think? *You* tell *me*.'

Reichert related how the Earl occasionally carried around with him a bundle of old issues of the scandal sheet *Hollywood Confidential*. Most of them contained gossip stories of Grace Kelly's involvement with a married movie star. One of her lovers was Ray Milland, who starred with her in *Dial M for Murder*. Grace and Milland, who had been happily married for thirty years, set up home together.

The Earl was constantly chuckling, it seems, about the reaction of Grace's father, Jack Kelly, on hearing of the engagement between his Hollywood queen daughter and Rainier. It was a disparaging, 'I don't want any broken-down Prince who's head of a country that nobody ever heard of marrying my daughter.' Most people in the US had no idea where Monaco was, and even much of the overseas press mistook it for Morocco.

By the late 1970s, the Rainiers had gone a lot further than simply having separate beds: they were sleeping in different countries. Grace was spending much of her time in Paris. So, too, was the Earl.

When Grace was spending a lot of time in Paris, though still the wife of Prince Rainier, she was in her forties. The Earl was eight years her junior and she had always shown a propensity for older men. However, a documentary film director, Robert Dornhelm, who frequently wined and dined Grace, told the French press that he thought having affairs with 'toy boys' would 'do her good'.

When the Earl was drinking one night in Cannes and this story was floated teasingly into the conversation, Reichert asked, 'Do you know if he took the advice of that Hungarian guy?' The Earl is reputed to have replied, with a mischievous wink, 'Well, I know she had one toy boy in

Paris. The same one as she had at her palace in Monaco from time to time.'

On his more mundane travels, such as when staying alone in Hove, which together with Brighton formed one sprawling conurbation area on the UK's south coast, some fifty-five miles from the centre of London, the Earl began booking a woman from one of Brighton's largest escort agencies.

Using the name plain Anthony Shaftesbury, he made his choice by phone. A man went through the personal details of the women available. 'She sounds perfect,' he said, as soon as one of the escorts was outlined as Spanish. The price he was quoted was £200 and he was told 'anything further' would have to be negotiated 'between the two of you' and was 'nothing to do with the agency'. The Earl knew the routine. Up from the deepest Dorset countryside he may have been, but he was no greenhorn when it came to masterminding and financing infidelity; that kind of trading never daunted him.

The Earl was asked if he wished the 'young lady' to come to his room. The agency 'salesman' assumed that the potential client was in town on business or holiday and was staying in a hotel. The Earl replied that he wished to meet the Spanish lady in the lounge of the Grand Hotel on the seafront at around seven thirty and they would dine at eight. It was unusual for punters to spend money and time on a meal, especially at such a prestigious establishment. This was the hotel at which Tory grandees had stayed during autumn party conferences and where in 1984 the IRA had planted a bomb, almost killing Prime Minister Margaret Thatcher and most of her cabinet. Normally it was straight down to business for the escorts, a euphemism for prostitutes. But the Earl was an old-style gent, as courteous as he was a closet womaniser. He treated a call girl, provided she was foreign, with more respect than he had for any English female invited into the Royal Enclosure at Ascot, for example.

The Spanish escort was impressed by his gallantry and impeccable manners. He stood to greet her, shook her hand firmly, almost bowed, and pulled out a chair for her to sit on. She noted that he was drinking champagne and asked for similar. (This woman agreed to speak with me on the record, on the condition that I did not question her about her domestic life.) The Earl, in every aspect of life, was well aware that you never had a second chance to make a first impression. However, his solicitude was natural, not the least contrived. Conversation between them came easily. She asked him if he preferred to be addressed as Anthony or Tony. 'You choose,' he said. She replied that she thought he was much more an Anthony than a Tony. 'Then I'm your Anthony,' he said graciously.

Most of the men in the lounge and bar wore suits. The Earl was wearing a tweed jacket, corduroy trousers, heavy brown shoes, a check shirt with red tie, and a matching silk handkerchief in the breast pocket of his jacket. His speech was measured and precise, velvet-soft, but he was not the least condescending or patronising. Summing up, the Spanish escort said he was 'tall, a shade stooping, handsome and debonair, with a carefree air about him, no doubt a dazzler in his youth'. This would have been in 1997, when he was fifty-nine.

While he didn't pry into her private life, he did ask if she had a career, 'besides *this* work'.

Answering truthfully, she told him that by day she worked as a cashier in a Brighton bank.

'Oh, dear, that must be monotonous,' he said sympathetically.

'So can this be if I'm with the wrong kind of man,' she responded, quickly adding, 'but you're not one of those I'm thinking of.'

During the meal, they had white wine and red, finishing with cheese and biscuits, coffee and port for him, brandy for her. The whole time he was very attentive. 'It was as if we were on a proper date,' she recalled, 'and I think that's exactly how he wanted it. He had the trick of not appearing to notice anyone else in the room. His entire focus was on me. I had to pinch myself as a reminder of why I was there. It would have been easy to imagine I was the only woman in the world who meant anything to him. Crazy, I know, but that's the way he operated. Reflecting, I think it was something he'd consciously perfected, a technique that charmed the pants off women, though it was the charm of money that mattered most to an escort-agency girl.'

Back in the lounge, she asked him what he had planned for the rest of the evening. 'I had to know if he wanted bedroom business.'

Bashfully, he replied that he was hoping to spend 'some time' with her at his 'very comfortable' place in Hove. This was not the normal way her business was conducted. By this stage, battle lines had usually been drawn; she would know what the punter was eager for and she would have quoted a price, the amount depending on proclivity and estimated duration. Then would come the haggling over money.

But 'Mr Shaftesbury' was not a typical punter, so she had to conduct the transaction with stealth and circumspection. Therefore, she asked how long he expected her to stay. For the night, he replied, as if it was obvious. She explained that she had to be at work, in the bank, by nine in the morning. 'I'll need some sleep,' she laughed. 'I can't possibly stay beyond two o'clock.'

The Earl was disconsolate. He muttered something to the effect that he hated anything rushed and sordid. Rushing sex was what English women did, he complained. 'You are starting to come across as more English than Spanish.' This was stated as an insult. 'Continental women usually appreciate the art form in sexual communion,' he added. She vividly recalled the reference to 'sexual communion', a description she had never heard in her ten years in the UK, since leaving her home in Barcelona after the break-up of a long-running relationship with a married man.

'I accept you're a genuine working lady with a career to protect and you obviously understand responsibility,' something I admire greatly in people,' he praised her. 'And undoubtedly two a.m. is an improvement on the Cinderella deadline, I'll grant you that.'

The tension evaporated. Still, she was wary of how to broach the tricky subject of payment, but she need not have worried, because he sensed her dilemma and helped her out diplomatically. If two o'clock was the latest, then he would have to settle for that, for which he would give her a 'little something'.

This was not music to her ears. On the contrary, it sounded ominous. What did he mean by *a little something*? She leaned across and asked that very question, to which he replied, 'How would you feel about five hundred guineas?'

She was mystified. Despite working in a bank, she had never heard of *guineas* and thought it must be an obscure foreign currency. Seeing her bemusement, the Earl said, 'Very well, bog standard five hundred English pounds.' Now that *was* music to her ears.

However, the music was to become more of a soothing symphony when he added that he would be more than happy to hand over a grand if she could manage to stay for breakfast. Suddenly the spectre of arriving at the bank in the morning tired and enervated was washed away.

'Let's have breakfast together,' she said, won over by the carrot.

She carried a bulky bag; in it were condoms, a pair of handcuffs and a whip, the tools of her trade. 'But he wasn't into anything kinky,' she remembered.

He had wine at home and they sat and chatted cosily for most of the night, as if a domestic couple. At one point she asked him what he did for a living; she had presumed that he lived permanently in Hove, possibly divorced or as a widower. His answer made her think he was a vet. He said that his job was looking after animals and trying to improve their lives. He also mentioned restoring properties and his love of art, which she took as meaning they were his pastimes. It did not cross her mind that she was about to climb into bed with an Earl, a close associate of royalty, and one of the ten richest men in the whole UK, a very red-hot, blue-blooded aristocrat!

When finally they migrated into the bedroom, there was no aggressive lust from the Earl. Earlier, when he had made an excuse to leave the room, he had tactfully slipped £1,000 in £50 notes under the pillow that was to be *hers*.

They had sex just the once and he held her in his arms until daylight, both of them sleeping in spasms. Just before they had sex, she was puzzled when he murmured, 'I want you to mother me.' She had never encountered a 'mother fetish' before and did not know how to respond, so she went ahead as normal and the subject was never broached again.

Breakfast was nothing more than two sweetened black coffees each and over-the-counter painkillers for the hang-over headaches. The Earl called a taxi for her, remarking that he would be returning to bed. 'Lucky you,' she said. Then he squeezed a £20 note into her hand for the cab fare. This was the sort of customer a prostitute came across once in a lifetime, if she was fortunate. So just before hurrying out at 8.30, she cast her line for a further catch, saying she hoped the night had been as satisfying for him as it had been for her, and she would always be very glad to see him again. A Friday night would be preferable because she did not work on Saturdays at the bank, of course. 'You could have me for the weekend,' she offered temptingly.

That offer registered with the Earl because over the next

two or three years they did spend a number of weekends together, dining, wining, going for country walks and the theatre, eventually rounding-off the day in bed, their love-making relaxed and undemanding, though always with a reference to 'mother', something that was to become more predominant, a sexual trademark, in fact, in the final, harrowing years of his life.

At the end of each weekend, he gave the escort £5,000. His favourite little game was to say, 'Now tell me how much that is in guineas?'

No longer did she ask for payment in advance. 'I trusted him more than I ever would have a husband,' she said. 'He was very young at heart. If he'd asked me to marry him, I'd have said yes without a moment's hesitation – and not just because of his money. But I knew it was impossible – or I thought I knew.'

She was to learn of his true identity only when his photograph appeared in national newspapers and on TV a few years later. 'When I read the newspaper stories, it dawned on me that I'd squandered my chance. And just think: I would have been a countess! How about that? And, even more importantly, he'd still be alive.'

The Earl was living very dangerously. If any freelance journalist had picked up the scent of the Earl's libertine lifestyle, he would have made a killing in the tabloids, especially as it exposed a Shaftesbury, so celebrated for their moral crusading and rectitude, irrespective of what might have gone on behind closed doors and drawn drapes.

Walking on the wild and dark side was a trait of the Earl's

that surfaced whenever he was under stress, his way of fleeing the black holes in his life. Soon, however, he would escape once too often.

His luck was very near to running on empty.

6

HANGOVER
OF GRIEF

The apocalypse occurred in August 1999.

The wedding was taking place of the eldest son of the Earl's sister, Lady Frances Ashley-Cooper. With the ceremony over and the celebrations in full swing, amid the customary atmosphere of much happiness and joy, Françoise, the mother of the Earl and Lady Frances, died in France. A marriage and death on the same day made for a polarisation of emotions. Tears of joy flowed in equal quantities with those of sorrow, which, of course, were more potent than the champagne. The Earl's hangover of grief would never be relieved.

The news filtered through later that day and with the suddenness of an electric light being switched off, celebration turned to mourning. The light had indeed gone out for the Earl. He had known his mother was suffering from cancer, but she kept the truth of the prognosis from him, as ever always so protective. He was under the impression that she was in remission, maybe close to a complete cure. But he was living in a fool's paradise, his favourite hiding place.

The death of his mother was an arrow through the heart of the Earl from which he never recovered. After the mourning, came the grief, which assumed a life of its own, growing daily and manifesting itself in many ways, some more subtle than others.

'For my brother, her death was a catastrophe,' said Lady Frances. 'He adored her. She had been his protector and greatest admirer since the death of our father in 1947, when Anthony was eight and I was six. When our mother died, it was as though my brother had become an orphan at age sixty-one. Without her, he felt emotionally bereft. He lost his grip on reality.'

Most people by the age of sixty-one do not have a parent still living. If they do, they are conditioned to expect death to come cold-calling any day. Yet the Earl, who could and should have had so much sway in the running of the country, was totally unprepared and completely knocked off-kilter by one of life's inevitabilities. He was in utter irreversible denial of his personal loss.

In contrast, his sister was mature about the circumstances: life had to go on, the estate had to be managed, and everything had to be held together. Life and death were partners; one automatically led to the other. Country folk in general tend to be more aware of the cycle of life than most. The seasons impact on their lives much more than on urban dwellers. The lambing season heralded new beginnings, while the harvest and the march to the market symbolised the beginning of the end of the chain.

The British aristocracy had always been a breeding ground for stoicism and the stiff upper lip. Marking time or going in reverse were not realistic options after bereavement for this class. Of course there would be a period of grieving, but day-to-day management decisions had to be made that impacted on the lives of so many people dependent on the Shaftesbury estate for their livelihoods.

The Earl's reaction must have been very hard on his loyal wife, Christina. Whenever he had spirited himself away for a few days, apparently on a whim, she'd taken the reins without a blink. And when he returned, nothing had been neglected. He owed so much to Christina, she was his real rock, and yet it appeared that she was no compensation to him for his mother, who had remained the most important and dominant woman in his life. For a wife so dutiful as Christina, this must have been a cruel kick below the belt. The subliminal message could not possibly have been more explicit: she was second best, even to a ghost.

Françoise had taken a haunting torment with her to the grave. Despite her unerring love and intense attachment to her son, she had been under no illusion: she saw in him the roving eye of his father. The genes of a man seduced by a chorus girl lived on, of that she had been certain. The Earl's sexual wandering had trashed his first marriage. Françoise had prayed that his marriage to Christina would endure. Their two sons were now aged twenty-two and twenty. The family was a team; the Earl was the captain, supposedly.

But what kind of role model was her beloved son, whom she would have willingly protected with her own life? His mother had hoped that by now he would have burned off the fuel for casual flirting.

Françoise was right to go to her grave a worried woman. In many ways it was not surprising that her son was something of a wandering minstrel in spirit. His formative years had been very unsettled. Despite being born into one of Britain's most iconic families, he was rootless. The family's seat of power was in Dorset, but he, along with his sister, was very much a child of France and a Parisian by temperament. Like a yo-yo, he'd crossed the Channel to and from boarding school. During his school holidays, he would never be sure until the last moment where he would be staying. There had been so much uncertainty in his life, having begun with the premature death of his biological father. Instability must have moulded him more than his family appreciated. However, because of his relationship with his mother, he had a natural and easy rapport with women. He bonded with them because the female species had always been pivotal in his life, whereas the male, his father, had deserted him through death. Despite his attachment to his stepfather, his mother remained the dominant figure. Women were the backbone of his life, while men were the weakest link, which further confused him because of the greatness of his forefathers and their acknowledged strength of character and resilience. His fondness for women, born out of mother love, combined with his wandering restlessness, born out of his childhood, fashioned the man whose aberrant behaviour was to reverberate around the world, confounding almost everyone who had believed they *knew* him.

The 10th Earl's elder son, Anthony Nils Christian Ashley-Cooper, was reared as the heir. After Eton, he qualified as an accountant to help him master the financial intricacies of such a complicated working dynasty. Without this onerous responsibility that anchored his brother to Dorset, the younger brother, Nicholas Edmund, was a free agent to pursue a career as a music entrepreneur in New York. But fate had an odious twist in the tail brewing for him, too.

Following the death of his mother, the Earl retreated from his business duties and his family. Almost as a reflex action, he became a stranger at home and indifferent to management policies that needed either defining or refining. There were family conferences without him. Christina and the others were comforted by clichés: give him time, the acknowledged miracle healer of all woes; better the shock was immediate rather than delayed; tears shed now will leave him with a clear head for the future. No one seemed to have flagged up the possibility that he might be suffering a nervous breakdown, probably because those kinds of mental afflictions were not known to harass the strong and indomitable Shaftesburys. They were made of sterner stuff than straw, the backbone of the nation; that is how they had been brought up. The Shaftesburys were no softies. They were leaders, pioneers and crusaders, moral warriors; always had been, always would be. Indefatigable.

A mental breakdown was never diagnosed because the Earl did not think there was anything wrong with his health and so did not consult a doctor. However, in view of subsequent events, it is fair to speculate that he was dogged by some sort of mental and psychological disorder; primitive folk would have said that he had become possessed by the Devil's demons. When snapping under mental pressure, a person's vulnerability becomes magnified. And as already established, the Earl's weakness was women. Foreign women, especially. Racy women, preferred. *Outré* women were irresistible for him.

Less than six months after his mother's death, the Earl deserted his second wife and both his sons. As if bringing down the guillotine on his past life, he announced that he was relocating to France. Alone. In other words, he was not only dumping Christina and his two sons, but also the stately home, the art collection, the thousands of acres of land, the people who lived in the village and toiled on the estate, and all the tendrils of private enterprise that branched from St Giles House, the engine room of the historic Shaftesbury empire. One worker on the estate likened St Giles House to an octopus, from which a tangle of tentacles reached all over the globe. One can only surmise what a harrowing experience it must have been for the family: Disbelief? Anger? A sense of betrayal? Eruptions? Tears? Pleading? Hand-wringing? Despair? Despite their elevated social position, their emotions would have been similar to those of humbler families in meltdown.

However, no amount of reasoned supplication would drive the Earl into a U-turn. He was on a crash course towards his nemesis.

The Earl owned an apartment in Versailles, yet another region of France where he felt completely at ease. It was the history of the city, its culture and the world-renowned gardens that appealed so much to his artistic temperament. Versailles was founded by King Louis XIV, only to become the cradle of the French Revolution; in other words, a guillotine for royal heads. It was this revolutionary connection that was much of the allure to the Earl. Despite his ancestry, he saw himself as something of a rebel. In fact, the Shaftesburys, who pioneered radical progress and reform in England, were all social revolutionaries to some extent. This family generically had no patience for natural evolution, which was too slow for them. *Now or never, tomorrow is a day too late,* might well have been their crested motto.

The Earl had had a vision of re-creating the Gardens of Versailles at his estate in Wimborne St Giles. However, he believed it could be achieved only by someone with the expertise of André Le Nôtre, principal gardener to the Sun King, Louis XIV, the genius responsible for such a symmetrical and enchanting landscape like none other. Typical of the Earl's thinking, he would entrust such a project only to a French landscape designer, but he could see how tourists in their thousands – even millions – would flock to see a modern replica of such a showcase to artistic, scenic beauty. The Gardens of Versailles also had all the natural curves he so admired in women.

If only he had persevered with his fantasy, completion of 'The Versailles Gardens of Wimborne St Giles' could have coincided with the release of a 2014 movie, *A Little*

Chaos, starring Kate Winslet, the flimsy story of a period garden romp with the director, Alan Rickman, taking the part of Le Nôtre. What a missed opportunity for the Shaftesbury entrepreneurs!

But the Earl was now not there with plans for the future; he was concentrating on building a shrine to the past. Wimborne no longer figured in his future. With that in mind, he began filling two rooms of his Versailles apartment with furniture and other possessions from his mother's home.

'He used all the furniture, books and knick-knacks of our childhood in Paris,' said Lady Frances. 'It was a bit much.'

He confided in friends that this was a way of keeping alive his mother. Every time he went into the apartment, he was reunited with her, conscious of her presence. He would talk to her photographs and hope for spiritual guidance. At no point, though, did he believe he was hearing her voice, though it is a known fact that he consulted two mediums in Paris. One told him that his mother had been trying to contact him because she was concerned about his health and money problems. It did not take him long to conclude that they were both charlatans, as they took him for a Frenchman of modest means whose mother was imploring him to top up his pension pot for impending retirement and old age. When he explained to one that he worked on the land, she took him for a farm labourer, a country bumpkin in Paris who was sightseeing. She claimed his mother was trying to warn him about the perils of big, bad Paris for someone so unfamiliar with its wily ways.

Despite his undeniable attachment to Versailles, he disliked the city's layout and physical character because it had 'no soul'. Unlike most European towns and cities, the streets were built on a symmetrical grid system. In fact, Versailles was adopted as the blueprint for the construction of Washington DC and many other North American cities. That was the Earl's overriding objection to this historic city of kings: you could be walking or driving in any urban sprawl of the USA.

Although the Earl made regular pilgrimages to his Versailles apartment, he did not stay long. Apart from his mother, through her lifelong belongings, there was nothing there for him. His quest was for sensual and secular distractions, the ultimate *dolce vita*. Paris was his immediate playground. He was welcome in all the capital's prestigious hotels, plus the bars and bistros of pulsating Montmartre. Oh, how he was besotted by this one-time bohemian and raffish hotbed of Paris's intellectual underbelly, which hosted the Moulin Rouge, the Sacré-Coeur basilica, pimps and madams of the *noir*. The Earl had known this 'naughty' neighbourhood when it was still a honeypot for impoverished artists, painters and writers. He spent countless nights there in his younger days, drawn instinctively to the energetic nightlife, the fact that there was an outlet for every conceivable vagary. No one was left out of the mix. It was said that Parisians talked nostalgically about Montmartre the way New Yorkers rhapsodised about the Village.

Not being a disciple of New York, the Earl preferred to compare Montmartre with London's Soho – although he was adamant that really there was *no* comparison. At best, Soho was a poor – very poor – cousin. There was, though, one similarity, he agreed: both had become sanitised and gentrified since the 1960s, much to his chagrin. The bohemians had been priced out of Montmartre by the tourist trade.

What is known about the Earl's movements is that on leaving Versailles, after having established the shrine to his mother, he booked into the Hotel Terrass, Montmartre's only four-star hotel, situated between the Sacré-Coeur and the Moulin Rouge, in the cosmopolitan Pigalle district.

In many ways it was not surprising that he chose the Terrass with its art deco interior and nineteenth-century grandeur. Also on record is that he hired a call girl, who called herself Lucille, from a dating service run by one of Europe's doyenne of madams.

The rendezvous was arranged for the Maison Rose, an arty restaurant in Montmartre with a reputation for good, honest French cuisine. Lucille, a blonde in her early thirties, was 'dressed to please', as they say in the trade. This was no less than the Earl expected because he knew the madam had all her girls inspected before they embarked on an assignment. She impressed upon them that they were ambassadors of the agency. One bad grape could ruin a whole vineyard, she would preach to recruits; her girls were refined. The Earl was not taking a gamble in this respect. This was something he knew from personal experience and the madam's track record. There were no raddled faces – makeup applied thickly as a mask was not allowed. All the girls had to look virgin-fresh and conduct themselves decorously, unless paid to do otherwise!

By now the Earl was drinking heavily and chain-smoking.

Although he did not dress expensively, it was readily obvious to Lucille and other women of his casual acquaintance that he was a man of considerable means. In fact, Lucille had never encountered such spontaneous generosity from a client. One of his foibles was his predisposition for continuity with a prostitute if he believed there was chemistry between them. In this respect, he was socially conservative. He liked to be surrounded by the familiar, and this applied as much to people as objects and settings.

He enjoyed Lucille's company and therefore negotiated for exclusivity. Lucille was willing because it would guarantee her regular work for a few days, maybe weeks, but such an arrangement had to be done through the boss. The bottom line was that he wished to book Lucille for a week. The transaction wasn't simple, however. How many hours per day was he prepared to pay for her company? The answer was 24/7. That would be very costly, he was cautioned. Cost was not a consideration, he assured. There was another obstacle: Lucille would need to go home daily to change into clean clothes. Not necessary, said the Earl. He would buy her new outfits daily. In fact, he would buy her anything, including jewellery and other accessories.

During a phone conversation, the madam asked for Lucille to be put on the line. 'How do you feel about it?' Lucille was asked.

'Wonderful!' she replied. 'He's very kind and a real gentleman.'

Lucille was instructed to call the agency twice daily and to report where she was sleeping, as a security precaution.

With Lucille in agreement, it was just a question of finalising the finance. The agency's payment was demanded in advance and the Earl paid with plastic. He also promised that Lucille would receive her *gratuity* daily in cash. Deal done!

Lucille was born and brought up in Rouen. Her parents had divorced when she was eleven and her mother married again two years later. She hated her stepfather, who on several occasions had tried to sexually abuse her while her mother was out, but she'd fought him off. When she complained to her mother, she was not believed and was called a muck-stirring, little liar who was trying to cause trouble just because she had always sided with her biological father. The rift widened and home life became intolerable, resulting in Lucille walking out on her sixteenth birthday, without a goodbye, and heading for Paris.

Within two days and with only a basic education, she was working the streets. The Earl was a good listener. He enjoyed hearing people's stories about their lives and with Lucille he once again demonstrated his talent for making a woman, even a whore, feel as if she genuinely mattered. They strolled through the cobbled streets and alleys of Montmartre, and ventured along the Barbès-Rochechouart, a notoriously rough area, especially at night, the Earl's penchant for recklessness and living on the edge coming to the fore again. Later, when drink and drugs were to rule his life, his sense of immortality was to be his undoing

One quirk of the Earl's quickly registered with Lucille: his infatuation with the 'pleasure palaces' of Paris before they were outlawed, ironically by a reformed prostitute who had gone into politics after World War II. But the Earl knew the name and location of every lavish bordello that had catered for kings, princes, heads of state, political notables, aristocrats, priests and even popes. Lucille, in contrast, knew nothing whatsoever of the background of the trade in which she worked, so the Earl took her on a grand guided tour, as if he was a brothel tourist guide, pointing out where each sex emporium had stood majestically and what had made it different from the rest.

He lamented that the 'Last Days of Rome'-style sexual gluttony had been banished from the City of Light by prosaic puritans. In so many ways, for him, the lights had gone out in Paris, which was still the City of Light but no longer the City of Enlightenment. He was literally obsessed with the carnal adventures of King Edward VII, when he was 'Bertie', Prince of Wales, before coming to the throne on the death of his mother, Queen Victoria.

Outside the Moulin Rouge, he told Lucille about the Prince's love for the Folies Bergère and how he would stand to toast the dancers with champagne, while the breast-gyrating chorus girls waved to him enthusiastically. He remarked that the two of them were standing on hallowed ground, where kings, sheiks and princes had gone before. Relating the Prince's eating habits, he recalled that he would sometimes dine with a couple of prostitutes in his private suites at his favourite bordello or at the Café Anglais, where the top-of-the-bill English call girl, Cora Pearl, was once served naked and covered in cream as the dessert for a party of super-rich revellers. Lucille found it hard to believe, commenting that it must have triggered an international scandal, but all the time the Earl was shaking his head. 'When in Rome, do as the Romans do,' he laughed, 'and when in Paris, do what the Parisians do.' And hedonism was what the Parisians had always done best, he asserted.

Paris was the acknowledged and acclaimed city of sin, where any pleasure of the flesh was acceptable. In the nineteenth century, the press did not publish 'intrusive' stories about the lives of aristocrats the way they did so 'shamelessly' today, he expanded. Newspapers were then concerned with important matters of state and international affairs – not trivial, bed-hopping affairs.

He was 'deliciously drunk' by then, as Lucille put it when talking to me, on a roll about palatial brothels, prostitutes who were venerated like current Hollywood starlets, and how presidents, dictators and other heads of state ruled from *maisons de tolérance*, state-controlled legal brothels, during the Napoleonic era.

The Earl was frank about his identity. His rebellion included mirroring Bertie, Prince of Wales, who had been delighted to be recognised and would not entertain the proposition of trying to party incognito. Equally, the Earl was open about his title, but Lucille did not believe him, though she kept her disbelief to herself. For a start, she was convinced that he was a Frenchman and not British; after all, his accent was perfect and he never struggled to find a word. All his habits and mannerisms were French. He understood French politics and the mores of the Parisians. She was not to know, of course, that he had been brought up in Paris, while simultaneously being the potential heir to a British aristocratic title with enormous territorial rights, virtually a principality in its own right.

Secondly, Lucille was unsure of the meaning of 'earl', although it obviously sounded grand. But where did it come in the pecking order of the British blue bloods? She assumed, wrongly, that an earl must be a member of the Royal Family. If so, it was unthinkable that he would be gallivanting around Paris openly with an escort girl and without bodyguards, often drunk, and gravitating to the red-light district of Montmartre, preoccupied with visiting the location of every grandiose brothel of the riotous cancan days, when the term 'bottoms up!' had a more functional meaning!

She tagged him a fabulist, with more money than sense, fun and harmless, someone who projected himself as more socially esteemed than he really was. She believed him a lonely dreamer and drifter who felt he had to buy company and affection, and that calling himself an earl gave him the sort of status he secretly craved. Despite his wealth, she actually felt rather sorry for him; once more he was being misread and underestimated. The problem for Lucille was that the truth, though staring her in the face, was too risible to be believed.

Le Chabanais, near the Bibliothèque Nationale, had always been Prince Bertie's brothel of choice, to the extent that he was often in residence there, with a personal valet and chef. Amazingly, in a country noted for its sexual extravagance and liberalism, the madam of the former Le Chabanais had been imported from Ireland. All her girls were chosen because they were lookalikes of international actresses of the period.

Starting at what would have been the entrance to Le Chabanais, the Earl asked Lucille to visualise the nightly scene inside what had been a cathedral of ungodliness, where Epicureanism (not Lucille's word) had been worshipped. Entrance had been reserved for royalty, the aristocracy and heads of state. Reservations had to be made well in advance, due to demand. When in residence, a bath filled with lukewarm champagne would be prepared for the Prince every evening, in which he would bathe and frolic for two hours with at least two prostitutes, handpicked by himself beforehand from a titillating beauty parade. His sexual gambolling would last from early evening until breakfast the following morning. All this was regaled to Lucille in a tone of reverence, as if the Earl was at a war memorial, paying his respect to fallen heroes. Lucille asked him if he wished he had lived in those heady days. 'No,' he replied, 'because if I had, I would have been dead long ago and not able to get up to mischief now with you.' He could be a real charmer.

Clearly his mind was very much on living life to the full, perhaps making up for the time he perceived as having been lost or squandered. If indeed that was his state of mind, it was not something his wife and sons would have wished to dwell on.

Taken at face value, the Earl's actions were disgraceful, dishonourable, selfish and wounding, but that is too simplistic. In my estimation, what was driving his bizarre and self-destructive behaviour was his undoubtedly unhinged mental condition. He had cracked. A fuse had blown. He was on the run, a fugitive from a future that was consuming him, sucking him dry and robbing him of the serene and taciturn existence for which he yearned: spending days watching owls and researching the habits and breeding grounds of rare bats, away from boring accountancy, balancing books and the night-and-day headaches of keeping afloat such a high-profile rural kingdom.

Equally, there can be no denying that, despite his devotion to nature, rustic simplicity and spiritual philanthropy, there was a baleful streak below the Earl's surface; it was not new and was deeply rooted in his complicated psyche.

So much for Victorian puritanism, he guffawed, still transfixed by the spot where Le Chabanais had once seduced so many of his social standing. Lucille smiled with him, though she did not fully understand. She had not been much of a scholar, and history, in particular, had never engaged her. But she had learned rudimentary English at school and it had improved considerably since having to entertain foreign tourists, for whom English was their mother tongue or second language.

Lucille took more notice when they reached the spot of the One-Two-Two bordello, at 122 Rue de Provence, near the Opéra, and the Earl began regaling her with the names of one-time habitués there: Humphrey Bogart, Cary Grant, Frank Sinatra and King Leopold III of Belgium. Sometimes they would merely drop in for a cocktail or to dine, maybe even escorting a genuine date, an heiress perhaps or leading lady in a movie being shot in Paris, who would be at ease among the stable of girls for hire, all of whom were tutored to display the politesse of a princess just out of a Swiss finishing school.

There were never less than sixty prostitutes – some legitimate actresses, *resting* between parts – on duty around-the-clock at the fashionable destination. The twenty-two bedrooms were individually themed, designed by theatre choreographers. There was a reconstruction of a wagon-lit, complete with sound effects and scenery that passed the windows to create the illusion of a thundering express train. Seats were decorated with white lace and equipped with vibrating springs. The 'Transatlantic Room' had a nautical flavour, with portholes, lifebelts and girls dressed as sailors. Another room replicated ancient Egypt, with a throne occupied by 'Cleopatra', who was billed as the star performer in the seven-storey ornate establishment. Cleopatra was the prize for royalty – but only at a royal price, of course. The Earl reeled off all this minutiae, saying to Lucille that there was a proud heritage to her chosen way of life and she should not be ashamed because her predecessors had been closer to the ruling classes than any banker, doctor or civil servant.

Queens may have been the power on – or behind – thrones, but harlots had been the *super-powers*, the Earl explained to Lucille, with a twinkle in his eye. Over a bottle of wine, coffees and croissants at a pavement café, he even wrote down for her some of the facts he had just been detailing – a sort of shopping-list of historical debauchery in Paris, to be learned and remembered as her homework!

"'Learn this and you can boast about your profession with your chin up to future customers," he said mischievously, as if my teacher,' Lucille reminisced. 'You know, I really do think he respected me. It wasn't put on. But there's no question that he was very mixed up.' From the One-Two-Two location, the next stop was the Sphinx.

For Lucille this was becoming akin to a book-at-bedtime serial, but she was intrigued by the Earl's storytelling and his depth of knowledge of an era when the elite of Paris whores had almost equal status with their sisters of the stage. Paris brothels were mainstream theatre. In the 1930s, there were more than 1,000 brothels in Paris, each one with a unique sales pitch. French politicians and British diplomats gravitated towards Le Sphinx, the Earl expounded. Marlene Dietrich often dined and drank there and enjoyed watching the comings and goings, chronicling in her diary little things that amused her. The writer Colette was in love with the Sphinx's madam, but often indulged in sexual encounters with the cabaret singer Polaire, generating much jealousy and numerous catfights, which drew boisterous spectators who emerged excitedly in various stages of undress from the bedrooms. 'Why cannot life be so carefree and frivolous today?' the Earl mourned.

Although Hitler outlawed all brothels during the Third Reich, the most elaborate ones of Paris survived and benefited from the patronage of Nazi officers throughout the Occupation. Hermann Goering, for example, had his own quarters at Chez Marguerite, a converted theatre close to Pigalle. 'Just around the corner from where we are now,' said the Earl. 'I'll show you.' And he did. 'How could an Englishman possibly know so much about Parisian prostitution history?' Lucille asked herself, still having doubts about his nationality. *Impossible!* Maybe he was making it all up, she considered, but that did not ring true either.

The clergy – French, British and Italian – patronised two brothels on Rue Saint Sulpice, situated on the arty Left Bank. The Earl said they would go there the following day. Lucille was pleased to be able to rest because her feet were aching, while the Earl was as frisky as a colt, which made her wonder if he was *on* anything, such as uppers, maybe cocaine, something she was familiar with. Numerous clients had offered her cocaine and she had accepted; the instant impact on her had been 'better' and much more gratifying than alcohol, and with no headache hangover. Since her introduction to cocaine, she had indulged spasmodically, but it was still expensive for her. Many of the girls with the agency knew dealers and turned tricks 'on the side' in return for coke.

Lucille asked the Earl if he used cocaine and his reaction was one of surprise. 'How would I know how to get my hands on stuff like that?' he had retorted somewhat indignantly, said Lucille. She replied that she understood cocaine had always been a 'high society' stimulant and was openly passed around at dinner parties, like the snuff of previous generations. Apparently, he seemed ignorant of the effects of cocaine, so Lucille explained that it gave you a 'kick' and 'lift', dissolved inhibitions and made life a laugh. 'Sounds like something I should have been on years ago,' he said, and wondered if she could 'get hold' of a sample for him to try.

No problem. She did not bother mentioning that it would

cost him because she knew what was a lot of money to her would be peanuts to him. So she called one of her friends, another girl on the books of the escort agency, who bought her own supplies from a pimp in Montmartre.

Lucille was told she could always find the pimp between noon and the early hours of the morning at a table of a piazza café, where he would be keeping an eye on his various flesh-properties. Lucille was advised to mention her friend's name and the madam of the agency as passwords. When Lucille reported to the Earl that she should be able to buy a sample for him to try, without a word he peeled off notes to the value of £500, saying something like, 'Will that be enough to get me started?' He was a caged bird flying free in the wild, at the mercy of a jungle crawling with predators. In many ways, he was so worldly, but he was not streetwise and was very much a lamb to the slaughter in the wrong hands.

Within half an hour, they were both sniffing coke and soon he was introducing Lucille in the bedroom to the old-fashioned waltz and persuading her to put on a cancan show for him, but without bloomers. Almost immediately he was hooked on the 'white witch powder' with its magical mood-changing qualities – and did not even notice that he had received no change from £500 for the very small quantity of pure but not crack cocaine.

When they had sex that night – and on subsequent occasions – it was the tour of the sites of the old brothels that inspired and excited him, along with constant references to his mother. Lucille was accustomed to role-playing for clients, but this was a new test for her: she was expected to be an *entertainer* at Le Chabanais, then the One-Two-Two, or the Sphinx. He is reputed to have bragged, while high on drink and drugs, that he had 'outdone Bertie' because he had shagged his way 'through the lot', albeit figuratively. But on climaxing, he would exclaim, 'Oh, mother!'

Next morning, they had breakfast at another pavement café: black coffee, croissants, cognacs (two each) and the new dish of the day for the Earl – cocaine. During breakfast, he chain-smoked as he read the London *Times* and the international edition of the *Herald Tribune*. Then, high on cognac and coke, it was off toe Rue Saint Sulpice on the Left Bank, where the narrow façade at number thirty-six used to be the entrance to the flamboyant Miss Betty's elaborate bordello, the clergymen's paradise on earth, where Roman-styled columns remained. At number fifteen, the name of another infamous madam, Alys, was tastefully inscribed in miniature mosaic tiles on the floor of the entrance hall.

They lunched leisurely in the sun – more cognac and cocaine – then off to a road near the Arc de Triomphe, where the garishly ornate Étoile de Kléber, affectionately nicknamed Madame Billy's, had deposed the One-Two-Two as the most lavish and pricey brothel in Paris when it opened in 1941. Wehrmacht officers and the French Gestapo, whose headquarters were nearby, ensured that Madame Billy's was supplied daily with champagne, caviar and an abundance of food, while the rest of the city starved. The legendary singer Édith Piaf had a permanent room there and entertained clients who paid for sex – and sometimes for a song during a bedroom romp. Her presence inevitably served as a magnet to other show-business celebrities. This history *lesson* interested Lucille as much as the riotous accounts of Bogart and Sinatra.

The Earl traced the demise of the *maisons de tolérance* for Lucille, though not in the didactic manner of a teacher, as once again they enacted scenes that aroused him.

Brothels in Paris were closed in 1946, mainly as an act of reprisal against the criminal underworld for collaborating with the Nazis. Many pimps had found sadistic work with the French Gestapo and the Bill to banish brothels was steered through Parliament by Marthe Richard, an erstwhile hooker. Someone should have shot her, Lucille suggested. The Earl considered this, then said that he was more an advocate of the guillotine than the bullet because it was uniquely French. It was even news to Lucille that the brothel emporiums had been declared historic monuments in the 1980s by the Ministry of Culture, affording them protected status, in recognition of their cultural contribution to Europe's self-designated capital of romance, although there had never been anything remotely romantic about the business of these over-glorified flesh markets, despite their allure to the 10th Earl of Shaftesbury.

7

A WOMAN'S
MAN

Lucille, who was so often the 10th Earl's paid-for companion in Paris, was the one woman who was prepared to share with me secrets of his sexual proclivities.

'You cannot begin to understand this without realising how besotted Tony was with his mother,' she explained, as our conversation continued. We were drinking coffee at a pavement café in the southern quarter of Pigalle and near the district known as Nouvelle Athènes (New Athens). Lucille's English was exquisite and spiced with her expressive French accent and animated gestures. She explained that all escort girls with the 'top' agencies in Paris and on the Riviera had to prove their fluency in English before being employed, because such a high percentage of clients were Americans or Arabs. The wealthy Arabs all spoke English as their 'natural second language'. Many attractive women, who were rejected by the 'high-class' agencies because of their poor education and lack of language skills, were advised to learn their trade in a lower league.

'Girls soon pick up English from foreign clients and after a few months they can re-apply to the agencies. It's all very civilised, like applying for a job with a corporation. You have to show that you're up to the job and can provide a high quality of service for the customer. After all, it's not cheap and it's important for clients to be satisfied and think they've got their money's worth. Sometimes you have to start at the bottom.' (From her expression, it seemed the veiled witticism was unintentional.)

Every table was occupied. The babble was endless and frenetic. No one gave us a second glance, as if we were invisible. 'In France, we respect people's space, especially in bars and restaurants,' she said. 'No one is going to bother trying to hear what we are saying. Eavesdropping is not the French way.'

The coffee was thick and black and served in a tiny cup. We must have talked for an hour and a half and had only the one drink each. In all that time, we weren't once pestered by a waiter.

'A lot of lies have been told about Tony, in the press and by other girls. He was a very tender and intelligent man, highly educated, and would never be violent, however drunk he was. He had enormous respect for women. He was very much a woman's man. Most people would wonder why he had to pay for sex, because many women would have given it freely to him, I imagine. He was so likeable, so lovable. You had to know him really well and have earned his trust to appreciate why paying for sex was necessary for him.

'Something else you should be aware of: Tony loved this city and he loved France. But not as much as he loved his mother. He loved her much more than he did his wife, more than anybody else. It is impossible to emphasise that too much, because it was responsible for his sexual behaviour, too.'

The first few times they had sex, she found the experience 'creepy', not because of any depravity on the Earl's part but due to his penchant for pillow talk of a nature she had never before encountered. 'I shall never forget the first occasion. As I was undressing, he commented on my figure, as men often do, to release any tension or just for something to say. They think you need to be flattered and wooed. They forget it's not a date. Seduction doesn't come into it. As soon as money changes hands, the deal's done. The meter's running. But usually they'll say something like, "You have a fantastic figure" and you know they're aroused. But it wasn't like that with Tony. He was already in bed with the covers pulled up to his neck and he followed me with his eyes and would suddenly say, "You remind me of my mother."'

She continued: 'Take it from me, that's not the normal conversation you have in the bedroom with a client. Quite honestly, I didn't know what to say. I must admit that, at that moment, I did think he was rather strange and I did wonder what kind of sex he was into. But you have to remember that I was with him on a long-term-booking basis and I'd been assured he was harmless. And then he said, "But my mother had a better figure than yours; that's when I was young, of course, a little boy." I was stunned. Again I didn't know what to say. I was sort of out of my…what do you call it?'

'Comfort zone,' I prompted her.

'Yes, that's it. He must have noted something wary or confused in my expression because he quickly said, "Please forgive me. I didn't mean to be rude. You are a very attractive lady." I'll always remember that he said *lady* as if he really meant it. He never treated me like dirt because of my profession. He was blushing boyishly when he said, "But, to me, my mother was the most beautiful person in the world, even as she aged, even the day she died. It didn't matter to me how others saw her. My eyes saw what they wanted to see." That was the gist of what he said, in his own words as I can best recall them.

'There were tears in his eyes and I felt sad for him. I was in my underwear and I sat on the edge of the bed and asked him if he wanted to talk some more about her. He held my hand and said, "You're very understanding, Lucille. I feel I can be open with you and you won't laugh at me."

'Whatever he'd said, I wouldn't have laughed, unless it was meant as a joke, when you have to pretend to be amused. We're not paid to insult clients but to indulge them.'

Apparently, he confided in Lucille that, when he was about fifteen, he had sexual desires towards his mother that he never attempted to pursue, of course. This was becoming very Freudian. Sigmund Freud's theory was that most young men, especially in adolescence, subconsciously fantasised about making love to their mother (known as the Oedipus complex). In his lifetime, there were more people who dismissed him as a degenerate crank than those who hailed him as enlightened. However, it seemed that Freud may very well have got it right when it came to the 10th Earl of Shaftesbury.

The Oedipus complex derived its name from Greek mythology. Oedipus, a young man, killed his father in order to marry his mother. The desire was to possess his mother exclusively and to rid himself of his father, to eliminate competition. Oedipus feared that if his father learned of his machinations, the mother figure would be removed from his reach, so he had to act first.

'This is one of Freud's most controversial ideas and one that many people reject outright,' psychologist Saul McLeod wrote in a medical paper in 2008. 'Freud believed that life was built around tension and pleasure. Freud also believed that all tension was due to the build-up of libido (sexual energy) and that all pleasure came from its discharge.

'In describing human personality-development as psychosexual, Freud meant to convey that what develops is the way in which sexual energy accumulates and is discharged as we mature biologically. Freud stressed that the first five years of life are crucial to the formation of adult personality.'

Conflict between frustrated wishes and social norms exists, which could easily have applied to the 10th Earl and his feuding inner self.

'The ego and superego develop in order to exercise this

control and direct the need for gratification into socially acceptable channels,' McLeod continued. 'Freud explored the human mind more thoroughly than any other who came before him... He was one of the most influential people of the twentieth century and his enduring legacy has influenced not only psychology, but also art, literature and even the way people bring up their children.

'Freud's lexicon has become embedded within the vocabulary of Western society. Words he introduced through his theories are now used by everyday people, such as anal (personality), libido, denial, repression, cathartic, Freudian slip and neurotic.'

A tenuous link between Freud and the Shaftesburys is the theory headlined 'Eros', an instinct that helps people to survive, directing life-sustaining activities such as respiration, eating and sex, the internationally famous psychoanalyst claimed in 1925. And Eros stands larger than life today in central London, reminding us mainly of the 7th Earl of Shaftesbury but subliminally also of Freud, the psyche-trespasser, who fervently believed that the unconscious mind governs behaviour to a greater degree than the majority of people suspect. As McLeod said, 'Indeed, the goal of psychoanalysis is to make the unconscious conscious.'

A sound argument can certainly be made for the 10th Earl having been guided by remote control, as surely as any self-destruct missile, unaware of the consequences of his actions or, indeed, the provenance of the incentives.

Psychoanalysis aside, Lucille was not shocked by anything

the Earl confided. 'I've heard a lot worse, believe me. What *was* new was undressing in front of a man, who was paying for sex with me, and have him gushing about another woman, albeit his mother. I did begin to wonder if all he wanted was to talk. Talkers rather than doers are more common than you might suppose. But it's a different sort of release for them. If that was the case with Tony, I didn't mind. Let's be frank, it would be easy money. And it was our first time together and I didn't think I'd ever become genuinely fond of him, nor of any client. We were always told never to allow it to become personal; it's just business, intimate business, but still business. Like a nurse, you can't afford to get emotionally involved. But we are all human, you know.'

For a moment she was defensive, although I was doing nothing more than playing the good listener and occasionally tossing a pebble into the pond to see where the ripples would spread.

'I did feel awkward when he stroked my arm, saying, 'Your skin is as soft as M when she was as young as you.'

If Lucille's account can be believed, the 10th Earl (Tony to her, and all his family and friends), he craved more than anything else to be mothered and pampered. I see no reason for doubting this version. She was not being paid, there was no pressure to 'deliver the dirt', and she was more protector of the Earl than predator. Unlike the other protagonist of this narrative, she was anxious to minimise the Earl's dependency on sex, drugs and alcohol. Her sympathetic depiction of the Earl dovetailed strikingly with another woman's recollections.

Lucille, of course, was not required to *mother* the Earl unless it was paid for, as an integral part of the fantasy package. If he drank too much, that was his choice, as long as it did not lead to violence. His health was not her concern. Lucille's outlook was exactly the same when it came to recreational drugs. They both used cocaine, so she was not offended by this habit as long as, once again, the Earl was in reasonable control of his behaviour and faculties and made no attempt to harm her. But, as she stressed, she was not a nursemaid. She enjoyed his company because he was considerate, generous – of spirit as well as materially – intelligent and cultured.

In 2010, Lucille gave up prostitution; she was not trying to promote her services via the interview. She was employed by the EC in Brussels as an interpreter and showed me her credentials. She was fluent in five foreign languages and also moonlighted as an interpreter for a number of book publishers, a remarkable achievement considering her very basic early education. After fleeing her childhood home, she had pursued further education in Paris.

When we met in Paris, she was on vacation. The rendezvous was arranged by the former proprietor of an escort agency, and the only conditions were no photographs and anonymity. *Lucille* was her escort sobriquet. I have deliberately gone into considerable detail about her background so you can judge how much reliance to place on her narrative. For me, it had the merit of plausibility, considering the considerable evidence produced in French courts about the Earl's fixation with his mother. The Earl's sister, Lady Frances, who has spoken about the Earl's dependency on his mother, said, 'For my brother, her [their mother's] death was a catastrophe. He adored her. She had been his protector and greatest admirer...' The Freudian connection and concept looms large, I suggest.

It also appears that there was a structure to the Earl's serial sexual encounters when in France, featuring repetitive visits to the sites of old haunts of ill-repute and other historic landmarks associated with the bawdy Napoleonic years. More conventional cultural attractions, concerts and art galleries, were not neglected; his entertainment was broad-based and eclectic.

At the end of the day, he liked to be tucked up in bed by Lucille and have a chapter of a book read to him in French. His favourite bedtime reads were anything about Napoleon Bonaparte. 'He always had books with him about Napoleon,' said Lucille. 'He had so much knowledge of French history. That was another of his obsessions.

'A prostitute sees a man as he really is. When Tony had sex, he wanted to talk about his mother. That's not something he would have been able to do with his wife; she'd think him mad or a pervert. From the first time, I could see that Tony was far away, in another place, another bedroom, when we were having sex. He was so remote, glassy-eyed, with someone else. Some men will close their eyes and imagine they're doing it with a youthful Brigitte Bardot or Marilyn Monroe. For me, that was fine. Of course, there will be those who will say that Tony was warped and dissolute, but I didn't see him that way at all. He had hang-ups – don't we all? – and I think he'd finally accepted that he didn't fit in any more with his traditional life. He drank in order to become a different person, to assume a new identity.'

Lucille explained that with champagne in him, he was more convivial and less shy, and that cocaine changed him even more, giving him zest. 'Often he said to me that he bored even himself until alcohol hit his head,' she recounted. 'Drink and drugs gave him a personality transplant. Several times I told him, sincerely, that he was very interesting and not in the least boring, but I knew he didn't believe me. In that respect, he was too smart for his own good. Because I was being paid to please him, he assumed I'd always be saying what I thought he wanted to hear, which put me in a no-win situation when it came to frankness with him.'

On the subject of his mother, she said that he told her that when his mother died, he lost the real love of his life. 'His way of putting it was that he lost his lungs; you know, she was his oxygen. Something else he said, which I hope won't hurt his family, was, "I always wished I could have married my mother. She was always the perfect woman in my eyes." His eyes became watery as he said, "But, spiritually, I was married to her from puberty. My real wives were mere companions."

He was grateful for his wife in England for giving him two sons, and he was devoted to the boys and very proud of them. But he didn't like dwelling on the life he'd left behind because it made him twitchy; it was baggage he'd dumped, rather than having mislaid. He'd thrown it away and didn't want any kind person finding it for him and giving it back. He was riddled with guilt because he saw himself as such a failure: the belief that he was such a deserter and a bore caused so much self-loathing that drink and drugs were his refuge, the only things that made living with himself tolerable, I think.'

Before they had sex, the Earl would kiss a photo of his mother three times and that was the cue to pull back the bedcovers. 'He would always be naked at that point,' she recalled. 'Without saying a word, he'd hand me the photo. I knew my role; it didn't take much learning. I'd hold the photo against my face, so that mother was looking at son. Then I'd go down on him. This was the ritual, without variation.

'Whatever you may think, there was nothing dirty or disgusting in it. You should hear some of the things an escort is asked to do! The Earl was sweet. As I went down on him, I'd say, "My! My! You have grown into a big boy." He'd just groan and neither of us would utter another word until it was over, when he would say, almost reverently, "Thank you, *mère*." He'd always split the sentence between English and French. But the most important word, the last, would always be in French.'

Very often sex with Tony had a cultural theme, she explained. 'There were the visits to all the locations of the palatial brothel emporiums of the Victorian days (as Tony called them, emphasising his British side). Those places were a constant sexual stimulant to him. This historic thread to his libido was illustrated by our trip to Corsica. We were chatting in bed, after sex, when he said, "How would you like to fly with me to Corsica?"

'I said, "When?"

'He looked at his watch and replied, "Today." It was already gone midnight.

'"How long for?" I asked.

'"Maybe a week."

'I said I'd have to get clearance from my boss, but he said to leave it to him and he'd fix it with her. And he did.'

The next morning, before breakfast, Tony had booked them on an Air Corsica flight from Orly. He also reserved a room for them at the Hotel Napoleon, which was in a quiet side street in the old centre of Ajaccio, the Corsican capital.

'Over breakfast, he said, "We're going to the birthplace of France's greatest ever leader." I knew who he was talking about because he was always hungry for more reading material about Napoleon Bonaparte. But from all the discussions we ever had about Napoleon, it was clear that the military gifts of the great man didn't concern him that much. I understood perfectly why we were going to stay at the Hotel Napoleon. He couldn't resist anything with the slightest connection, however tenuous, with the once-upon-a-time emperor.

'I can remember on the flight he asked me if I could guess why Napoleon had legalised state-run brothels. "So he would benefit from being able to make use of them free of charge," I joked, though I hadn't a clue.

'"No, because he considered whores were essential to any civilised society," he educated me. "He planned to have brothels all over his empire." And that was to include all over Britain because Napoleon, according to the word of Tony, couldn't conceive a future without France not having conquered the British. I have a sneaky feeling that Tony wished Waterloo [the battle] had gone the other way. Not that he was unpatriotic, but he did say he agreed with Napoleon that brothels save respectable women – that included me, I guess! – from being pestered and assaulted. Tony sneered when recalling that it was an ex-prostitute who spoiled Napoleon's good social work and outlawed *maisons de tolérance*.'

The fact that Napoleon had lost his virginity to a whore, she recounted, was a source of delight and comfort to Tony. It made the two of them sort of kindred spirits.

'This may sound crazy, throughout my entire experience with Tony, he treated me as if I really was his Countess. You see, the truth is that I was more to him than just a woman to fuck. I was his companion, not a commodity. We talked and behaved like a normal couple: that tells you a lot about Tony and his approach to life. I never felt that I was with him just to do a job, to fulfil a contract. He bought me presents and nothing was too much trouble for him, but that didn't colour my judgment of him.'

On their second day in Corsica, they visited Napoleon's first home, a four-storey house in Ajaccio that is now a museum, Maison Bonaparte. They hired a car and on the second day drove north into the mountains to find another property that had been owned by 'Boney'.

In the coastal town of Calvi, he remarked that had he been forty years younger, then the French Foreign Legion would have offered him the 'perfect escape from' from the pressures that imprisoned him. The Legion's parachute regiment had been based in Calvi. Over dinner, he said, 'But forty years ago I didn't want to lose myself. I had my mother when she was in full bloom.'

Even for those few days in Corsica, he had packed a complete portfolio of photographs of his mother. 'He displayed several of them in the bedroom and the nightly sex routine was adhered to rigidly,' said Lucille.

On the return flight, the Earl spent most of his time talking again about Bonaparte and impressing upon Lucille that the stories of Napoleon hailing from coarse peasant stock were nothing more than English propaganda and that he had actually been born into aristocracy. If the Earl had lived long enough to read Stephen Clarke's book, *1000 Years of Annoying the French,* published in 2010, he would have been mortified by one reference to 'Boney's' alleged upbringing: '*Of course, as far as Parisian marquis was concerned, the noblest Corsican was about as aristocratic as a chamber pot…*'

What also emerged on that flight from Corsica was the link between Napoleon Bonaparte and the Earl's fascination with the Riviera, which was not just about the climate. The Earl rhapsodised about Napoleon having been appointed Inspector General of Coastal Defences for the whole of the Côte d'Azur, as a reward for his military success at Toulon. With the appointment came a luxury villa just outside Antibes, which perhaps explains why that particular fashionable Mediterranean resort was so special to the Earl.

It seems that there was a quirky roadmap to the last years of the Earl's life, in which history and culture were his erotica and he was guided by a sort of sexual satnav.

8

CONVERGING
ON CANNES

Jamila M'Barek had been very busy since arriving back in
France from Tunisia. Her night of sex, champagne and
drugs on board a yacht at Saint-Tropez in her first twenty-
four hours on the French Riviera had proved to be the
gateway to easy street. From that heady beginning, she had
not gone in search of work: money had come to her. She
was inundated with propositions. If she did have a problem,
it was making a choice from all the lucrative daily offers. She
joked with friends that she needed a secretary and booking
agent. One acid retort she received was that other girls like
her already had that sort of service but the providers went by
the name of pimps.

Young, wealthy layabouts wanted to date her, but they
were off her radar; she was after top-drawer *business*. Older,
richer men desired her as an accessory. Now they *did*

interest her. The big sex deals were nearly always sealed on the water, in motor yachts or cabin cruisers. Balding, flabby fifty-something tycoons, into their third or fourth jaded marriage and weary of their umpteenth mistress, jockeyed for her company, and would crudely bid against one another. Having acquired the right to paw a beautiful ingénue over dinner on deck with a dozen or so other couples at the table was a boost to the ego of the cholesterol-clogged men, their hearts frequently reliant on pacemakers, who circulated in a world in which everything could be bought if you had sufficient capital to beat the opposition.

Most of the women at those dinner bashes were hired commodities, as was Jamila. It was essential to the boat-master that he had the most desirable female of the bunch on his lap. Cocaine was available as freely on tap as the champagne; they went together like drugs and dealers. Within just a few days in Saint-Tropez, Jamila discovered she could name her own price. The equivalent of £3,000 for a night soon became a ballpark figure.

After a five-course feast, including rich caviar, buckets of bubbly, several rounds of top-quality coke and sickly liqueurs – the women mostly topless – the older men (as perceived by Jamila) were often beyond rising to the demands of sex. In the morning, probably just before noon, they would stir and the communal drunken snoring (hours too late for a dawn chorus) would cease. Bleary-eyed and fragile, most of the *oldies,* who Jamila rarely spent the night with, would awake with blank memories of the night but assume they must have fallen asleep after exhausting themselves in the sack with carnal aplomb. One punter, who spent his life cruising the seas, hardly ever venturing on land, bluntly asked her, 'So how many times did we do it?'

'Six,' she lied.

'Was it good?'

'It blew my brain.'

'It certainly did mine. I can't remember a damned thing!'

They had not done *it* once, of course, and for this she received something in the region of £5,000. This was a yarn she retold in the bars many times.

Jamila had not been on the Côte d'Azur long when she was introduced to Dutch businessman Raf Schouten, who offered her genuine romantic dates. She saw prospects in a steady relationship with a prosperous man, in his forties, who was not obese or ugly. She was already pregnant when he proposed marriage after just six months of dating and living together for a trial period. She had landed her first really big catch and probably could not believe her luck. She would have a home, on the Riviera, an anchor, security, respectability, and a legitimate stake in her husband's business portfolio. Soon she gave birth to a son, Raf, quickly followed by a daughter, Kiara.

The marriage was stormy, mainly because of Jamila's independent nights out on the town. Her husband, something of an innocent in the sexual melting pot of the Côte d'Azur, soon had substantial evidence that his wife was working as a prostitute, despite the luxurious lifestyle into which she had married. When he tackled her on the thorny subject, she lost her temper and tried to make him the guilty partner, accusing him of spying on her and trying to keep her tethered to kitchen and bed.

Still he had not elicited a straight answer from her. Where was she going at night until the early hours of the following morning? What was she up to? Why was she neglecting the children? Retaliating, she screamed at him that she had never wanted children and it was none of his business.

After that poisonous spat, the marriage was a shipwreck. When he announced that he was divorcing her after barely three years, she clapped her hands derisively, again mocking his manhood and warning that she would ensure she milked him for every franc to which she was legally entitled.

Following the acrimonious split and divorce, Jamila had little time for her children, then aged three and four. They were a burden and cramped her style, so they were quickly placed on the Riviera with their paternal grandmother, who happily took over. The loving upbringing they received was down to their caring grandmother, who never tried to deter Jamila from seeing her children. But she rarely visited and when she did, it was tantamount to a politician's whistle-stop tour.

Still hankering after a career as an actress, Jamila took off for Paris, not short of money now. Always using the first name Sarah, by which she was even known to her children, she went looking for a theatrical agent. She boasted that she had been on an acting course in Paris, after living for a while in Switzerland, though I was unable to uncover any record to substantiate either of those assertions.

However, she did meet Catherine Gurtler, a madam

who managed a number of top-of-the-range escorts. She recognised the potential in Jamila, but not as a conventional actress, though she would be giving performances that tested her talent for improvisation. Prostitution continued to appeal to Jamila's laziness and partiality for easy money. It was a life choice that suited her. There were no auditions, no early mornings, no long periods of being out of work between parts, and no cash-flow difficulties: payment was instant, cash in the hand, no waiting for a cheque in the mail after an agent had extracted his or her cut. So it was a no-brainer for Jamila. She was in such demand that she could have worked seven days a week, afternoons, evenings and nights. All-nighters made for the biggest paydays.

Gurtler was one of the new breed of madams who embrace modern technology, advertising and trading on the Internet, and also exploiting quality newspapers, especially the *International Herald Tribune.* This modus operandi enabled her to operate simultaneously in several countries, never mind cities, without her base being known to the authorities, although she mainly resided in Geneva. She was not committing a crime, so she was never a 'person of interest' to vice squads.

But as fast as Jamila earned, so she spent, and her easy come, easy go lifestyle began to catch up with her. When she was offered a photo shoot for *Playboy* magazine, she jumped at the opportunity and was ecstatic when copies of her posing nude appeared in print worldwide. She really deluded herself into believing that this was her breakthrough to stardom, achieved without any hard labour: no training, no beginning at the bottom and working her way to the top, no waiting tables to scrape together a living until offered another part. In her delusional mind, this was going straight in with an Oscar. But in this instance there was no mouthwatering follow-up. The Hollywood big fish were not biting and she was now thirty-three years old. A look in the mirror told her the cruel truth. The years of drugs, alcohol, skin-disregard and client hopping had taken their toll. She was living non-stop in the fast lane and the mileage on the clock was accumulating commensurately.

Gurtler stressed to Jamila that the hottest money for a looker like her was to be made in Cannes, especially during the annual International Film Festival in May, the preceding two weeks and the fortnight following. For a call girl in Jamila's class, May in Cannes was the same as December was for retailers during the pre-Christmas bonanza.

So, in appreciation of the matriarchal *wisdom* of Gurtler's economic advice, Jamila returned to the Riviera, this time basing herself in Cannes. Via her online network, Gurtler managed girls in Paris and throughout France.

Hollywood's big names were always jetting in and out of Cannes year-round, but particularly in spring for the film festival – harvest time for the premier-league hookers. Gurtler's name and contact numbers were in the little black books of most Hollywood aides, minders who invariably hid behind designer shades, even at midnight. Gurtler, or a similar operator, would be contacted by one of the aides, saying that a *special* girl was required for the night by a discerning gentleman who would be referred to as Mr Smith, Mr Jones,

Mr Bigshot, whatever. The transaction would be negotiated and sealed without the client's involvement. Rarely was there a dispute over the charge. There was a regular format to the arrangements: the woman would go directly to the client's room. Champagne would already be in an ice bucket, mostly in a penthouse-type suite. The hooker would have been given strict instructions regarding what to wear. Fluency in the English language was essential, a factor that worked in favour of women like Jamila. After a couple of glasses of champagne, the client would make his assessment: if the escort was not to his liking, she would be rewarded with a modest tip and sent on her way. The aide would express his disappointment to the despatcher and a new 'consignment' would be organised; it really was as clinical and tasteless as that. However, if the escort made a positive impression, then money would be discussed convivially. Usually the bartering would begin with a blunt, 'What is your fee?'

Jamila always started by asking for the equivalent of $10,000. Usually the client would chuckle and shake his head, calling her a 'dreamer'. Jamila would smile sweetly, stressing that she was 'worth it'. Obviously she watched a lot of TV adverts.

'How can I be sure?' might well be the client's response, to which Jamila was always up to the challenge of the repartee: 'Only one way to find out, suck it and see!' That line, she would boast to Gurtler, was always the clincher. It never failed to hasten the wheeling and dealing, even if she had to settle for a pruned fee. This money would all be for Jamila, tax-free and not to be shared with the agency, which had already extracted its charge from the middleman, the aide.

Hookers like Jamila soon built up a reputation with the Hollywood jet set. Her name was circulated among the high rollers, so she was frequently requested by name – Sarah. She never failed to arrive for business without a stash of cocaine, which she shared freely, ensuring all inhibitions were soon 'Gone with the Wind', an in-joke among the Tinseltown fraternity. Happy, drug-high punters were generous payers.

During Festival week, Jamila would be familiar with at least 50 per cent of the men she serviced, having seen them many times on TV and the big screen. She played a game with herself as she travelled by cab to a plush hotel: who would the Mr Smith, Mr Jones or Mr Bigshot really be this time? Jamila and the client would never leave the room together. Dinner was always ordered via room service and when it arrived, she would discreetly disappear into the bathroom.

In court in 2007, and under oath, Jamila named superstars George Clooney and Bruce Willis as among her clients; also former Wimbledon tennis champion of champions Bjorn Borg and Prince Albert II of Monaco. All these men denied knowing her, let alone having shared her bed.

By 1998, the Earl was virtually detached from his family and estate. In all but name, he had assumed a new identity, certainly a new public persona. He had moved on from Lucille and many other similar young women of the night to become seriously attached to a twenty-nine-year-old French model, Nathalie Lions. Nothing of the country squire remained, even, or especially, when it came to his attire. At sixty-three, he had morphed into a classic Riviera playboy. He dressed in black leather trousers, pink silk shirt, mock crocodile loafers, a gold chain dangling around his neck on to his exposed chest, and large red and black shades.

He flew Nathalie first class to the Riviera, Barbados, Miami, Los Angeles and London, where he delighted in showing her off to old acquaintances, who could not believe that this was the same serious-minded, reticent 10th Earl of Shaftesbury for whom they had had so much respect just a few years previously. It was as if he had turned into Faust, having sold his soul to the demon Mephistopheles.

Everywhere he went, Nathalie was on his arm. One night he was seen in Bellini's bar in fashionable Kensington, south-west London, where he put on an exaggerated display of writing two or three cheques for her to bank and spend. People who had known the reserved Earl for decades were speechless at the transformation; he was a complete stranger to them. He soon acquired many hangers-on, all of them after his money. When some old friends tried to talk politics, he brushed them aside, saying, 'To hell with that boring stuff, where's the party?'

Some were so alarmed that they phoned the Earl's elder son, Anthony, to see if everything was 'all right' with his father. It was mortifying for Anthony to learn that his father was back in Britain with a much younger woman in tow, and not that far away in London, but had made no effort to visit the family and the estate of which he was still, of course, the official master. These phone conversations were very awkward for all parties. The callers tried to be circumspect, while alerting the Earl's heir to his father's roistering, embarrassing, decadent behaviour. They could not bring themselves to disclose that the Earl was introducing Nathalie as the next Countess of Shaftesbury, as soon as he had 'rid' himself of that 'old harridan' who ran the place 'like Colditz'. This was obviously drug and drink-fuelled vitriol and such a fallacious characterisation of his wife, Christina, whose warmth and kindness elicited the best in others. After all, the Earl had seen fit to entrust her with the onerous responsibilities that he had ditched. Son Anthony would have been heartbroken to hear his father trashing his mother in this way in bawdy company in a public bar.

Anthony accepted that these callers were well-meaning folk, old stalwarts who were genuinely concerned for the family, its honour and perpetuity.

After a few days of sampling London's nightlife, including pubs in the King's Road, the couple took off for Nice, as if the UK had nothing left for them.

At the beginning of their relationship, Nathalie, like Lucille, had questioned the Earl's validity, believing he was romancing to impress, though there was no doubting the money he had at his disposal: that was unmistakably real. Now, though, all that scepticism had vaporised. She had seen his official title on the cheques she had been given and on correspondence; in addition, she had met a number of his grandee cohorts. He was the real deal. And he was proposing marriage, offering her fairy-tale dreams of living somewhere resembling a castle, making her a countess, hosting magnificent balls, attended by prime ministers, princes and presidents. Of course there would be nothing stuffy about the modern-day flings he had in mind; partridge and pheasant might still be on the menu, but no doubt the Earl's darker side was dwelling on his proclivities for cocaine, unlimited champagne and bed-hopping.

The Earl made up his befuddled mind that he and Christina must be divorced. He was in a hurry to clear the path for his marriage to the much younger and vivacious Nathalie; he was rapidly becoming addicted to sex and drugs. Rising at noon, lighting his first cigarette of the day, downing two glasses of champagne before a black coffee, then having a sniff of cocaine, followed by a luscious soak in a deep, bubbly bath with a woman, and he was ready for the remainder of the swinging day. What a difference from having to be up at dawn in dark, chilly Dorset, and all the headaches that couldn't be relieved with a couple of aspirins. And everyone so glum! No gaiety, so many burdens, no exhilarating 'white magic', and no unrestrained self-indulgent sex with a variety of women. Wimborne St Giles was not missed. Here was a phenomenon, a man recycled into someone unrecognisable from his past sixty-odd years and with the transmutation so rapid; it was as if he had undergone a brain transplant and a completely different person had hijacked his body.

In order to precipitate the divorce, he readily admitted serial infidelity. His first marriage had ended, as you will recall, due to his admission of adultery with an anonymous woman (more light will be shed on that later), so there was a certain element of déjà vu here. Christina had obviously suffered more than enough. Despite being Swedish by birth, Britain had become her true home. Being the daughter of an ambassador, she knew all about duty, obligation and diplomacy, plus the importance of upholding dignity. And she had no intention of turning her back on the Shaftesbury estate and her sons, particularly Anthony, who had been dumped in the mire as much as she, having to perform the role of Earl but without the title. In truth, they had been left in an invidious position, but they were down-to-earth grafters. No one on that estate, other than the 10th Earl himself, was going to capitulate. The battle would continue without the General.

Of course, Anthony was distraught for his mother and they both did as much as possible to comfort one another. But no rational thought process could prepare them for what was going on, beyond the fact that they had been deserted and the illustrious Shaftesbury name was in danger of being dragged through the mud and ridiculed.

The Earl had first met Nathalie in a lingerie shop in Geneva: he had gone in to buy exotic underwear for another woman, with whom he was sleeping. What evolved was a smooth, classic chat-up and pick-up. The knickers went to Nathalie instead of the originally intended recipient.

In London, while doing the rounds, he introduced Nathalie to everyone as a member of the royal house of Savoy. The Earl is reputed to have given her cheques amounting to a total value of more than £1 million. He also bought her a £100,000 Rolex watch and an Audi TT sports car.

One friend tried to put a different spin on the Earl's

behaviour, arguing that he was grotesquely misunderstood and that, in fact, he was driven by the instinct of his eminent progenitors, in particular the 7th Earl, and that his family philanthropy was perpetuated through him. In this respect, they said, his passions included rescuing lap dancers from depravity and the Devil. This was a rather risible attempt to portray him as a Gladstonian figure, a contemporary and political ally of the 7th Earl, who ventured on to the mean streets to counsel and redeem fallen women – *allegedly*. The problem with the rather hilarious hypothesis is that the women the 10th Earl hooked up with were not lap dancers, and he pursued a salacious way of life, participating in orgies and using cocaine. A curious way to go about redemption!

His French lawyer, Thierry Bensaude, offered a more obscure spin, describing the Earl as a 'philosophical adventurer in society'. Certainly he was an adventurer, embarking on risk after risk and endless pleasure-seeking, no matter what the cost, to both his assets and his honour, but it is difficult to see where anything 'philosophical' fitted in, except in the sense of, *whatever will be, will be, and I might as well go out with a bang!*

He was divorced from Christina in 2000 and by then his decision-making had become erratic and blurred by drink and drugs. Hardly having time to catch his breath, he became engaged to be married to Nathalie, but just as suddenly called it off when a tabloid newspaper revealed her as a 'Penthouse Pet', a model who had posed naked for *Penthouse* magazine, and a former *Sun* newspaper Page Three pin-up with silicone-enhanced breasts. It is difficult to fathom why he was so incandescent about Nathalie appearing unclothed in a magazine with a worldwide circulation. Much more credible is that someone else had strayed on to his radar and was titillating his sexual taste buds.

From living recklessly, he was now about to embark on a perilous course that would send him hurtling towards his sinister and macabre destiny. The die was cast...

9

ATTRACTED
TO BREASTS

The Earl was first drawn to Cannes by yet another story relating to Bertie, Prince of Wales, who had become King Edward VII on the death of his mother, Queen Victoria. As the monarch, he could no longer frequent Le Chabanais and other licentious 'playhouses' of Paris, but he could not resist a trip to Cannes in 1903 just to ogle the towering architectural domes, believed to have been modelled on the breasts of the famous courtesan 'La Belle Otero', which sat atop the Carlton Hotel that dominated the palm-fringed bay.

Those 'breasts' are still an architectural showpiece today and the Earl flew south to Nice, then by road to Cannes, just to photograph this masterpiece of workmanship after reading about the former king's fascination with them. He already had a home in Nice and, of course, had been to the Côte d'Azur many times on holiday. But it was only in his post-fifty years that he learned of 'Dirty Bertie's' connection with the Carlton, where the Earl had actually stayed on numerous occasions but had never bothered to examine the roof. The domes are an integral part of the famous Cannes skyline, but their significance had never before been brought to his notice.

Breasts and Bertie were a union too nostalgic for the Earl to bypass and so he fired away with his camera to add to his collection of material on the royal rogue, who actually became a much-loved king, responsible for the Entente Cordiale, the seed of which was no doubt planted in a sumptuous French brothel, the site of which had been visited by the Earl on his quirky pilgrimage with Lucille.

With his engagement to Nathalie dead and buried beyond resurrection, he was soon on the prowl again. And Cannes could be even more tempting than Paris for a man on the loose with little but sex, champagne and cocaine on his mind, especially one so ridiculously rich and remarkably well-preserved for his age, and with a recently acquired self-destruct outlook.

Eager for new female company he phoned the trusted Catherine Gurtler, his ever-reliable broker. Gurtler advertised her escort agency in the *International Herald Tribune*, one of the Earl's daily reads, and it was through this newspaper that he had first discovered her services. Now, whichever region of France he happened to find himself in, he always turned to Gurtler to find female company, although he did have the contact details on his mobile of a pimp in Nice as a back-up.

On a miserable day in February 2002, he told Gurtler that

she had previously supplied him with an escort going by the working name of Sophie and that she had been very much to his taste. The Earl was one of Gurtler's regular clients – if not the most regular – so his business meant a lot to her. Apologetically, she informed him that 'regretfully' Sophie was not available; in other words, she had already been booked by another client, though it was not put to him quite that bluntly. But, the Earl was lucky because, by pure chance, an even more gorgeous and vibrant young *lady*, of excellent breeding who was an extrovert conversationalist, could be at his disposal. So went the sales pitch, so smooth that he must have felt relieved to have missed out on his first choice because it was leading to such a serendipitous encounter. The substitute, he was told, was called Sarah and once seen she would never be forgotten. True enough.

It was also hinted that once he had been with Sarah, Sophie would be washed from his memory. Also true, sadly for the Earl.

However, *serendipitous* was most certainly not the right word. Sarah was, of course, Jamila M'Barek, and the Earl's destiny was just about to take a deadly nosedive. He had reached a point in his life when he had become as endangered as the *Titanic*, heading for an iceberg.

Cannes conjures up images of glamour: movie stars gracing red carpets, millionaire playboys sunning themselves on yachts, bronzed beauties tanning on silky sand, sentinel palm trees rustling in a whispering breeze, gourmet food and magnums of champagne in ice buckets at every restaurant table.

Back in 1834, Cannes was a sleepy village, built around a bay; nearly all the inhabitants were fishermen and their families. Then along came Britain's Lord Henry Brougham, who was captivated by what he saw, and its potential, and put down roots. As soon as other British noblemen heard about Brougham's 'conquest', they began rolling in, quickly followed by well-heeled Russians, Americans and an assortment of Euro-aristocrats. Cannes was on a roll.

The popular picture today of Cannes is not fraudulent when it comes to the parts shown in holiday brochures and James Bond-type movies, often showing La Croisette, where superstars like George Clooney, Brad Pitt, Angelina Jolie, Pierce Brosnan, Harrison Ford and Madonna are fêted as they smile and wave to their adoring fans, engulfed by the world's media and a battery of cameras. But that is a small, rarefied quarter of Cannes. There is a much darker and sinister side to this hedonistic playground.

Just a few hundred yards away and there was a very different landscape, where you ventured at your peril after dark and could be forgiven for imagining you had wandered, with the help of a time-machine, into 1950s Soho or an unlit alley of cut-throat Tangier. One windowless bar was advertised as the ideal destination for an 'intimate evening'. Step inside and you immediately engaged with what was on offer: a bar-full of attractive women looking for company and a good time – at *your* expense. There was a large dance-floor, two bars and a backroom with video screens. Outside, among the shadows, lurked the dealers, furtive figures, some of them pimps who also had a financial investment in a girl or two inside the bar.

Trade became brisk as the evening gathered momentum. It was not a place to be alone, signalling vulnerability. This is all contrapuntal to the mythology of the Côte d'Azur coastline. As one British newspaper, the *Guardian,* reported in 2007, 'This is supposed to be the land of men in unbuttoned white shirts leaning on Lamborghinis, of beautiful, sophisticated women, of champagne parties on multi-million-pound yachts, of lavender plantations and villas perched on red cliffs above the blue waters...'

Neither was this seedy district where you would expect to encounter an ageing British Earl, six foot one and as ramrod erect as a guardsman, when not slouched over a bar or a whore, cigarette dangling between his fingers, champagne stains down his garish pink shirt and his brain engulfed by a fog of drugs. But Shaftesbury was there, sometimes as regularly as the pimps and dealers, one of the props of this social decay and decadence. The man who loved rural wildlife had been seduced by the lowest form of urban wildlife.

In a labyrinth of narrow alleys, where all kinds of nefarious transactions took place after sunset, there were numerous bars, some catering exclusively for gays. One such establishment was noted as a 'crossover' bar, though one gay guide described it as 'more hetero than homo, depending on the night'.

This rough quarter of Cannes is relevant to the narrative. When Jamila did not have a booking from an escort agency, she worked among the demi-monde as a hostess in one of the myriad pick-up joints. Jamila's brother, Mohammed M'Barek, was also on the scene. Married and the father of young children, he was in and out of work, with no real trade. He was an unstable and unreliable character, noted for his short-fuse temper, impressionable and something of a Walter Mitty character. When in Cannes, he was always pleading poverty and badgering Jamila for handouts. Mostly she obliged, though reluctantly. He would promise to repay her as soon as his luck changed, but she knew it would never happen, accepting that the money she handed him was a gift, not a loan. Despite their brother–sister blood relationship, there was always an element of fear and friction.

Jamila was by far the stronger personality of the two. She had fine-tuned her tunnel vision. As much as possible, she mapped out her life, and she had one overriding goal – to become rich. Breaking into the movies was still an ambition, but becoming famous was secondary to making a fortune. If fame brought with it riches, then fine. But if there was more money in an option that ruled out celebrity status, then it was no contest: that would be her choice. All her acquaintances recognised that she was money-motivated. Psychologists doubtlessly would have attributed her relentless pursuit of money to her deprived childhood. I am sure, even if it was subconscious, she had made a pact with herself that she would never be poor again. Whatever it took.

Mohammed was a drifter, usually within the netherworld of any city to which, by chance, he gravitated. A former part-time professional footballer until his psychopathic tendencies excluded him from contact sports, he had no game plan beyond day-to-day existence. He lived by his wits, a definite handicap because he was not endowed with many. He was swarthy and bulky, so at least there was always strong-arm work available for him as a minder or bouncer in 'Dodge City', the nickname among the smart set of Cannes for the no-go area.

Paradoxically, the Earl was as much a drifter as Mohammed, but on a completely different level. Both were losers, but neither would have recognised this facet of their similarity. The only real difference in this respect was that the Earl had so much to lose, while Mohammed had so little.

Although Mohammed was constantly mixing with ruthless dealers, he preferred to sponge cocaine off Jamila, even if he had enough money to buy a supply on the street. Understandably, Jamila felt used, which in a way was ironic because no one exploited people for their own ends more than she did. This is where the fear factor came into the relationship with her brother: she was wary of conflict with him because of his mood-swings, caused by drugs and mental instability, and how little it took to make him detonate. Usurers gave him casual employment as a factotum and bully-boy debt collector. Sometimes he would make illegal deliveries for underworld bosses, many of whom were living in luxury on the Riviera, brushing shoulders with the legitimate rich and royal. Occasionally he would do favours for wives, some quite respectable, whose husbands were cheating on them. These women did not want a divorce or the cost of legal fees, so for a much more modest outlay and a one-off payment, he would use his fists to teach erring husbands a bloody lesson. Thuggery was a safety valve for his many grievances.

Jamila, never one to miss a trick (an unintentional pun), appreciated the potential advantage of keeping Mohammed on side. The day would come when she was able to make use of his strength...

Jamila was forty-one years old when Gurtler despatched her to do business with the Earl. Highly relevant in regards to what was to evolve were the conversations between Jamila and Gurtler before this defining day. Jamila was neurotically fixated about her future. She kept asking Gurtler how many more years she could hope to keep trading on the very demanding Riviera sex circuit, where annually there was so much fresh female flesh on the market; all of it so much younger than Jamila and fired with youthful ambition, fame and fortune the goal, whatever the cost.

Gurtler tried to reassure Jamila, stressing that there was no substitute for experience and, in any case, she continued to look much younger than her years. For some time to come, Jamila would enjoy an edge over her ever-increasing rivals, said Gurtler, feeding Jamila what she wanted to hear. The psychology of managing escorts was little different from that of a football coach towards his or her players: belief in themselves was all-important and would lead to improved performance, whether on the field or, where escorts were concerned, in bed.

As for the long-term, Gurtler emphasised to Jamila that so much would depend on how well she cared for herself, and in particular to avoid more skin damage and reduce the alcohol intake. Her flesh was losing much of its tone, mainly due to excessive sunbathing on yachts, the beach and poolside at the villas sprinkled around the backdrop of red hills. Jamila confided in Gurtler that she was tired of the rat race, the different men and their countless vagaries. In her whinge, she went on to say that once you had seen one penis, you had experienced them all.

Obviously Jamila was threading her way through a maze of self-doubt and she told Gurtler that it was time she found a super-rich sugar daddy so that she could stop having to play the field for a decent income.

Gurtler was later to place on public record that Jamila was 'obsessed with money'. Along with others, Gurtler wondered what Jamila was doing with all the vast sums of cash she had been pocketing nightly. It had become as much a drug to her as cocaine, a ratcheting process of dependency.

Yet she always seemed desperate for another urgent cash-infusion. Money for cocaine was a constant outgoing, of course, but it was frequently an expense funded by punters as a gift on top of the fee for sex. True, she was providing a modicum of upkeep for her children, but there was never a flourish of generosity. Maybe Mohammed was digging deep into her cache? Certainly she was not saving for retirement; prostitutes tend not to have pension pots. Her cash-haemorrhage was a mystery.

Bearing in mind their heart-to-heart chats, Gurtler expressed the opinion that Jamila's encounter with the Earl could be her golden opportunity. He was a sybaritic British aristocrat, divorced, and he favoured a special relationship with a hooker if the chemistry was right, Gurtler told Jamila. He had a proclivity for what he termed 'exotic women'.

Gurtler had a gut feeling that Jamila might well strike gold. 'The rest is up to you,' she said prophetically.

Because she was going on a date with a randy British earl, who was addicted to sex, cocaine and alcohol, Jamila focused on meticulous preparation, presenting herself as a red-carpet stunner. And the result was an instant knockout. From the moment they shook hands and kissed, mouth-to-cheek Continental-style, he fell for her as if a trapdoor had suddenly been sprung open beneath him. Not one to falter in front of goal, Jamila swept him off his feet.

The Earl's comment to Gurtler after that original encounter was that he wanted Jamila to himself for 'every minute of every day'.

Jamila anticipated that a British lord of one of Europe's cornice families would hang out at the fashionable hotspots, but this perfectly understandable assumption was way off the mark. The Earl yearned for a run – not a walk – on the wild side. And Jamila was the perfect tour guide for the unwholesome underbelly of Cannes. She trawled him around all the 'alternative' bars, obtained cocaine for him, and kept him on a permanent high with all the drugs, drink and sex he could handle. She was prepared to indulge in any form of role-playing, no matter how outré.

The Earl remained unbelievably infatuated, while she had all the native cunning learned from her rotten childhood and no scruples about her strategy to secure lifelong affluence. Here was a life-changing opportunity that she intended to seize it by the throat. For her strategy to work, it was essential for the Earl to always be gagging for more, so she played hard to get. But not *too* hard! She gave, then took away, pretending at times not to be available, as if there was stiff competition, but then allowing herself to be bribed by him into cancelling any other rendezvous so that she could be with him. She kept him guessing, so that his interest and competitive, predatory spirit never waned. The *bribes* were gargantuan, running into thousands of pounds a time, until he was caught in the eye of a woman-made vortex, an unbalancing, swirling mixture of romance and avarice. The emotional cocktail was heady. He thought he was in love and Jamila undoubtedly pumped oxygen into that belief.

The speed at which the relationship burgeoned was staggering, like a runaway juggernaut, brakes dismantled, crashing relentlessly through every obstacle placed in its path. Having first met in February 2002, by the spring, marriage was already on the agenda, pushed along by Jamila and with little resistance from the Earl.

In fact, the Earl was so besotted that he was eager to show off his new bride-to-be to family and friends. He sincerely hoped that his sons would accept her and a lunch rendezvous was arranged at an Italian restaurant in west London for Jamila to meet the Earl's younger son, Nicholas, who was at that time twenty-three. Just the two of them would be present.

Although the Shaftesbury clan had no idea that the Earl was contemplating marriage, the lunch was an unmitigated disaster. From the moment they shook hands, the encounter was combative and bruising, pugilism with words that lasted only one round. This is Nicholas's brief and pithy recollection of that watershed meeting: 'Instantaneously, I saw her as someone who was out to get everything she possibly could.'

Jamila wasted no time listing items and possessions belonging to the estate that could be transferred to France. When Nicholas balked against any such prospect, she retorted abrasively, 'Oh, you just want to keep everything for yourself,' he recalled.

'At that point it became obvious to me that she was someone who was manipulating my father, so I walked out,' Nicholas added. Lunch was over – and Jamila was left with the bill. It was small beer compared to the price she was later to pay. In any case, the tab was eventually picked up by the Earl, having been passed on by a furious Jamila, who was unused to being rebuffed so unceremoniously by a young man.

The elder brother, Anthony, had not attended because he, with his mother and Lady Frances, were occupied with pressing management issues at Wimborne St Giles. Nicholas was seen as the expendable one for such a showdown because he was not a member of the management team, nor was he heir to the ancestral title. Also, he was the worldly and streetwise scion, despite his comparatively tender age. He could spot a phoney in crowded Times Square, it was said about him, apposite because New York was his base.

Official records show that Nicholas, just like his father and brother, attended Eton College. What was not public knowledge at that time was the fact that he had been expelled from Eton when he was sixteen for landing in trouble with the police over drugs.

'A group of us got cautioned, up in London, by the police,'

he explained. 'Pot was found in the car. That was the tipping point. I was already a marked student.

'As a child, you want your father to be indomitable, showing you the way. My father was never that figure. I could have gone in a horribly different direction. But I vowed to myself, there and then, that I would never let myself go too much out of control again. I've been in control ever since.' The tragedy is that his father did not have the strength of character of his wife and sons. Instead of the father setting an example, it was the other way round.

After being booted out of Eton, Nicholas was accepted at another highly-rated public school, Canford, which nestles inconspicuously and riverside in rustic Dorset, between the coastal, urban sprawl of Bournemouth and Poole and the quaint minster town of Wimborne, only a few miles from the Shaftesbury estate. From Canford, he went to Manchester University, reading economics and social policies, but his real passion was music, and it was that which enticed him to New York, where he quickly made a name for himself as a promoter and DJ. Within a very short time, he was in constant demand. He managed a trendy club, Arcspace, a venue noteworthy for its lack of a drinks licence. Crowds were drawn to the club for the quality of the music and dancing rather than the opportunity to get legless on drink and/or drugs.

The electronic music scene was his speciality and he soon had a faithful following among discerning New Yorkers. He organised a series of music events, was recognised in the business community as a successful entrepreneur and was constantly booked as a home DJ for celebratory occasions, such as weddings, anniversaries and engagements.

So Nicholas was not someone to be hoodwinked by the likes of Jamila. And his report to his brother and mother was ominous. They were left in no doubt that storm clouds were gathering. Thunder and lightning were on the horizon and the Shaftesbury name and its lineage was threatened.

10

A TRAP
IS SPRUNG

Jamila wanted a quick shotgun wedding. *Strike while he is hot*, was a motto she had learned from all her man-manipulating days on the game.

Christina had divorced the Earl and he had been as keen as Jamila to tie the knot, but something instinctive made him hesitate. He was to tell a woman a couple of years later that 'something wasn't just right', that he could not 'put a finger on it, but smelt a rat'. Jamila, the very large and voracious rat, sensed that she was about to lose the catch of a lifetime. She had him cornered, but he was wriggling. Something had to be done quickly and decisively to prevent the Earl from escaping the hook.

We can only speculate over what induced this ambivalence in the Earl. Maybe he pondered on the way they had initially come together, and here he was on the brink of making a countess out of a seasoned call girl – a greater challenge, surely, than Bernard Shaw's epic melodrama, *Pygmalion,* which, at least, was recognised as far-fetched fiction. Then there were the shady bars and dodgy dealers she consorted with so intimately; though, in that respect, they had become two of a kind, birds of a feather. Hypocrisy is renowned for inducing self-deception.

The Earl was also aware that Jamila had not severed her connection with Gurtler; why not, if she was genuinely ready to settle down as a one-man woman, enjoying marital togetherness?

Clearly the Earl was lonely. Superficially, this seems a contradiction, because wherever he went, he always had company. But the companionship was bought. He was surrounded by *friends* as long as he was throwing about his money, buying all the drinks and meals. His pack of followers was nothing more than hangers-on, birds of prey just waiting to swoop. Jamila warned him that he was being taken for a sucker. What a smart move! This was a distraction, intended to make her appear solicitous and protective, someone he needed on his side, a *loving* friend, not foe. In truth, she wanted to plug the flow of money to others so that it could instead be channelled her way.

Although the Earl vetoed a spring wedding, there were never arguments about the date – or anything else, for that matter. The Earl never remonstrated; squabbling was not his style. By nature, he was passive, the complete opposite of Jamila. When someone pointed out to him this difference in temperament, he fell back on the old cliché of opposite poles attracting.

The weeks rolled by. The Earl had come off the boil. The impetus was just not there any longer. By now, Jamila was desperate. As so often in the past, she gambled everything on her native cunning, which had always served her so well. Beneath the haze of drugs, the Earl was still an English gentleman, of the old school, who believed in behaving honourably, especially towards women, his weak spot in this situation. So she told him that she had a special announcement to make and insisted they go for a romantic dinner in the Grand Hotel, under the towering breast-like domes that fascinated the Earl so much.

Because the Earl smoked and drank so much, plus ingesting cocaine daily, he never had much of an appetite, and so nibbled at his salad that evening. A waiter poured the champagne for them. The moment had come for Jamila to roll the dice. Her theatrical timing was perfect.

'A toast,' she said, raising her glass. The Earl blinked quizzically. They clinked glasses. *What's going on?* he must have been thinking. With her free hand, she reached across the table to run a finger tantalisingly over his lips, whispering, 'Let's drink to the three of us.'

The Earl fluttered his eyes, face blank. Still he had not cottoned on. 'Three of us?' he intoned.

'You're not usually this slow catching on,' she said playfully. 'Darling, I'm pregnant. I'm having *your* baby. You're the father. Since the day we met, I've never been unfaithful to you. Please say you're as thrilled as I am.'

For a moment, he was speechless. When the implication finally dawned on him, he said, 'Are you certain?'

'The test is positive,' she said. 'I've suspected for a week or two, but didn't want to say anything until I was sure. This is such a magical moment!'

This whole scene was recreated months later by the Earl for another woman who had become a major player in the drama that drip by drip was unfolding.

Suddenly the Earl beamed and his chest swelled. This was something he had not allowed for entering the equation: to be a father again after well over twenty years.

Jamila emphasised that they must plan for the future. 'If it's a boy, he will go to Eton, it's a Shaftesbury tradition,' said the Earl.

'And if it's a girl?'

'Then somewhere like Heathfield or Roedean, followed by a Swiss finishing school. But we're getting ahead of ourselves.'

Now it was Jamila's turn to look clueless.

'First we must marry. Without delay. We can't have you going around pregnant without a wedding ring on your finger.'

She cooed appropriately.

The champagne was quickly finished. Another bottle was ordered. Pointing to the bubbly, the Earl told Jamila that there would be 'no more of this' for several months, not until after the birth. Abstinence was not something she had bargained for.

No matter, Jamila had netted her man. She had relied on the Earl's old-fashioned, British rectitude. Smart psychology.

Apart from the Earl's later recollections, that particular

dinner conversation was recalled by Jamila for Gurtler's benefit on the phone. 'I really am going to be a countess,' she burbled. 'I can't thank you enough for being the original match-maker.'

The Earl decreed that his sons would have to be informed forthwith, a tricky task. This set off alarm bells in Jamila's scheming head. She feared Nicholas, and rightly so. He was clever and astute. More to the point, he was already hostile towards her. He was not a young man malleable in the wily hands of a seductive sorceress and Jamila had no doubt that Nicholas would turn his elder brother against her, if, indeed, that had not already been done. The brothers were the last frontier to be crossed. Bypass them, and Jamila was on a home run.

She agreed with her husband-to-be that his family should be notified, but pleaded with him not to leave her alone, because this was a very emotional and sensitive time for a woman. He duly promised to correspond with his sons and sister by letter; it was not the sort of personal and confidential information an aristocrat would entrust to email or a text message, which would be such bad form.

Nicholas is on record saying that the news that his father and Jamila were to marry hit him like a 'bombshell'. He added, 'It was head-in-the-hands time. She pretended she was pregnant, which was a great card to play; you know, the old trick.'

What will never be explained is why the couple chose to be married in Hilversum in the Netherlands. They were living together on the Riviera, so what was the pull of the

Netherlands in damp, murky winter? One could understand romantic Paris, especially considering the Earl's attachment to the city in which he had been raised. But Hilversum! It was the beginning of winter, cold in northern Europe but still mild and sunny on France's south coast. Maybe they both considered it advisable to be away from their old stamping grounds and dubious contacts on the Côte d'Azur. Jamila, most of all, was anxious that nothing should spoil the day for which she had plotted so assiduously and for so long. Now it was really going to happen.

There could be another more rational and sentimental reason for the Earl choosing the Netherlands for the wedding. As mentioned earlier in the book, the 3rd Earl of Shaftesbury had emigrated to the Netherlands on health grounds, though he had soon moved south to a more kindly climate. The Netherlands had particularly appealed to the 3rd Earl because of the country's tolerance and free-thinking attitude and it is very likely that the 10th Earl identified with this philosophy and was following in the footsteps of an ancestor with whom he shared a special affinity. There is no escaping the fact that the 10th Earl was a romantic and tended to be steered more by sentimentality than common sense.

Thirty-one kilometres southeast of Amsterdam, Hilversum is part of Randstad, one of the largest conurbations of Europe. With a population of around 85,000 in 2002, Hilversum was dubbed throughout the Netherlands as 'Media City' because it was the hub of the country's TV and radio broadcasting. Radio Netherlands, aired from Hilversum, had been listened to via shortwave since the 1920s.

Despite its national importance, the town had never been granted city status, and locally the city centre is called '*het dorp*' – the village. If the idea was for a low-key, safe-from-the-media wedding, then choosing a radio and TV mecca was a curious choice. There was something else, too: in that same year, Media Park was the scene of the assassination of politician Pim Fortuyn, a hot-headed anti-Islamist racist. Race issues were rearing their ugly heads. Jamila had changed her name long ago to Sarah in an effort to expunge her Arabic heritage, which made the selection of Hilversum an even more extraordinary preference for such a special occasion. Only two people knew for certain the answer to the mystery and one of them is unable to divulge, and the other has never been willing to, so far.

On 5 November 2002, Jamila became the official new Countess of Shaftesbury. She had pulled it off, while Nathalie Lions had been ruled out for being a 'Penthouse Pet'. Yet Jamila had posed naked for *Playboy*, which, for some inexplicable reason, had been overlooked as inconsequential by the Earl.

Not lost on the Shaftesburys at Wimborne St Giles, meanwhile, was the significance of the date of the wedding: 5 November, Guy Fawkes Day. The anniversary of a devious plot to bring down an institution!

The title went to Jamila's head quicker than the champagne and cocaine. Even Gurtler was instructed to address her as Countess and to curtsy whenever they met. 'Absurd!' Gurtler guffawed. 'She was drunk on imagined power and wealth. She was no lady and would never be. She couldn't handle it.'

But top of the agenda for Jamila was that she should live in the luxury befitting a countess, especially as there was a child on the way. The Earl approved and set out making immediate provision to ensure that her lifestyle was commensurate with her new social status. She even thought that a countess should always wear a tiara in public – even to the hairdresser (hilarious but true). In many ways, this narrative could transcend genres – from tragedy to comedy – were it not so blatantly tragic. Clearly the whore-countess was delusional.

For starters, she wanted her own substantial property that was separate from the matrimonial home and in her name only – a rather odd request for a newly wed, one might reasonably think. But the Earl ceded to her entreaty and readily splashed out £500,000 on an apartment in Cannes for her, acknowledging that, although married, they both needed their own space. He enjoyed travelling, especially between his various bases, while Jamila wished to remain rooted in Cannes for the time being, so she claimed.

A countess with child could not be expected to take care of herself, so domestic staff were employed, on the Earl's personal payroll, of course. Jamila had also fallen in love with a windmill that had been converted into a cosy home, in the Gers region of south-west France. Around this time, the Earl was showering his new wife with gifts, money no object. He hated seeing her depressed and sullen, something of which she was only too well aware and mercilessly exploited. Seeing her brooding over a period of days, he suddenly took off on his own and purchased the windmill, buying it in Jamila's name and presenting her with the keys. Apparently, he accepted the idea of the windmill being a place where the three of them could retreat for summer vacations, fleeing the madding crowds of the Riviera.

Jamila did not have transport, so he bought her a four-by-four vehicle. Housekeeping money was set at £8,000 a month, although the extent of Jamila's cooking was limited to boiling eggs and making toast and coffee. They invariably ate out for lunch and dinner, quite often for breakfast, too. Sometimes separately.

However, Jamila was not confident about her legal position should her husband die, so she questioned the Earl about his will. Obviously it was a delicate matter, but it had to be discussed considering their age difference. As it stood, the estate would go to Anthony as the heir and a large proportion of the other properties to Nicholas, while the money and investments would be divided among the family. Jamila railed against the whole arrangement, which she declared unacceptable. Where did she fit into this equation? As the current countess, she was entitled to the bulk, she argued, no doubt stressing that this was not a question of greed but a matter of protocol and equity.

Apparently, the Earl was sympathetic to her concerns and quickly amended his will to leave her £4 million, plus his villa in Nice and the apartment in Versailles, the shrine to his mother, which contained artefacts and antique furniture that were worth a small fortune, a *large* fortune to Jamila before her newly-acquired social elevation. These changes were an interim, an insurance, he assured Jamila, so that she was instantly shielded from penury should he drop dead from a heart-attack; more substantial codicils would follow when his chief accountant had furnished him with an up-to-date inventory. There would have to be several meetings with his London solicitor, occasions he dreaded because of the need to be fairly sober and to resist cocaine for several monotonous hours.

Jamila seems to have spent much of her time resenting being the Countess of Shaftesbury and not yet active in the administration of her kingdom. Her philosophy was simple: what was her husband's was now also hers. She had not even set one foot or eyes on the estate. The Earl had been very sketchy and vague with his depictions of his rural kingdom, probably because, in the practical sense, he had disowned it and wanted it expunged from his psyche, and also due to the constant mist shrouding his befuddled brain. At times, though, his clarity of thought was exceptional.

He had talked about St Giles House as the epicentre of the Shaftesbury dominion, a stately home with twenty bedrooms, the finest private library in the entire UK, an art collection valued at millions of pounds, and stables, all set among 9,000 acres of woodland and undulating fields of fertile farmland. *Epicentre* was an appropriate definition of the estate because it was the core of the Earl's personal earthquake.

Typical of the Earl and his state of mind, he did not have any photographs or memorabilia with him of the extensive territory he owned. Jamila probably had visions of a turreted castle, such as seen among the pine forests of France, where she would have an automatic right to host banquets and perhaps even entertain members of the British Royal

Family. She was determined, as soon as possible, to assert her position, which meant a visit to *her* estate, where she would put everyone in their rightful place, especially the elder son, Anthony, and the Earl's ex-wife, Christina, should she have the temerity to show her face.

When the Earl heard of her plans, he recognised her right but was keen to avoid being caught in any crossfire and so chose not to accompany her. He would stay at his place in Hove, Sussex, while Jamila went about her bossy business. She cajoled him into hiring a chauffeur-driven Rolls-Royce for her, so that she could sweep into Wimborne St Giles in regal fashion, creating a stir.

Nicholas, in New York, chuckled at the shock he presumed Jamila would feel on her arrival at St Giles House. Unknown to her, and probably even the Earl, this historic property had in 2001 been recorded on the Register of buildings at risk, due to neglect that had allowed it to decline and decay. Buildings recorded on the Grade I list included those of 'exceptional interest, sometimes considered internationally important'. Jamila was unaware that the house had not been lived in properly for about sixty years. The Earl's grandfather had been the last to occupy the house in permanent residence. Since then, the family had occupied more modest and modern properties scattered around the village.

Anthony greeted her coolly, which was reciprocated. No love lost from the off. Scowling perpetually, Jamila strutted around St Giles House with Anthony in tow, as if he was her butler or footman, a downstairs minion straight out of *Downton Abbey*. 'She wanted to see everything,' said Nicholas, who had been briefed by Anthony within minutes of her leaving. 'That would have been quite a reality check for her, this fallen-down house. Apparently, she pointed at the paintings, saying, "We'll take all those."'

Anthony was enjoying himself. 'Sorry, you can't,' he said, according to Nicholas. 'Those are in trust for the children.'

Nicholas said, 'She got more and more irritated by how little there was to get her hands on.'

Finally, she flounced out, petulantly saying, 'We'll see about that. I'm going to have everything checked-out legally. Mark my words!' She was not interested in seeing any of the land and animals.

As the Rolls drove through the village, she spotted a farm labourer trundling along the roadside and ordered the chauffeur to stop, whereupon she alighted and beckoned with a finger for the workman to approach her, which he did desultorily. She asked him if he knew who she was. Of course he did not and said as much. So she introduced herself as the Countess of Shaftesbury, chatelaine of all that could be surveyed, and beyond.

He took off his cap, not as a mark of respect but to scratch his head. 'That's funny, you're not the countess I've known for donkey's years,' he said. Now she really was nettled, trying to impress upon him that she was the *new* and *rightful* countess, the only bona fide one now, but he would have none of it. He knew the *real* countess and so did the rest of the village, and that was final, he said, dismissing her as if she was an imposter.

As a parting shot, Jamila warned that 'everyone around

here' would be seeing a lot more of her and that they had 'better watch out'. She had expected to be received with awe and deference, with male villagers raising their caps or touching their forelocks, while the women curtsied. Her attitude and the quips she made were overheard by the chauffeur, much to his amusement. Although only a brief snapshot, it demonstrated how ordinary country folk could instantly identify the wheat from the chaff.

The Earl and Countess Jamila returned to France. Despite everything that Jamila had already accrued from the marriage, she was far from satisfied. As ever, she wanted more. The domestic staff in Cannes heard Jamila constantly losing her temper, though the Earl, as taciturn as ever, never retaliated. Jamila mocked him, accusing him of not being a 'proper aristocrat' and that his stately home was a 'rotting dump'. She even derided his sons for being 'ill-bred', rather rich coming from her. Neither did the workers 'know their place', presumably because no one had bowed or curtsied to her. When she was not openly rowing, she was bickering, always on the warpath over something. All the time she was forgetting that her husband had no interest in anything that happened in Wimborne St Giles.

Within just a few weeks of the wedding in the Netherlands, it was apparent that the marriage was on shaky ground. The Earl began spending more time alone, along the coast in Nice. He complained to his drinking chums that his wife was behaving strangely, aggressive and more like a predator than a partner. It appears that for a while he brainwashed himself into dismissing Jamila's hostility towards him as hormonal, directly related to the *pregnancy*. All would be harmonious, he kidded himself, somewhat optimistically, after the birth. In the meantime, he was anxious that Jamila received the very best pre-natal care.

On one visit to his wife, when he stayed a few days, he was overheard by a maid saying that he planned on booking Jamila into the finest maternity unit in Europe that 'money could buy'. No expense would be spared for this child. This was something that cheered up Jamila, providing her with the opportunist cue to ask for more money so that she could start investing in baby necessities. Despite everything he had already given her, the £4 million and the extravagant monthly allowance, the Earl spontaneously signed more cheques for her to cash at intervals, without a single specific question about what the money would buy. It seems that while she was his countess, then it was his duty to treat her as an inviolable goddess.

Now we come to what must be seen as the most surreal angle in the disintegration of this clearly unworkable marriage. Jamila, the Countess of Shaftesbury, called Gurtler to announce that she was ready to resume as a call girl escort. To say that Gurtler was speechless would be an understatement, though she quickly recovered from her bewilderment and didn't pry too much. Having a genuine countess on the books was indeed an unexpected sales promotion. There was one condition, however, imposed by Jamila: Gurtler must not advertise a 'British countess for hire' in her *International Herald Tribune* advert because it would almost certainly be spotted by the Earl.

So Jamila was back on the game, while continuing to celebrate her pregnancy with her husband. The bookings poured in. She rented her body on millionaires' yachts, yet she was a millionaire, too, in her own right, and probably worth more than most of the punters when adding to her own sizeable nest egg the invisible assets and investments attached to the Shaftesbury estate. Yet here she was prostituting herself, as if it was as much in her blood as the addiction for cocaine. She even oversaw orgies in her Cannes apartment, after sending home the staff. Sometimes the sex parties would last two or three days, with everyone high on every conceivable combination of drink and drugs. The Earl could have shown up at any moment and this outrageous gamble must have given her a perverse buzz. It was a dance on the high wire. Russian roulette. A roll in a barrel over Niagara Falls. And as with all gamblers, the stakes had to get higher and higher until at the brink of bursting; as with drug addiction, the dose needed to raised by ever-increasing increments. Unable to resist flirting with danger, she was as self-destructive as the Earl, which was probably the only real thing they had in common.

Incredibly, the zany conduct of Jamila was matched by the Earl. While Jamila was being booked out by Gurtler, the escort agency proprietor was also procuring girls for the Earl. She, the matchmaker in the middle, had to be careful that she did not inadvertently arrange a sex tryst between the Earl and his wife!

The Earl would often dine with his escort at The African Queen restaurant at St-Jean-Cap-Ferrat, where Hollywood superstar Jack Nicholson moored his yacht year-round. In fact, whenever Nicholson was vacationing on the Riviera and ventured ashore, he, too, would invariably eat at The African Queen, although no one ever took any notice of him. There was never any sudden ambush by the paparazzi. This indifference to the famous by the residents of the Riviera was an attraction to Nicholson, Brad Pitt and Johnny Depp, who all lived nearby in unmolested peace, and was also a plus factor for the Earl. No one was fawned over just because they were a film star or an aristocrat; such people were so common to the region, they were part of the scenery.

The inevitable showdown between the Earl and Jamila came when she should have been at least seven months pregnant and there was still no sign of her carrying a child. The Earl confronted her at home in Cannes. In his subdued manner, he accused her of tricking him into marriage. She flew into a rage, keeping to the script that attack was the best form of defence, and all of this was overheard by staff in the kitchen. She denied lying to him, but claimed there was no baby now because she had undergone an abortion. He did not believe her.

'Are you calling me a liar?' she screamed.

'Yes,' he replied equably. Then he asked for the reason for the abortion when they were so affluent.

'Do I really have to tell you?' she yelled. 'You're an alcoholic. You're hooked on drugs. On top of everything else, you're sex mad, a pervert. What kind of father would you make, apart from a lousy one? What sort of example would you be to a child?' According to witnesses, she had just been sniffing cocaine before the Earl's arrival and had drunk a whole bottle of champagne.

'You've made a fool of me,' he said quietly but bitterly.

This reconstruction of the dialogue during this bust-up was put together by the police from statements taken from Jamila's domestic staff and was presumed to be a fair interpretation of the verbal savaging.

As a consequence, in April 2004, the Earl phoned his wife from Nice to say that they were officially separated and he planned to divorce her. The marriage was over, after less than two years.

'You'll be sorry,' she warned. This was no idle threat.

The clock was ticking.

11

THE
DYING EMBERS

The Earl began drinking more heavily than ever. He trawled the hostess bars of Cannes, Nice and Antibes. By now he was also sufficiently streetwise to conduct his own drug transactions. In his mid-sixties, he was rocking again, having sex with bar girls and escorts, seemingly strapped to a crazy, carousel lifestyle that was spinning ever faster and faster, perpetuating a vertiginous existence of drugs, drink and casual sexual encounters.

In order to preserve his sexual performance and prowess while ingesting so much alcohol, he used maximum-dose Viagra and was reputed to go considerably over the daily limit with his erectile pill-popping. Sex so dominated his life now that he was also paying for regular shots of testosterone. If he had been living in the USA, his physician would almost certainly have referred him to a sex-addiction clinic, such as the one where Michael Douglas was treated so successfully and proved that there was life after sexual suicide.

Jamila's brother, Mohammed, had moved from the south of France to live in Munich, Germany. He had debts and enemies to escape from, but he still visited his sister in Cannes, especially when in dire need of cash. When she called Mohammed to tell him that she and the Earl had split and he was divorcing her, he raged that once again she was spoiling everything. 'What's the matter with you?' he remarked, adding, 'We were on to such a good thing'. The reference to *we* convinced Jamila that, all along, her brother had seen himself as a major beneficiary in her marriage. He instructed his sister to seek a reconciliation, flattering her by saying that if she worked her magic on the 'old boy' his resolve would melt in no time at all.

From her later statements, it appears that Jamila vowed she would 'give it a go'. And she did. She fired off loving text messages, which the Earl stored in his mobile's memory but ignored. So she called him. 'But he was as cold as a corpse towards me,' she said later, with irony. For the Earl, there was no going back. He had been duped into marriage and he could no longer believe a word his estranged wife uttered. Despite his chaotic lifestyle at this point in the dying embers of his days, there were still moments – often unbelievably long periods – when he reasoned with astonishing clarity. Perhaps by now his body was tolerating the alcohol and cocaine to such an extent that he needed the combination in his blood in order to be *normal*.

While bar crawling in April 2004, he bought drinks in

the Golden Gate, one of his old-time favourite haunts, for attractive new acquaintance Nadia Orch, a thirty-three-year-old mother of two children. They talked and drank late into the night. Nadia, like Jamila's father, was Moroccan by birth.

By now, as an habitué of these back-street bars, Shaftesbury's sobriquet was 'Earl' to doormen, bartenders and the demi-monde. He was the big spender, the Brit with the upper-crust French accent – who could buy the Riviera to add to his other holdings, if he so chose, so went the myth that engulfed this bigger-than-life figure.

There had been a lot of jealous women – Nadia was not one of them, however – from the wrong side of town when Jamila snared 'old money bags', removing him from circulation and causing a mini-recession for the other bar girls. News travelled fast on the netherworld jungle-drums. Jamila had been seen in hotspots with different men; 'Earl' had been dating Gurtler's girls. The marriage was a mirage. 'Earl' was once more on the prowl and up for grabs. Not unnaturally, everyone wanted a slice of him. To some women, he was a generous gentleman; to the callous he was a sucker, ever ripe for the taking.

Nadia's lifestyle had been shaped by her circumstances: raising two children alone in a millionaires' playground like Cannes was horrendously expensive. She was in France to escape poverty, not to bring it with her as part of her baggage. She was determined that her children should be smartly dressed, well fed, and educated to a standard that qualified them for a profession and freed them from society's underbelly. These were the issues that Nadia and 'Earl' chatted about convivially during that first meeting. Nadia was very different from Jamila and the Earl warmed to her.

The feeling was mutual. They were surrounded by bawdy chat-up talk. Sex deals were being brokered. Money was exchanging hands. So, too, drugs. But this mellow long-running conversation, punctuated by orders for more drinks, was on a higher plane and a relationship was born.

That night, the Earl slept with Nadia at her stone cottage in Vence, another town situated on the coast, between Nice and Antibes. They discussed at length his marriages. Errant husbands had a tendency to return to their wives when the cost of divorce fully dawned on them. But the Earl was adamant: there would be no going back, he had no love left for Jamila, and he had already alerted her that divorce was a fait accompli.

Here again was a classic example of the Earl's repetitive impulsiveness. He dived into the deep-end of relationships with the immaturity of a schoolboy with a crush on a girl in the same class. Sex had become an imperative of his daily life, a necessity as much as food, drink and oxygen. But there always had to be affection, his anchor or mooring, while one-off, casual sex with other women was a snack between proper meals. However, Nadia was very soon more distressed by the Earl's drinking than by anything else he did.

Her concerns were reflected in what Nicholas, now the 12th Earl of Shaftesbury, had to say: 'My father was always drunk by lunch. It was as bad as that. There were a lot of spirits, a lot of wine. Initially, drink was a bolstering tool, but then it became a crutch. He never got violent or mad; he just withdrew. It was incredibly difficult for my mother. But she decided early on that she was going to stick around and safeguard the estate for me and Anthony. If it wasn't for her, a lot of this wouldn't be here.

'But one of the things that is often skated over is how much respect and loyalty the people on the estate had for my father. There was a huge fondness for him, until the drink started to take over and dominate his personality. He was a very charming man and spent many years doing amazing things with the estate and running this place very well.'

His father, he said, was a gentle soul who suffered from alcoholism and depression, and he used alcohol as a way of curing the pain and loneliness of his childhood: 'My earliest memory is of him clasping my hand and telling me how much he loved me and he never stopped saying how much he loved me and how proud he was of me. For this reason, we never stopped trying to help my father and protect him from the world around him.'

The Earl's lonely childhood, especially after his father's premature death, could account for his obsessional requisite for infinite female company. It is very Freudian and no one will ever know for certain, but his behaviour does suggest that many of the women in his life were, to some degree, mother substitutes, despite belonging to the demi-monde. They were French, like his mother, and they shared certain traits, particularly their strong wills and single-mindedness. Despite his own pragmatism, he was attracted to the opposite in women, those who most mirrored his mother, though not in her morals.

Nadia was strong-willed, but also fiercely caring. She craved a conventional home life, in which her children would grow up with security.

The town of Vence was built in the hills of the Alpes Maritimes department in the Provence-Alpes-Côte d'Azur region. Originally, Vence had been a medieval walled village. It is famous for its refreshing and alleged rejuvenating water that can be drawn from several hygienic fountains. The appeal for the Earl, apart from Nadia's presence, of course, was the town's history and architecture. The cathedral was built in the fourth century on the site of a Roman temple. A castle had been transformed into a modern art museum. The Earl was inspired by the knowledge that he and Nadia were living in the town where author DH Lawrence had lived; so, too, were Anglicist Émile Delavenay, and Jacques Morali, of disco music fame (Village People and 'YMCA'), who was born in Paris and buried in Vence. And with Nicholas promoting electronic music in New York, this connection probably bridged the Atlantic for the Earl, forging a spiritual proximity with his younger son.

Although a small town, with a population of only 19,000, the Earl was content there with Nadia, but he remained restless, an inherent chink in his makeup, probably enhanced by the drink and drugs. Nadia had no quarrel with his comings and goings — in fact, it helped to keep fresh their relationship — but she did disapprove of his excessive drinking, which led to several stand-offs (it cannot be stressed enough that the Earl never rowed). However, wherever he was in the world, he would always call Nadia several times every day, as a matter of ritual.

It seems that the Earl had never formally asked Nadia if she would marry him as soon as the divorce from Jamila was finalised, but frequently he would refer to future times when she was his wife, Nadia explained. Also according to Nadia, they both took it for granted that they would be married as soon as legally possible. If either of them had reservations about marriage, it was Nadia. She was genuinely frightened by his incessant drinking – not for her safety but for *his* health. After he had been away, once or twice she told him not to bother 'coming home' if he was drunk.

It seems that becoming a countess was no great pull for Nadia. Certainly she enjoyed the Earl's financial generosity, but a social position among the British aristocracy was meaningless to her. After all, the Earl had no intention of returning to the UK to live. France was his country of residence; it was Nadia's too. The Shaftesbury empire was nothing but a haunting demon for the Earl, so their future was always be in the south of France.

Marriage to the Earl promised financial security for the remainder of Nadia's life, but she was insistent that she was not looking for a marriage of convenience. There had to be love, respect and trust. They both had foibles and had erred in the past, but their joint failures could be used as building blocks for the future, she hoped. Nadia sought a commitment from the Earl that he would drastically reduce his daily alcohol consumption. She probably had no concept of how impossible it was for an inveterate alcoholic to conquer his addiction without professional counselling, plus the desire to kick the habit.

Throughout October 2004, a flurry of calls took place between Jamila and her wayward brother, Mohammed. This was established through phone company records. At this time, the Earl had been in Hove, Sussex, for several days, but, as ever, had been in regular contact with Nadia. He suggested that they take a ten-day holiday in Antibes before winter really set in with damp and murky weather. She was excited by the prospect and prepared for the vacation in fashionable Antibes, which was only a few miles away, and wondered if *her* Tony (the way she referred to the Earl) had news for her of his divorce and if he might be in a position to pop the question and propose a wedding date.

On 3 November, the Earl flew into Nice, the busiest airport in France outside Paris. English aristocrats had owned property in Nice for two or more centuries. Called Nice la Belle (Nice the Beautiful), it boasts the fifth largest population in France. There was the Promenade des Anglais ('the walkway of the English'), which said it all really. Like so many of the wealthy British gentry before him, the Earl was lured by Nice's natural beauty, mild climate, clean air and soft light that had for generations appealed to artists.

From the airport, the Earl phoned Nadia. Picture the scene: Nadia was all packed and ready to set off. Antibes, here we come! But the moment she answered the phone, she knew that the Earl was disgustingly drunk. After all the heart-to-heart discussions and pillow talk pledges to drastically reduce his drinking, temptation had got the better of him. He could not even abstain long enough to start the holiday sober.

Nadia was desperately disappointed, as much as being angry. She emphatically refused to go with him. He offered to go to their home in Vence to 'talk it over'. Her abrasive response was to tell him not to bother because she did not want to see him until he was sober. She then hung up. He called three or four times in quick succession, but she did not pick up.

So what did the Earl do? With the holiday in ruins before it began, he was led by his own internal navigation system, which directed him straight to Cannes and the tawdry bars. After doing the rounds, throwing around his money, he then did something strange, even for him. From his mobile, he called a fortune teller, Martine Dupre-Cordier, in Menton, reasonably close to Cannes, saying he wanted a reading – *urgently*. She replied that she had an available slot the following day. But for a reason known only to him, he was not prepared to wait until the following day for an appointment. It should be remembered that the 1st Earl of Shaftesbury consulted fortune tellers. The 10th Earl was aware of every little nuance and peccadillo of his ancestors. Maybe he wondered what the number one in the bloodline had gained from messages from sibyls. He never lost his appetite for knowledge and new experiences.

'It has to be today,' he implored. 'As soon as possible. Now!'

Despite having drunk sufficient alcohol to render most people unconscious, he was intelligible, said Martine. Although the French were renowned for their alcohol-consumption, second only to Luxemburg in the European league of big tipplers, it was a rare sight to see anyone who could not hold his/her liquor, mainly because their drinking was taken slowly over a long period. David Hampshire wrote tongue-in-cheek in his book, *Living and Working in France,* 'As every French person knows, intelligence, sexual prowess and driving skills are all greatly enhanced by a few stiff drinks.'

So Martine relented and agreed to a one-hour session at a fee of 50 euros, as long as he was prompt. He hired a taxi at a cost of 300 euros and politely shook hands with the fortune teller, thanking her profusely for giving up her time when obviously she was working overtime. As always, he was charming, and Martine was dazzled by his politesse. She was delighted that she had made a special concession for him.

As soon as the session began, he enlightened Martine about his relationship with Nadia and explained that he was there because he wanted to know if Nadia was pregnant and if she wasn't, would she bear his child in the future. This begs the question, of course, as to whether he was plagued by the memory of how Jamila had trapped him into marriage. If Nadia were to become pregnant, would the child be a girl, he further wanted to know. The reason for this addition to the original question is incomprehensible. It must be borne in mind that he had been drinking all day and his very presence at a fortune teller's was inexplicable and irrational. Her answers, for what they were worth, did not please him. She could not see a future for him with Nadia and therefore the question of a child did not arise.

Disgruntled, he mentioned that he was divorcing his wife.

'When I told him that it might not be so easy, he said he had not come to hear bad things,' Martine recollected. He offered her considerably more money to continue, but she declined it, believing that he was trying to bribe her into seeing a rosy future for him; in other words, he wanted to be told what he hoped to hear. But Martine would not compromise her integrity, so he departed disappointed.

So it was back to Cannes again by taxi for the nomadic Earl and straight to one of his old haunts, Le Barracuda, where he downed a load more, finally tottering out into the night that was halfway between midnight and dawn. At least he did not have a woman with him, but he was sufficiently coherent to check into the £130-a-night Noga Hilton Hotel on the brightly lit seafront 'Strip'.

In the morning, after a breakfast of sweetened black coffee, miniature vodkas from the room's mini-bar, and painkillers for a thumping headache, he was soon on top form. He phoned Jamila and invited her to have lunch with him at the hotel so they could discuss the divorce settlement in more detail. She accepted. Then he called Nadia.

As he sounded sober, she was much more agreeable than the previous day and wondered if they might now salvage the holiday, but by then the plan had been amended. He was going to have lunch with Jamila at the Hilton. It was imperative to have this meeting in a public place so that no lies could be told about his behaviour, he explained.

Nadia naturally was saddened that the holiday appeared to have been cancelled, or at least been put on hold, especially in order for the Earl to entertain Jamila, but her mood changed when he emphasised that the one-dimensional purpose of the lunch was to push along the divorce proceedings so that they could soon be married. A reconciliation was not on the agenda, he assured her. Now Nadia was euphoric and wished him luck.

'See you,' she said. A casual valediction, bristling with so much poignancy.

Jamila, however, stood him up. So instead of lunch for two, it was drinks for one.

Eventually, he phoned Jamila to find out why she had missed lunch without even having the courtesy to call him. Her story was that the subject was too sensitive for a busy restaurant, according to the account he related to Nadia. Many of the issues to be sorted were very confidential. How could they possibly be frank and explicit with so many strangers around? Also on her mind was that the next day, 5 November 2004, would be their second wedding anniversary. She was emotional, she told him, and hoped that he understood her sentimentality. At least they could be civil to one another, she later claimed to have pleaded, while suggesting that he visit her on their anniversary at the apartment he had bought for her, a place that housed so many fond, endearing memories. They could reminisce over the good times with a drink or two before getting down to the sordid business of winding-up their marriage. Reluctantly, he agreed, something that proved to be the defining moment in this rollercoaster saga.

The next day, on 5 November, the Earl headed for Avenue Maréchal Koenig, situated at the foot of La Californie, an exclusive residential cornucopia of Cannes, with a spectacular backdrop of red hills that seemed ablaze in the brilliant sunlight. He opened the double gates and walked nonchalantly up the pebbled path and to the first floor, an approach he had made hundreds of times before. Jamila was waiting for him. They kissed on the threshold, not passionately, just a polite French-greeting kiss: a peck on each cheek, equivalent to a sedate British handshake.

Despite the time of year, the Earl was dressed for summer: black T-shirt, a pair of baggy old jeans and scruffy trainers. It seems that he had not shaved and his hair was a tangled mess, according to Jamila's unflattering description.

The Earl was not in a sentimental mood. Jamila said it was readily transparent that he had been drinking again. She offered him a glass of wine and, naturally, he accepted, but he would not drink a toast to the future or their past together. Then it was down to business

The Earl announced that it was his intention to cancel Jamila's monthly allowance forthwith, something he had confided in Nadia. Jamila warned that he would 'not get away with that' and she would oppose him all the way, through her lawyer. This divorce was going to cost *him,* not *her,* she stressed combatively. He would not be walking all over her. She was still the Countess of Shaftesbury and taking that from her would come at a very high price.

She would be fighting for half the estate or 50 per cent of its value. Jamila was to contend that he laughed at her scornfully. She also claimed that it was soon apparent no common ground existed that would enable further discussion or agreement and so they parted icily. The only settlement reached was that the issues would be left to their respective lawyers.

Now, the countdown to calamity had reached its climax; the clock had stopped ticking.

12

DEADLY
SILENCE

Nadia waited for the Earl to call. But he did not and 5, 6 and 7 November passed without any contact from him. She tried reaching him between ten and twenty times each day. He did not answer. This was totally out of character – since their first night together, he had never failed to call Nadia at least twice a day, even when under the influence of his customary cocktail of drink and drugs. The Earl was almost robotic in some of his habits. Drinking at all hours was one example; keeping in touch with the current love of his life was another.

Nadia became frantic. She had landline numbers for his portfolio of properties – in, for example, Nice, Paris, Versailles, Hove and, of course, Wimborne St Giles. She tried phoning them all, except the estate, just in case Christina answered.

She heard nothing but ring sounds. As a last resort, she

decided to call the management office of the estate in Wimborne St Giles, which occupied one wing of St Giles House. No, the Earl was not there, they said. He had not been seen for many months. No, they could not help her with his whereabouts. Of course the name Nadia Orch meant nothing to them.

Nadia couldn't settle. She did not sleep. 'Tony [the Earl] didn't answer his phone any more,' she told the local media later. 'I was worried. I called again and again. This wasn't like him. I was sure something bad had happened. You get a feeling about these things, vibes. Bad vibes. Mostly he was attentive and such a generous man. People took advantage of his generosity, though.

'I feared so much that his excessive drinking could spoil everything. I thought refusing to see him until he was sober might help to straighten him out, bring him to his senses and prove how much he really loved me. "If you really love me as much as you say, then stop getting drunk," I said. "Do it for me." But it was hard for him. Hard for both of us. I did my best to understand him. He'd been drinking heavily for so many years. Long before it was common knowledge that he had an alcohol problem, he was a secret drinker. But he was very open about everything with me.

'No matter how much he'd had to drink, he was always very sweet and never abusive. When drunk, he wasn't the kind of man who would become violent or insulting. He had such good manners; that's why he was accepted in every establishment in Cannes, whatever his condition. Even if he could hardly stand up, he was still a gentleman. He was the most loveable man on earth, even in the bad times, and there were many of those.'

When all Nadia's efforts to reach the Earl failed, she contacted his Nice-based lawyer, Thierry Bensaude, who also had not heard from the Earl for a while, but he initially wasn't apprehensive. Like everyone else associated with the Earl, he knew all about his impulsive disappearances, only for him to reappear after a few days to continue a previous conversation as if he'd merely gone off to buy another round of drinks rather than taking a week-long hiatus. He was confident that the Earl would surface very soon. Nadia was not at all sure.

A 'dark shadow' had been cast over Nadia's life. Emotionally ragged, she had no one to turn to. Because she was not married, or even engaged, to the Earl, the local police in Vence did not take her enquiries seriously. After all, he was still married to someone else and they had only Nadia's word that he was divorcing Jamila. Probably they suspected that the Earl and Jamila were together again and Nadia was out in the cold. One could appreciate their perspective. There was not a shred of evidence to suggest that the Earl had come to any harm.

Ten days after the Earl's wedding anniversary and his visit to Jamila, he was still off everyone's radar. Nadia again called Mr Bensaude. Now he too was uneasy. He had been making his own enquiries through people who always had a hotline to the Earl and the outcome was another mysterious dead end.

Consequently, on 15 November, Mr Bensaude filed

an official missing person's report with the Nice police. Right from the outset this was recognised and conducted as a high-profile case, not one to be filed away to gather dust and await developments. The French police were pro-active and ready to work in conjunction with foreign law enforcement agencies including Interpol. Naturally, the first step was to have all the Earl's properties checked to ensure that he had not been taken seriously ill and collapsed in one of them. This meant coordinating with the police in Cannes, Paris, Versailles and Hove, and also Winfrith, the county headquarters of the Dorset Constabulary in England.

Despite the planned holiday in Antibes, the Earl had also been expected at his flat in Adelaide Crescent, Hove on 10 November, when he was meant to be conducting some legal business. This was confusing because if he had gone to Antibes with Nadia on 3 November for ten days, he couldn't possibly have been in Hove, England for the tenth. Nothing quite added up, but the police were soon to discover to their irritation that chaos was a recurring theme in the Earl's complicated life.

Mr Bensaude spoke by phone with Anthony, the Earl's elder son, who at the outset was not unduly worried. They chatted at length about where the Earl might be. The consensus was that he may well have been taken ill and was in hospital somewhere, possibly outside France and the UK. Because of the Earl's aggressive drinking, liver or heart disease were high probabilities, though, in either event, surely someone would have been contacted – Anthony, Lady Frances, one of his lawyers, the Countess (Jamila) or even Nadia. More likely, then, he had suffered a head injury, falling while intoxicated, and was unconscious or struggling with amnesia.

These were frustrating and tense times for everyone close to the Earl. Daily, Anthony spoke with the police in Nice, who were coordinating the search. A forced entry had been made into all properties and the Earl was not in any of them, which was both good and bad news.

When Anthony was advised that, on 18 November, there would be a nationwide appeal in France for information about the whereabouts of the Earl, he sensed the investigation was moving into a new phase. The tempo was being stepped up. The time had come for Nicholas to be fully apprised.

'I was sitting in a café in New York when Anthony rang,' said Nicholas. 'He said, "Dad has gone missing. We're slightly worried." He hadn't shown up for something. There was a sense of shit, something's happened here, because you always felt that something was going to happen.'

The public appeal went ahead and elicited several calls, but nothing that could be called a positive lead. The fact that the outcome from the public appeal by the police was disappointing should have come as no surprise to anyone with knowledge of the French public's attitude towards the law enforcement agencies. A survey conducted around the time of the Earl's disappearance revealed that the police were loathed by the public and considered a lower life form than prostitutes. By comparison, politicians were highly trusted and respected. However, when it came to voting, the abstentionists were by far the largest party!

Now that the police knew the Earl was not in any of his

residences, or in a hospital, so it seemed, the logical approach was to piece together his final movements before vanishing apparently into the ether. Mr Bensaude provided details of the Earl's matrimonial imbroglio and his petition for divorce. Nadia told the police about their argument and cancelled vacation, plus her lover's intended visit to his estranged wife Jamila, to 'clear the air' about annulling the monthly allowance and trying to speed up the process of dissolving the marriage.

What Nadia was unable to tell the police was whether the appointment with Jamila had gone ahead. 'I waited for a call from him, but it didn't come,' Nadia recalled weepily. 'Day after day we had been chatting repeatedly, lovingly, on and off, then complete silence. It was as if he'd dropped off the edge of the world. Everything stopped so suddenly. My life came to a standstill.'

Phone records showed that the Earl's mobile had been inactive since 5 November, the cut-off date. Everything had to revolve around that pivotal day. Guy Fawkes Day. The gunpowder plot. What kind of fireworks had engulfed the Earl? Domestic pyrotechnics or something bigger?

Jamila was interviewed at her home, the luxury apartment given to her as a present by her husband. She confirmed that the Earl had visited her, by appointment, on their second wedding anniversary. They had been alone and the meeting had been strained but civil. He had been drinking, as usual, but knew what he was doing and saying. She said that she was offended by his plan to end her monthly allowance. She considered his proposal unfair and demeaning, and intended to resist through her lawyer. They had kissed when he had arrived but not when he left.

Jamila was asked specifically about his condition when departing. No different from when he turned up, she said. Had she any idea where he was going next? No, but probably to one of the bars, she supposed. 'Or to his new woman!' she added. She suggested that they visit Le Barracuda and the Golden Gate, predicting that someone in one of those bars almost certainly saw him later in the day, especially that night.

She was questioned about ownership of the apartment, to which she replied, 'It's mine. No one can take this place from me. It was a wedding present from my husband, when all he ever wanted to do was please me. I soon found out, however, that there's nothing ever constant in the life of my husband. He's unstable. He is very rich and you do know that I am a genuine countess, don't you?' They had not known, and said as much. However, they did know a lot of other things about her, none of it flattering.

They picked up on her remark that the Earl was 'unstable' and asked her to elaborate. 'He's unreliable,' she explained. 'He changes his mind by the minute. You never know what he's going to do next. He makes plans, then changes them on a whim. When he's reasonably sober first thing in the morning, he'll make a decision, but by the afternoon, when he's drunk, he'll have forgotten all about his earlier intentions. You cannot believe a word he says because every day he's so drunk.'

She was thanked for her assistance, to which she said something like, 'Anytime. Just drop by.'

On the doorstep, one of the detectives thought of something else. Had she tried phoning the Earl since 5 November?

'No,' she replied. 'Why should I? I had nothing left to say to him. The next move was up to him.'

Jamila M'Barek, a countess! That was likely grounds for guffaws and swearing among the lower ranks of police officers when the detectives returned to their police station. What was the world coming to?

Jamila had been correct in one important assertion: the Earl was a regular in all the haunts where you would not expect to encounter an aristocrat. However, this line of inquiry soon ran out of steam. No one had seen him for days. And he was not someone you would forget. It was impossible to pin down bar owners, their staff and customers to a day or time of a last sighting. Many could not recall what they had done or who they had seen the night before. In this hazy environment of booze and drugs, a revolving door of tipplers came and went. Here was a very special kind of netherworld where the anarchists and dropouts were millionaires or billionaires. The Earl had become a multi-millionaire misfit in society. *He* was not so much missed as his money. Single-handedly, he had made a significant impact on the black economies of Cannes and Nice.

The police were not making any headway. Nadia was the one person who admitted having recently fallen out with the Earl. Also, the police had only her word that she had not seen him since his return to Nice and the aborted vacation. She had also been the one person pushing for an investigation right from day one of his disappearance. But could that have been a smokescreen to divert attention away from her?

The police had to keep an open mind and consider every possibility. So they called on Nadia at her cottage. She was fraught and frenetic, but apparently pleased that, at last, some action was taking place. She showed them around her home. The Earl had left behind a few belongings in the bedroom and bathroom, nothing of value or apparent consequence. The hoovering eyes of the officers sucked in everything. There was nothing to suggest that violence had occurred in any of the rooms, but Nadia would have had plenty of time to tidy up. But what possible motive could she have to harm the Earl? She was the one person who stood to gain most by keeping him alive.

The Earl's Nice-based lawyer had verified that his titled English client was divorcing Jamila so that he could marry Nadia, making her his new countess. Financially, Nadia would also gain immensely, not to mention her legal stake in properties and land, as long as the marriage was sealed. With the Earl out of the way, she was a loser. So if Nadia had harmed the Earl, it would have occurred only in a fit of rage; she would have been damaging her own prospects, tantamount to self-immolation. And if she had killed the Earl, how could she have disposed of the body? No one had heard a disturbance. Neither had the Earl been seen around Nadia's neighbourhood in November. Although making character judgments was a lottery, the police did not see Nadia as having a violent disposition. Against her, however, was the fact she remained a 'person of interest'.

Nadia willingly gave all her mobile details so that the police could run a check on her incoming and outgoing calls, plus texts. Her calls also produced a map of her movements, the equivalent of leaving a jungle trail that could be followed. The subsequent information gathered from the network provider substantiated Nadia's statement. The police quickly concluded that Nadia's distress was sincere and that she really cared about the Earl's safety. She pleaded with them to 'find him, whatever it takes'. One officer told me there was panic in her eyes and voice. It was not just the money that she was missing. Clearly the relationship had been a special one, despite the age gap.

Very soon the Shaftesbury family had dismissed the notion that the Earl was on one of his benders or mysterious vanishing tricks from which he would emerge unscathed and recharged. Anthony flew to France for a meeting with Commander Brunache, who had taken charge of the investigation. Brunache was highly rated in the police force and had an impeccable record. He was as shrewd as any villain and his clear-up rate was envied by his peers, of which there were few. A face-to-face meeting was helpful for both men. The Commander was able to garner from Anthony the kind of information about the Earl that had not been forthcoming from anyone in France.

So many of the people the police interviewed on the Riviera had their own dubious interests to protect. Anthony was candid. He acknowledged the truth in scandal stories about his father's out-of-control drinking and racy lifestyle. Drugs were a different matter. If the Earl had indeed become a cocaine user, or addict even, he said, the downward spiral must have commenced after he decamped to France, following his mother's death. As for womanising, well, yes, that had been an unfortunate peccadillo throughout his adult life, but only with non-British women; his real penchant was for French females, especially those of doubtful propriety but exuding a vibrant personality. Angels of the devil were his weakness. The Earl's sons knew their father much better than he knew himself.

Brunache assured Anthony that the Earl's disappearance was being taken 'very seriously'. He was frank with Anthony. 'There are a number of possible explanations for your father's disappearance,' he said. 'We are exploring all possibilities. He could have decided to disappear; people do that. He may have committed suicide or he could be a victim of crime.'

Suicide seemed unlikely. No note had been found anywhere. And surely a body would have come to light by now had he taken his own life, even if he had gone out to sea and jumped overboard. If he had done something like that, where was the boat? Of course, he could have been assisted by someone else, maybe even murdered that way, but once again, where was the corpse? It would have been washed ashore somewhere along the southern shores; the tides would have taken care of that.

Was he a Lord Lucan copycat? This theory had legs and it was soon a runner!

Lucan, as mentioned in the prologue, had disappeared into oblivion in 1974 after murdering his children's nanny, Sandra Rivett. France had almost certainly been Lucan's first port of call in his elaborate escape. It had been thirty years since that astounding vanishing act. The police and press had always been convinced that Lucan must have received help from a number of powerful people. The 10th Earl of Shaftesbury would have been in his thirties when Lucan had done his infamous runner. They would not have been friends, not even casual acquaintances. But the Earl might easily have become privy to the modus operandi and he certainly had millions more pounds to pay conspirators than Lucan, who was virtually broke. If anything had suddenly become too much for the Earl to bear, after a slow, progressive burn, might he not have tried the Lucan formula – the lords' escape?

Helen O'Brien, former owner, with her husband, of the Eve Club in London's West End, was already living in Nice. All her club members at the Eve had been aristocrats and leading politicians. There was also the fact that she had spied for British Intelligence and was acquainted with the Earl. They had met a couple of times for cocktails in Nice. If anyone had a genuine clue as to the fate of Lucan –and maybe even the Earl – it was Helen, who died in 2005, having outlived her husband.

This theory was tasty. But did it pass the litmus test of logic? The Commander did not think so. Lucan was a killer. The Earl was a pacifist. Lucan was deeply in debt through his gambling. The Earl was loaded, despite his extravagant living. Lucan faced dying in gaol. The Earl faced marriage to an exuberant young beauty who gave him immeasurable pleasure.

Of course an alcoholic and cocaine addict was liable to

behave irrationally, but this was a very compelling reason for Brunache's cynicism towards the Lucan syndrome. A clear head and glacial detachment were required to pull off a Lucan-type stunt. The Earl was emotional and his head was normally only completely clear for a couple of hours in the morning. Also, the Earl was gregarious when he had been drinking and sniffing and was not a loner like Lucan, despite a disparaging assessment to the contrary by the very biased Jamila. Hence, Brunache's instincts steered him away from James Bond storylines.

In Wimborne St Giles parish church, the Rev. David Paskin led prayers for a 'happy outcome' to the conundrum. 'Everyone is anxious and concerned,' he told reporters. 'It's the unknown that's so worrying. Lady Shaftesbury (Christina) is very concerned.' Officially, of course, Christina was now the Dowager Countess of Shaftesbury, but no one in Dorset accepted Jamila, especially those with close links to the Shaftesbury family.

Meanwhile, the French press were in a feeding frenzy. There was little reference, though, to the Earl's wealth; his title was the selling factor. To fully understand this it is necessary to be au fait with French culture. In his book, *Living and Working in France,* David Hampshire wrote, 'In many ways the French are even more class and status conscious than the British (it was the Normans who introduced class into Britain, with classes ranging from the aristocracy – *les grandes familles,* otherwise known as the guillotined or shortened classes – and upper bourgeoisie, through the middle and lower bourgeoisie to the workers and peasantry). The French class system is based on birthright rather than wealth and money does not determine or buy status.' A missing aristocrat was front-page headline news in France, even if he was a pauper, which the Earl most certainly was not, of course.

This culture also influenced the attitude of the police. This is not to suggest that the French police would have ignored the report of a missing peasant, but it is fair to conclude that the response would not have been so dynamic.

Lady Frances, the Earl's sister, sought an input from Detective Chief Superintendent Graham Cox, the head of Sussex CID, as the Earl had a base in Hove in Sussex. After listening to Lady Frances's narrative, Cox liaised with Commander Brunache in France.

A month after the Earl had been reported missing by Nadia, Cox announced that he and his force were treating the case as one of murder. Simultaneously, Brunache publicly declared that he agreed with Cox, 'due to the lack of a ransom demand or evidence of fraud'.

The Earl had numerous credit cards but none had been used. Since 4 November, there had been no transactions involving any of the Earl's many bank accounts, no money had been withdrawn or transferred. If he was still alive, how was he surviving?

Still, there remained an element of uncertainty and a sliver of hope that he might not be dead and could be rescued. 'While there was no body, there was hope,' Brunache reasoned optimistically. He was a naturally upbeat leader, one who would pluck a positive from a graveyard of negatives.

In a further statement, Jamila told how she had warned

her husband about the 'bad company' he kept and the risks he was taking. A very strong theory was that the Earl had been kidnapped by Russian or North African gangsters who were plotting to steal his fortune or demand an astronomical ransom. Giving credence to this theory, Jamila claimed that she had returned one day to her Cannes apartment to find her husband in the company of a 'large Arab and two Arab women who were rifling through the wardrobes'.

The Earl, according to Jamila, was standing on a stool, singing and dancing, 'making a fool of himself'. The women had departed with a 'car-load' of Jamila's clothes, if she could be believed.

The Earl, of course, was not around to contradict the yarn. Certainly the possibility of kidnapping was highly possible. Most people with the Earl's sort of status and opulence kept either a low profile or plenty of bodyguards. The Earl kept neither. The police could see that he was a prime target; but, if so, why the silence from the kidnappers? Why no ransom demand? The family's original suspicions were in tune with this possible scenario.

Violent crime was on the increase throughout France, but especially in the south. In fact, the Mediterranean coast had become one of the most corrupt and crime-ridden regions in all Europe, worse than any city or area of the UK: so beautiful, yet so bad, a mirror image of many of the glamorous women who contributed so much to the allure of the Côte d'Azur. Gang warfare was rife and escalating, particularly in Cannes and Marseille.

Within the underworld operating on the Riviera, the

most dangerous by far was the French mafia, known as Le Milieu. Marseille had been linked to organised crime, drug trafficking (previously immortalised in the Hollywood blockbuster *The French Connection,* starring Gene Hackman), money-laundering, armed robbery and prostitution. Now gangsters had expanded further east along the coast, polluting the swinging resorts of Nice, Cannes, St Tropez and Antibes. There are no prizes for guessing why: as rats are attracted to garbage, so the mafia is drawn to money – especially easy money. The nouveau riche, with their swanky yachts and sporty cars, used drugs, especially cocaine, as if weaned on them; it was their daily bread. The market was there. Demand was ravenous and perpetual, and like oxygen, the requirement was year-round.

In the past, a motley collection of southern gangs had traded on only their own turf, content to be limited to a single patch, as if owning a vegetable allotment, cultivating rackets that yielded a modest annual return. But the mafia did not function that way. With the beefed-up rackets so lucrative, they wanted it all. The dealers of old had been comparatively small-time hoodlums. If armed, it would have been with a flick knife at most. Everything changed with the mafia invasion. They stormed in with guns and military-styled raids and ambushes. Bodies were washed up. This was a ruthless takeover. Anyone resisting went out in a blitz of bullets. Some simply disappeared quietly and mysteriously, the way the Earl had done.

Before too long, the old dealers had been absorbed by the mafia, who had flics (cops) on their payroll and so suffered less interference by the law. Quickly they doubled and trebled the street value of their illegal commodities.

People like the Earl, however, were not deterred by price. The Earl would have had no idea of the going rate of cocaine. He would not haggle. Whatever the price quoted, he would pay, and he was just one of many users of that ilk on the Riviera. The mafia looked on them as juicy grapes in a vineyard: ripe for the picking – and all year, not just for a season. Occasionally other gangs tried to poach and then there would be bloodshed. Sometimes innocent people were caught in the crossfire, like the Earl. Maybe the Earl was indeed one such victim?

By the 1990s, kidnapping had also become a big earner. This racket morphed out of crimes carried out by scoundrels known as 'Highwaymen of the South'. A typical way of operating was to pose as cops and set up a roadblock. Motorists would stop and be robbed of all their money, credit cards and other valuables. Often they were even made to strip and were abandoned naked on the roadside at night.

Before the police had even processed reports of such crimes, the stolen cars would already be on ferries to North Africa. But for the mafia, highway robbery was too small beer to be bothered with. Kidnapping multi-millionaires and demanding ransoms for their release had gold-standard appeal as a perpetuating business plan for organised French crime. It was within this context that Brunache had to evaluate the Earl's disappearance. He desperately needed a lead, something vestigial to show where the trail began.

The Commander had taken seriously Jamila's allegations

about the Earl and possible threats to him from gangsters. So his questioning was forensic. What had she said to her husband after the Arabs had left? She had replied that she wanted to know what they were doing in *her* apartment (the Earl, of course, had a key). But he would not discuss it, said Jamila. He was 'bombed' again. He just wanted sex. The Commander was puzzled. How many of her clothes had the women run off with?

'A wardrobe full.'

'And you just accepted it?'

'The clothes had been paid for by my husband and he said, "Don't fuss so. I'll replace them for you. Get me a drink."'

Then came the million-dollar question. How did she know that the Arab man was a gangster? Her reply was that it was a 'known fact' in the bars.

'So what was his name?' She did not know.

'What criminal activity did he specialise in?'

'Drugs, robbery and fraud.'

'Had he served time in gaol?' She was unable to answer that question too.

'Who knows. When these people are not around for some weeks or months, who knows where they've been. These people come and go. That's how it is down here. Surely you know that?'

Had she seen the Arab and the women before? – 'Yes, in the bars.'

Paradoxically, Jamila's story struck a chord of plausibility. In the days leading to the Earl's disappearance, he had complained that a number of his antiques and some money had been stolen. Brunache was not immediately in the loop on this matter, and to appreciate the reason for that it is necessary to understand the French policing system.

There are three main police forces: the police nationale, the gendarmerie nationale and the Compagnie Républicaine de Sécurité (CRS). The formal way of addressing French policemen is *monsieur l'agent*, but on the street they are commonly called *flics*. The Interior Ministry oversees the police nationale, known as agents de police. Their brief is dealing with all crime within the jurisdiction of their respective police stations and these officers are mostly seen in towns and distinguished by shiny, silver buttons on their uniforms. In rain and fog, and at night, they wear white caps and capes in order to be readily identified.

In contrast, the gendarmerie nationale is army controlled under the Ministry of Defence umbrella. These officers wear blue uniform, traditional kepi and gold buttons. Their beat is the national arena (like a Flying Squad), investigating offences often associated with organised crime (such as the mafia) and rural mob violence, and carrying out mountain rescue operations and air patrols along the coasts, looking for drug-smugglers and illegal immigrants in boats. A broad remit that frequently crosses into the territory of other forces. The CRS are basically the riot police, controlling demonstrations and rebellions.

However, in addition to these three main groups, nearly all cities and towns of a reasonable size have their own municipal force – police municipal corps urbain – for investigating petty crime, traffic offences, road accidents and hooliganism. As in the UK, neighbourhood policing is seen as the enlightened way forward.

Normally, the local officers did not carry weapons, unlike those of the three main arms of law enforcement. There are also special forces, such as the 'police judiciaire' (PJ), which is the equivalent of the UK's Criminal Investigation Department (CID).

The Earl's complaint of theft was bogged down in the files of the municipal force of Nice. France is the most bureaucratic country in the entire world. Whatever a citizen is applying for through the civil service, on average ninety-eight forms have to be completed in quintuplicate, then signed by forty-seven officials in thirty-one different government departments – just, for example, a disabled driver's parking badge! Similar bureaucratic madness is prevalent in the police departments, readily explaining why any complaint of theft has to be made in person at the local police station and a detailed report (*déclaration de vol/plainte* filed. The complainant is given a copy of the report to keep as a record. Initially, the Earl had tried to make his report by phone, dialling 17 – the emergency number in France – but was told that nothing could be done without him making a personal appearance and spending between two and three hours form-filling.

His disappearance, possible kidnapping and even murder, came very much into the domain of the PJ and the police nationale. These were elite forces, and overlapping with lower-ranking agencies was rare, which fully explained the delay in making the connection with the theft allegation, which, in any event, had not been properly filed. But in relation to the Earl's disappearance, was the alleged theft merely a diversion anyway?

Regarding kidnappings, there was another headache for Brunache: when the victim was very rich and/or powerful, often the family or employers secretly hired private negotiators and behind-the-scene deals were brokered to secure a release without either the police or press hearing about the clandestine trade-off. Frequently, the police were not even informed after a ransom had been paid and the victim liberated. Brunache had to be confident that Anthony had not contracted mercenaries or private hostage-brokers to try to free his father.

The Earl's heir was adamant: there had been no ransom demand, although he and the family had been anticipating one. He also gave his word that the investigation would be left to the French police, in whom he had every confidence.

The mafia were never slow when it came to issuing ransom demands, so, if the Earl had been kidnapped, the police were sceptical that gangsters affiliated to organised crime were responsible. International terrorists operated differently, however. For a start, money was not always the objective. More often, politics was the underlying motive. And those cabals were sometime content to *sit on* their catch for weeks or months, to stretch the suspense, before breaking silence – and then maybe even to stage a public execution, as seen so often in the Middle East in recent years.

Despite the dilemma and many plausible possibilities, Brunache soon concluded that terrorists were unlikely to have been instrumental in whatever had happened to the

Earl. However, the involvement of organised crime was still a viable possibility. Had it not been for his lifestyle, the Earl's domestic situation would have been the main attraction for the police right from the outset. One of the golden rules for anyone in Paris or on the south coast was never to flash around money. The Earl had committed that cardinal sin daily, whenever in Paris and certainly on the Riviera. He lived as if he believed himself immune and immortal. Despite his unique grasp of every region of France, he either overestimated his own instincts or underestimated the dark motives of people of whom he was fearless.

Putting aside the more exotic theories, Brunache began focusing on who would benefit from the Earl's death, always a sound starting point. Not Nadia. Not any of the drug dealers. Not the owners of bars or restaurants. Not the proprietors of escort agencies. Nor the whores. Brunache was left with two people: Anthony, the Earl's elder son and heir, and Jamila, the whore-countess who was on her way to being sidelined if the Earl lived to see the divorce go through. Inevitably, codicils would have been added to the Earl's will to exclude Jamila after the divorce. The allowance was to be stopped and she would have no portion of the estate. After all, they had been married for only two years, and Jamila had never made any contribution to the running of the estate. Quite literally, she had only ever been a sleeping partner.

Brunache liaised with Superintendent Cox in Sussex. Both agreed that with no signposts indicating they should be exploring other routes, Jamila had to be the prime suspect.

But without a body, they were stymied. However, another long-shot possibility existed, something else to whet the appetite of the French investigators.

Scotland Yard had been keeping a watching brief, not taking an active role but ready to assist if asked. The French authorities knew all about the Lord Lucan case because he was still on the official international 'wanted' list. But there was another case, possibly more relevant, that the new generation of French detectives might not have been familiar with.

'Parallel cases' were always worth considering because they could be blueprints for subsequent mimic crimes. The case file passed to the police in Nice by Scotland Yard was that of senior UK Member of Parliament John Stonehouse, who went missing on 20 November 1974. (Strange how the month of November kept popping up! The Earl was last seen on 5 November. On 15 November, he was reported missing. On 18 November, the police issued a public appeal. And on 20 November 1974, a neatly folded pile of Stonehouse's clothes was found on a beach in Miami, Florida, where he was on holiday. Just a coincidence, no doubt.)

When Stonehouse failed to return to his hotel and there was still no sign of him a couple of days later, the Miami Beach police presumed he had gone swimming and drowned or had been savaged and devoured by a shark. There seemed no other plausible explanation and solemn obituaries appeared in all British national newspapers. A tribute was paid by Prime Minister Harold Wilson. Stonehouse had been Minister of State for Technology and Postmaster General in

Labour governments. At one time he was even seen as a potential future prime minister.

Unfortunately, outside politics he had become a rogue dealer, setting up a chain of dodgy companies, one of them a bogus international charity, purportedly for flood-devastated Bangladesh but really for lining his own pockets. As his financial quagmire thickened and he became increasingly bogged down, so he resorted to deceptive, creative accounting. And he had not died in the sea off Florida.

While the US Coastguard was searching the south Atlantic for a body, Stonehouse was winging his way first-class to Australia, travelling on a false passport with a new identity. Waiting for him in Sydney was his ex-Parliamentary Secretary and current mistress, Sheila Buckley.

In a further twist, Stonehouse bore a striking resemblance to the missing Lord Lucan. Several Australians contacted the police to say they were sure they had spotted Lucan, who was still wanted in the UK for murder. This fitted neatly with the Scotland Yard hunters' theory, who had earmarked South Africa or Australia as the two most likely countries Lucan might have headed for, if still alive. The Riviera was another strong possibility, because of the ritzy casinos in Cannes, Nice and Monte Carlo.

Following further tip-offs, the Australian police arrested Stonehouse on Christmas Eve, 1974, convinced they had netted Lord Lucan, a major coup for them. A comic sketch appeared later of Stonehouse being made to drop his trousers. Lucan had a six-inch scar on the inside of his right thigh. There was no such scar on the man they had in custody.

Initially, the police were disappointed, but they soon learned that their catch was still a big one. However, it was another six months before Stonehouse was deported to the UK: during the interim, he unsuccessfully sought asylum in Sweden and Mauritius. Eventually, he was tried at the Old Bailey on twenty-one charges of fraud, theft, forgery, conspiracy to defraud, causing a false police investigation and wasting police time. On conviction, he was sentenced to seven years in gaol.

It was not until more than twenty years after Stonehouse's death in 1988 that the Australian 'catch' was revealed as far larger than anyone could have possibly imagined at the time: since 1962 and throughout his entire House of Commons career as a senior minister, Stonehouse had been a paid Communist spy, selling secrets about the government's plans and technical military information.

Police psychologists in France added their input into the Earl's disappearance. All people under severe stress had a snapping point. The amount of pressure a person could shoulder varied. However, there was a common thread. When people 'broke', the urge was to run, not just to flee from the unbearable mental load but to escape from themselves. They craved to be anyone other than who they were. They wished to be reborn, to wipe clean the slate and make a fresh start. And the only way that could be achieved was by faking death and re-emerging as a completely different person. It had been done, certainly by a number of high-ranking Nazis. But 'death' followed by instant resurrection required money – a lot of it – and it was therefore an option available only to a limited number of people.

The shrinks believed that the Earl had slipped into the high-risk category for a Stonehouse-type emulation. His life was a tangled mess, comparable to a domestic Spaghetti Junction. He had fled from his onerous responsibilities in the UK, unloading all the burdens on to his young son, the loyal wife he betrayed and divorced, and his doughty sister. His alcoholism, drug-consumption and sexual incontinence were all symptoms of escapism, but that had a limited lifespan of its own. The next stage without professional intervention would be death from liver failure, coronary disease or an overdose – or any combination of the three. There was the distinct chance, the shrinks believed, that he could have 'disowned himself completely' and resorted to reinvention. The Earl certainly had enough money to give it a try.

Against this theory was the fact that for rebirth much preparation was required. Long before Stonehouse had staged his 'death' in Miami, he had set up a worldwide network of bank accounts in his soon-to-be-assumed new identity. There had been financial transactions so money would be available to draw upon as soon as he arrived in Australia. No money had been transferred out of any of the Earl's bank accounts in France or the UK. All his clothes, passport and credit cards were in his Nice home. Nothing appeared removed. It was obvious he had clearly expected to be returning. If he had done yet another runner, it had been without preparation, a spur of the moment, reflex response to something foreboding and intimidating.

The Stonehouse storyline had Hollywood seductiveness and tinsel, but it did not gain traction with Brunache. He was certain that the Earl's fate was much more down to earth and prosaic.

The circumstantial evidence against Jamila was far too flimsy. True, Jamila seemed to have been the last person to spend time with the Earl before he vanished, but this was insubstantial when applied to a man with the reputation of a rake, hooked on cocaine and also addicted to hookers. The fact that Jamila had a police record was meaningless too. Every citizen of France has a police record, even if it is blank. This was another example of France's obsession with bureaucracy. Much is held on file about everyone, even if unrelated to crime. The public call this intrusion their 'Big Brother with the long nose'!

The absence of a body would be argued by the defence as evidence that that was no crime. How could the police refute a proposition that the Earl might have sailed off into the sunset with a coterie of fellow aristocrats, currently in a stupor on one of the seven seas? They could not. Also, French law made it more difficult for the police to go on non-specific explorations against suspects. Everyone arrested had a statutory right to a lawyer within three hours and were not obliged to answer a single question. Silence by suspects could not be held against them, which differs from amended English law.

The French justice system is inquisitorial. Suspects are interrogated by an independent examining magistrate. This can commence only after access to a lawyer has been granted to the detainee and the right to silence still remains. So although the Shaftesbury family were hungry for action, the softly-softly-to-catch-a-monkey approach made sense.

Find the body became the police mantra. In the meantime, Jamila was giving media interviews as the countess who had been deserted by her British aristocrat husband on their wedding anniversary. Changing tack, she then feared that he might have had a heart attack and be lying dead out in the wild, rotting like a penniless vagabond with no family, with his loved ones unable to give him a proper burial. Her conjecture apparently changed by the day. Her favourite, which was to be repeated many times, was that the Shaftesburys were somehow behind the Earl's disappearance. She had never been accepted by the family, she declared, which at least had the merit of truth. The family were afraid that the Earl would 'blow' the Shaftesbury fortune. There was also truth in that. She would never be accepted on the estate as the chatelaine and rightful Countess of Shaftesbury and stepmother of the two sons despite the indisputable legality of her position.

But she did not stop there. She accused 'unknown persons' connected to the Shaftesburys of having paid for the Earl to be kidnapped, flown to the UK, probably in a light aircraft from Nice that could have landed within the grounds of St Giles House, where he was being held a 'prisoner', or he might have been admitted to a detox clinic against his will, in England, guarded at all times to ensure that he did not abscond. 'Aristocrats will do anything to safeguard their status and heritage,' she told the press. 'That is why in France we guillotined them all!' There was also the possibility that the

Earl had been sectioned in the UK for his errant behaviour, supposedly for his own safety, she further maintained in one of her many scattergun rants.

Son Anthony was kept informed of Jamila's sweeping accusations and outbursts, which he treated with contempt. So did the police. Detectives were working unobtrusively and methodically, out of the spotlight, garnering evidence through modern technology. Less sophisticated, so far, was the search by uniformed officers and the Gendarmerie nationale. The countryside around Cannes and Nice posed a daunting challenge for a body hunt – as arduous in its own way, if not more so, than the Australian outback.

Vence, Nadia's hometown was central to the region where dogs and helicopters were deployed. Vence typified the communities and landscape inland from the Mediterranean. In fact, all development in the Côte d'Azur amounted to a strip along the coastline. There were few buildings ten miles inland of the Mediterranean. The late Sidney Sheldon treated his readers to a vivid description in his 1996 novel, *Morning, Noon & Night*, when he wrote of Vence as 'weaving its ancient magic on a hilltop in the Alpes-Maritimes, situated inland between Cannes and Nice. It is surrounded by a spectacular and enchanting landscape of hills and valleys covered with flowers, orchards and pine forests. The village itself, a cornucopia of artists' studios, galleries and wonderful antique shops, is a magnet for tourists from all over the world.'

For mile after mile there are red hills, plunging valleys and deep ravines, woodland, jacaranda trees, olive groves, shrub land, and the all-pervasive perfume of lavender and jasmine.

But the winters are becoming harsher, the mistrals sharper. Not so long ago, snow was a rare spectacle, but now it was a regular sight in winter, perishing plants and bemusing the natives the way it would if it became a feature of southern Florida. Cicadas and lizards were in hibernation. And the chilly weather was hampering the searchers, especially as the police had no real map reference to focus on.

'All we could do was take Cannes as the last place where the Earl had been seen and to fan out from there,' said Brunache. But the Earl could also have been disposed of in any of the urban conurbations, so there was no great momentum or enthusiasm behind the rural exploration. He could even have still been alive, living with a new identity in his beloved Corsica, with assets that he had stashed away years previously. The permutations were incalculable.

'More hopeless than looking for a needle in a haystack on our estate,' son Anthony lamented. 'But I'm positive there's one person who could lead us straight to my father.' He had Jamila in mind, of course. And he was biased with bile, it must be admitted.

In February the following year, 2005, there was a development that caught everyone off-guard. Jamila had an 'emotional' breakdown and was admitted to a psychiatric hospital. She was said to be hysterical and required sedating. And while under sedation, she began muttering some alarming revelations, which staff believed the police should hear about without delay. Hence, detectives were Jamila's first visitors, though they were not armed with flowers, fruit or chocolates.

In all solved criminal cases, there is a breakthrough moment, though it is not always recognised at the time; this one was, however. At last the first cracks were beginning to show. Brunache was rubbing his hands because he already knew considerably more than he was leaking to the public domain. The net had been cast wide. Now it was narrowing. He was beginning to see more than one spider almost in his web.

Sometimes with murder, as in dancing, it takes two to tango.

13

LADY
MACBETH

A doctor and nurse reported to detectives that Jamila had been verbally 'wandering', mumbling about her husband's death, saying she was to blame and it was all a terrible mistake. At one point, when apparently feverish, she muttered, 'He shouldn't have died; that wasn't meant to happen... If only he hadn't been so stubborn and demanding... I wanted to stop it happening... It was so horrible... I panicked... I blame myself... I feel so guilty.' This apparent catharsis was repeated over and over, so staff were able to cobble it together for the record.

Brunache was unimpressed. The so-called 'wandering' — or rambling — was rather too well structured. The sentences were precise, as if coming from a very clear head. Many of the highly paid call girls of the Riviera had police clients who were treated to freebies in exchange for tip-offs relating to law-enforcement action. He suspected that Jamila already knew the net was tightening. The *nervous breakdown* was an artifice, designed to buy her breathing space, the hardened murder investigators reasoned, and the 'wanderings' were no such thing, rather a calculated tactical manoeuvre by an ice-hearted Lady Macbeth. But what was her game? Where was this apparent self-incrimination leading? Of one thing they were certain: along the way there would be a get-out clause for herself, her parachute.

Commander Brunache ordered a round-the-clock watch on Jamila at the psychiatric hospital. As soon as doctors declared her fit enough to be discharged, she was driven along the coast to police headquarters in Nice, where Brunache was waiting for her. The interview was to be conducted in a room fitted with state-of-the-art audio and video recording equipment.

There was expectancy among all the senior murder inves-tigators in Nice: 25 February 2005 was to be a momentous day. A breakthrough day! That was the mood.

The Commander proceeded courteously and cautiously, beginning by saying, in French, of course, that he believed Jamila wanted to ease the burden that had been making her ill. She had been saying disturbing things in hospital and now was her chance to clear the air and end her misery.

Jamila vacillated, so Brunache teased her along, putting to her the mutterings hospital staff had overheard. Still she wavered. None of that could be believed, she said. She had been talking gibberish. Carefully crafted gibberish, thought Brunache. None of her psychiatric wanderings could be held against her, she maintained, because they were symptoms of her mental condition.

Brunache's antenna was on a wavelength matched by few officers. He picked up signals that would be missed by most investigators. He believed that Jamila was playing a game of cat and mouse with them. So he played along. She must have considered herself the cat. Brunache allowed her to continue thinking that she was toying with mice. In reality, if not exactly a mouse, Jamila was a pussycat, while Brunache was a big cat – lion-big, king of the crime-busting jungle.

She asked for specific comments she had made in hospital to be read to her. Brunache obliged, although he had no doubt that every word she had uttered had been scrupulously edited in her brain before being released to her mouth. Behind his implacable exterior, he must have been smiling to himself. She was canny, he had to acknowledge almost admiringly, but more fox than cat, such a manipulator, her skill doubtlessly honed on the escort circuit on which all the men were branded mugs. Unbeknown to her, however, she had met her match.

'Did I mention my brother?' she asked, her voice laced with innocence.

'Not that I've heard,' said Brunache. 'Perhaps now is the time to tell us everything.' And all the while he was saying to himself, *She knows we're on to her, so what's her line going to be? Which way is she going to jump or wriggle?*

Finally, she said, 'I don't want to do this, but I can't live with it any longer. It's making me so ill. It landed me in hospital. I will go permanently insane if I don't bring closure to this mess.'

Brunache sat back, ruminating, like a poker player studying the upturned cards on the table and wondering what else was in the pack. *I must give her the rope to hang herself with,* he was thinking (incidentally, the death penalty was abolished in France in 1981).

For several minutes Jamila talked about betrayal and how families should always stick together. But there was a limit, especially when, she said, you had 'a brother who was a dangerous head case'.

Ah! Brunache now began to see where this was heading. This was going to be a watered-down confession. Not really a confession at all, but a slimy exercise in passing the buck.

As if driven to despair by the weight of someone else's guilt she had been shouldering, her story came out in drops, like water from a dripping tap. She had lied, but only to protect her 'mad' brother, Mohammed, who had killed the Earl, something Brunache already knew; it was one of the behind-the-scenes secrets gleaned from a network of authorised police wiretaps (more about that later). The killing had not been planned, Jamila professed, though Brunache had evidence to the contrary. Mohammed had arrived unexpectedly at the apartment (another lie) on 5 November, 'horrifying' Jamila, because the Earl was due.

Brunache continued to listen, although he knew that Jamila had arranged for Mohammed to be there, having driven in his BMW all the way from Munich, where he was living with his wife and children.

Brunache was allowing her plenty of slack, letting her version be recorded before he began nibbling away at the edges, and before launching into a complete demolition job. Jamila had showed her brother into a bedroom, instructing him to stay there, 'no matter what'. She further told her brother, she claimed, 'This has nothing to do with you and I don't want you interfering. I don't want any trouble or unpleasantness. He shouldn't be here long. I'll get rid of him as quickly as possible.'

By now Jamila was in full flow. The Earl had reiterated that he intended putting a stop to Jamila's monthly allowance. She had protested, but he was not prepared to relent or compromise. He was going to marry Nadia and he wanted to reduce his outgoings as much as possible. 'In other words, I could go to hell,' Jamila said. 'He had used me, got all he wanted from me, which was nothing more than perverted sex, and now I was no more use to him.' She managed a couple of tears as she referred to herself as nothing more to the Earl than a spent cartridge or a used condom. Colourful rhetoric, which must have sounded well rehearsed.

The stage was still all Jamila's. She dropped her head. The prelude was over. Now to the nitty-gritty. Mohammed must have been listening to the conversation while smoking cannabis: she gave no indication at this point how she knew he was ingesting pot while hiding, though later explained that she had smelt it when the bedroom door opened.

Suddenly the bedroom door had burst open and Mohammed appeared, fuming, all fired up to 'protect' his sister from this 'arrogant monster'. He engaged in verbal combat with the Earl, calling him a rat and 'no gentleman', a 'disgrace' to his class and country. Jamila, trying to be the 'grown-up one' of the three, had endeavoured to 'cool things'.

The moment had been reached when Jamila was about to parachute out!

Just as Mohammed seemed to be responding to her pleas, the docile Earl physically attacked the much younger and muscular man, and a full-scale punch-up broke out. Jamila tried to intervene, but was pushed away. Unable to watch, she ran into the kitchen, hands to her ears to block the noise. Then there was silence.

When she ventured out of the kitchen, the Earl was motionless on the floor, with Mohammed crouched over him, giving mouth-to-mouth resuscitation. When the Earl failed to respond, Mohammed tried heart massage, still to no avail.

'Neither of us could believe my husband was dead,' she said, just before her head went into her hands. 'It was unreal. How could someone die that easily? He must have had a heart attack. Mohammed was just defending himself. There was blood on the floor, but I didn't know if it had come from my husband or brother. We were both in a state of shock. But there was nothing we could do for Tony. My brother was stumbling around in a daze, shaking his head. "He just went limp", he said.

'All Mohammed was doing was trying to hold him off. Admittedly, Mohammed should have stayed in the bedroom, but my husband started the fight. He was so drunk. He was in a drunken rage. I've never seen him like that before.

The drink and cocaine mixture must have damaged his health so much, especially for a man of his age. Despite our disagreement, I didn't want anything like this to happen. It was awful. And on our second wedding anniversary! So sad. Such a waste. And all so unnecessary. My brother went on his knees and prayed. I was sick.'

Jamila had reached a full stop. She probably thought she had done rather well. After all, how was anyone to dispute her story?

Brunache allowed the silence to become uncomfortable before saying simply, 'And then what?'

Jamila thought about this before answering, 'We didn't know what to do.'

'Did you send for an ambulance?'

'No.'

'Why not?'

'Because there was nothing anyone could do for him.'

'But the body had to be removed. Cause of death had to be established.'

Even before he had really started to test Jamila's account, Brunache knew how porous it was.

'We were in such a state, not thinking straight. Mohammed had been drinking as well as smoking cannabis.'

The picture Jamila was sketching was of two brawling drunks, both on drugs, with her caught helplessly in the middle.

The next question was another straightforward one: 'So what *did you* do with the body?'

Now Jamila's discomfort really was on show.

'My brother said it had to be removed from the apartment.'

'Of course…and that's what ambulances are for,' Brunache pointed out equably.

'I was forced into what happened next.'

'And what was that?'

'My brother said the body had to be put into the boot of his car. I didn't want any part of that and I said as much. I wanted to call the police because we had done no wrong. The death was an accident. Mohammed had been defending himself. But he said we wouldn't be believed.'

'Why not?'

'Because of where we were born. Because my husband was an aristocrat. People would say I was just after his money. You know how vicious people can be, especially when they're jealous. They hate the thought of someone from my background getting on in life.'

'Was the body put into the car boot?'

'Yes.'

Another simple question that elicited more incriminating admissions.

'We carried it to the car.' The *we* had turned them into partners in crime.

'Both of you?'

'Yes, but only because he forced me to.'

'What *force* did your brother use against you?'

'You have to understand that my brother's not right in the head. He can be very intimidating.'

Of course Jamila had not answered the question. 'You haven't described the force against you.'

The metaphoric noose was tightening.

'It was his manner. If I didn't help him, I would be the one blamed; that's what he said. No one would believe it was an accident and that it was my husband who'd brought about his own death. We had no witnesses. My past life would be dragged into it. The fact that I'm a countess wouldn't be taken into consideration. As a countess, I was socially equal to Tony, but that's not the way people would see it, especially with my husband's family stirring up trouble.'

'So you helped your brother?'

Head lowered again; extended pause, then, 'Yes. I told him it was a stupid thing to do. Telling the truth always pays.'

There followed questions about how they were able to carry the body from the first floor to the car. The answer was that it was a risk that had to be taken when it was dark and 'well after midnight'. Mohammed had not driven off until dawn. Now she was shaking all over and feared she would be re-admitted to the psychiatric hospital, saying, 'I don't want to go back there.'

'You won't be,' Brunache assured her, the double entendre no doubt intended.

The next question was yet another million-dollar one: where had the Earl's body been taken?

Jamila denied all knowledge. She insisted her brother had driven off alone with the dead Earl. She had no idea what he did with the body. It had been three months since the Earl was killed and did she *really* expect the police to believe that, in all that time, she and her brother had never spoken about what had been done with the body, Brunache scoffed.

Nevertheless, Jamila stubbornly stuck to her account. She had played no role in the killing of her husband. She was not at the scene when the 'tragedy' occurred, there had been no pre-planning, the death was accidental, and it was under duress that she had aided her brother in loading the body into his car. She flagged up the fact that she was afraid of her brother because of his psychopathic tendencies. As for what Mohammed did with the Earl, she preferred not to have that information. It was 'too awful' for her to think about. Although it was a 'terrible accident', of course she wished it had never happened. 'If only we could turn back the clock, I wouldn't have let my husband into the apartment while Mohammed was there,' she wailed. 'It could have been averted, but hindsight is useless.'

She had been terrified of the consequences if she failed to follow her brother's orders to the letter. There could be no denying that Brunache was up against an artful adversary, just the sort of cerebral challenge he welcomed, a version of chess. The Earl had been the sacrifice, but Brunache had no intention of being checkmated. And he would most certainly not settle for stalemate, or a draw.

Although Brunache was no nearer to locating the body, he was already in a position to prove Jamila a liar, so he formally arrested her. That was on 25 February 2005. The following day, Mohammed was arrested at his home in Munich. He had been traced by Interpol and the German police had been keeping him under surveillance on behalf of the French authorities. Later, he was deported to France, where, under questioning, he supported most of Jamila's statement, but was adamant that he, too, had no idea where he had disposed of the body.

Of course the French police had more than enough to detain in custody both Jamila and her brother. So much now hinged on finding the Earl's body – the final frontier. While it remained missing, it was a barrier to a successful prosecution. This was Jamila's one ace in the hole. But was it enough?

As promised, the French police regularly updated the Earl's elder son, who now knew that he and Nicholas had lost their father in an act of bloody violence – a long way from the aristocratic world to which he was accustomed.

Almost as unnerving for Anthony was the realisation that, at the age of twenty-seven, he was now the 11th Earl of Shaftesbury.

14

THE RAGS
AROUND HIM

Jamila had always considered herself a girl of Cannes, while the 10th Earl had always preferred Nice. These preferences had already defined the character differences between husband and wife: joined at the hip in wedlock, yet poles apart in chemistry and culture.

The French writer Guy de Maupassant was so depressed in Cannes that he slit his throat. PG Wodehouse ridiculed the 'Petite C' – standing for 'Little Cannes' – as a 'loathly hole', while Rudyard Kipling mocked it as a 'music hall review'.

Cannes is flash, loud and meretricious. Foreigners – mostly Arabs and Russians – swan along the Croisette (four lanes with a central reservation and rustling palm trees) in Lamborghinis, Ferraris, Lotuses and the occasional black Bentley or yellow Rolls-Royce. In the seafront hotels, a bottle of lager could cost £15. On TV in the bedrooms of one hotel, the first thirteen TV channels are all in Arabic, the next bundle are Russian, somewhere around number twenty or twenty-one come two or three French programmes, and last of all, sort of slipped in as an afterthought, is the BBC's World News.

Cannes is not France. It has been conquered and turned into a Foreign Legion of the international super-rich. If you are a millionaire in Cannes, you are one of the poor! And if you need to ask the price of anything, then you should not be there.

If Cannes had a heart, its pulse would certainly be the Marina, where year-round floating palaces the size of some ships and bigger than ferries are moored. Many have six decks and boast ostentatious gold fittings. When you hear in Cannes that familiar tinkling sound in the evening from moored yachts, it is not coming from masts but elaborate chandeliers all over the decks. The majority of owners are Arabs or Russians, plus the occasional Texas oil magnate, software tycoon or Hollywood star. Apart from during the May International Film Festival, showbiz personalities tend to belong to Cannes's third division.

Some of these luxury cruisers cost £50 million. Neither is it unusual for a uniformed crew of thirty to be employed while in harbour as well as at sea. King Edward VII, when he was Prince of Wales, described Cannes as 'criminally posh'. Today, many people would agree that it is criminal, but it is doubtful that the adjective posh would spring to mind.

The casino is another garish attraction for the high rollers. No wonder Cannes is a paradise for prostitutes like Jamila, a countess with proof of her legitimate status in a town where the hookers virtually have a licence to print their own money.

By contrast, Nice is so very British and identified by sedate understatement; definitely the Earl's kind of town. Along the front, instead of Lamborghinis, there are roller-bladers, joggers and strolling dog walkers; in the sleepy old town, Vieux Nice, you'll find a flower and fruit market, and quaint courtyards and alleys.

The British community had collectively paid for the seafront-cum-boulevard, the raffish Promenade des Anglais. Robert Louis Stevenson had trotted into Nice on a donkey, while Oscar Wilde, just out of Reading Gaol, and Charles Dickens had arrived more conventionally by steamer. HG Wells conducted a typically discreet Nice romantic affair in the Negresco hotel, while Isadora Duncan was strangled by a scarf when it became tangled in a wheel of her sports car, after she had been dancing naked with a reptile. The dance had been very elegant, though. Even misanthropic Bernard Shaw had given his grumpy nod to Nice because it was so 'unpretentious' and 'civilised'. It is easy to see why the Earl was so comfortable there, while Jamila was much more at home in brazen Cannes.

The investigating magistrate, Catherine Bonnici, supported the police in refusing bail to either of the suspects. After all, they had confessed to being implicated in the Earl's death and even if it was accidental, his demise had been deliberately kept from the authorities and the body disposed of illegally.

Also, if released, they were likely to flee the country to North Africa and dissolve into a continent from which it would be virtually impossible to retrieve them.

Unknown to the arrested couple, the police had been busy tapping their phones for several weeks. Scanners had been used to listen to mobile conversations. Brunache had several aces in the hole, of which the prisoners were ignorant. Patience had finally paid off the day Jamila phoned her sister Naima. For a while it had been a normal sister-to-sister chat. The detectives monitoring and recording the call had been yawningly bored, until…Jamila suddenly began grumbling about having had to pay Mohammed 150,000 euros for his participation and silence. In a couple of blinks of their eyes, the detectives had gone from boredom to elation.

Jamila talked about 'blood money' during the conversation, and how her brother was untrustworthy, a walking time bomb. In a roundabout way, she insinuated that he would keep coming back 'for more' whenever he ran short. He was a greedy leech, but not to worry, she was going to fix him. He would not have a hold over her for much longer. Then she went into specific detail as to how she planned pinning her husband's death on her brother; something was said about the difficulty of her ruse without the body coming to light, whereupon Jamila was heard telling her sister that she knew *exactly* where the body was. When the time was right, she would find a way of leading the police to it, she said, perhaps by giving detectives a list of Mohammed's alleged favourite rural rambles. Most of his rambles were between low-life bars; there was not much difference between brother and sister. By the end of the call, the police were salivating. They had hit the jackpot.

The police now had proof that the Earl had definitely been murdered and that it was a conspiracy between sister and brother. This information was all accumulated before the arrests. The killing had clearly been premeditated. Jamila had paid her brother 'blood money' for lethal services rendered. Jamila's account was a tissue of lies. The killing was no accident. The Earl had been lured to his death. From the moment he had crossed the threshold into the apartment he was doomed; a dead man walking.

Brother and sister continued denying all knowledge of where the corpse had been dumped. If only Jamila had divulged the location over the phone while chatting with Naima, it would have been a wrap for the police. But unknown to the couple, they were slowly but inexorably drowning. Just a little more patience was required, said Brunache, congratulating his team. The pair in custody were living in a fool's paradise.

The police obtained permission to hack into the pair's online bank dealings – and there it was, 150,000 euros transferred from Jamila to Mohammed, just a week after the murder. Another nail in their coffins.

The detectives had also taken possession of both prisoners' mobile phones. The communications experts downloaded records from the GPS tracking devices in each handset. These records gave the police a catalogue of the movements of Jamila and Mohammed, plus map references of places where they had made calls or received them, from several weeks before the murder and in the days that followed, proving that the two had been in constant contact with one another. But this all took time. It was an assiduous, time-consuming process. None of it could be rushed. The data had to be processed, logged and then analysed. This was backroom, boffin-plodding detective work, not for the frontline action team.

Brunache was most interested in the out-of-town locations Jamila had been in the lead-up to the murder, while her brother was still in Germany. He had a hunch. It was a tedious assignment because nearly all Jamila's movements had been to and from bars or hotels. There were numerous days when she had been to four or five hotels in Cannes in the space of twenty-four hours. Some days she had been on cabin cruisers and even out to sea. But there were also drives into the wilderness and one location stood out like a precious stone among bling.

Two days before the murder, Jamila's mobile had been in rough terrain a few miles outside Cannes in the Alpes-Maritimes region. Brunache was ebullient. Jamila had moved around quite a bit that day in the countryside, but within a compact area. 'She was looking for the ideal spot to hide the body,' he speculated to his fellow senior officers. 'What else could she be doing out there? Not picnicking!'

Wasting no time, he assembled a specialist mountain-type search squad, a dual operation between the police and military. Methodically working from large-scale maps, they began covering every inch of the target zone that had been circled in red. Hundreds of bramble bushes had to be crawled under. There were hillside forests and dense undergrowth.

None of the land was even. Much of it was rocky, with rivers and streams criss-crossing the hazardous landscape.

On the second day they were concentrating on a valley around Théoule-sur-Mer when one of the officers shouted excitedly in French, 'Here! Here!' Others came running, scrambling and stumbling, kicking up dust into their eyes. Hidden partially beneath bramble and in the undergrowth of a ravine beside a riverbed were the unmistakable remains of a human body.

Much of the corpse had been eaten by scavengers, wild beasts such as foxes, wolves and field rats. A large amount of the clothing had been ripped and chewed. Newspapers reported that the Earl had been wearing an expensive made-to-measure Savile Row suit of the kind he would have worn to meet and entertain royalty. This was untrue. The rags around him had been a T-shirt and jeans. The trainers had disintegrated.

The date was 7 April 2005; the painstaking procedure had finally brought about the grim harvest that had eluded them for so long. The 10th Earl of Shaftesbury was no longer missing.

Later that same day, a police spokesman stood before reporters, TV and radio journalists, photographers and cameramen to announce triumphantly, 'As far as we are concerned, there is absolutely no doubt that it is him [the Earl].'

The police on the Riviera had plenty to celebrate that evening. They had earned the wine they sampled. There was no celebrating, however, in a little rural corner of England where the only grapes were of wrath.

The call from the Riviera had been taken by Anthony soon after the shredded body of his father had been unearthed. The tears that followed were a product of mixed emotions – sadness and relief. Only now could the process of closure begin. There was still a long way to go and a trial to be faced, but they had been living in a long, dark and seemingly endless tunnel and now there was light at the end. These were the thoughts articulated that evening by Anthony.

But he was so very wrong.

More cruel, unimaginable twists lurked in the script.

15

GHOULISH TALK

The body was even too ravaged for Anthony to positively identify his father. But eleven days after the search ended, DNA tests concluded with a positive result.

In May that year, 2005, Anthony, now the 11th Earl of Shaftesbury, flew to New York to be with his younger brother, Nicholas. They had so much to talk about. Firstly and probably most importantly, there was the funeral to be planned. This was a ghoulish discussion because they were unsure just how much there would be of their father to go into a coffin. Another unknown factor was how long they would have to wait for the French authorities to release for burial his precious few remains.

The brothers were very close. With only a year separating them, they were virtually twins. They had grown up together, played together, gone to school together, partied together, and participated in endurance sports. Now they needed each other more than ever. The blood tie would hold them together like an adhesive, giving them strength and keeping them sane. Physically, they were so alike; it was difficult for outsiders to distinguish one from the other. They were tall, dark-haired, slim, aristocratic and debonair, but without a flicker of arrogance. Both had healthy lifestyles and were determined to sidestep the pitfalls that had led to their father's unseemly downfall. In all external appearance, they were two super-fit scions, thoroughbred colts, set to carry the Shaftesbury torch for the next sixty or eighty years.

Despite their unmistakable similarity in looks and character, Anthony was undoubtedly the more serious of the two. This was to be expected because he had been reared and tutored as the heir, rather like a prince next in line to the royal throne; the difference between William and Harry. It was Anthony who was now solely responsible for the ancestral estate and the massive entrepreneurial operation that went with it. During their father's reign, there had been so much neglect and now, at such a tender age, twenty-seven, it was up to Anthony to be the saviour. And up for the challenge he was!

Since finishing his education, Anthony had devoted every working hour to learning how to manage an estate the size of the Shaftesbury's and with all its complexities and complications; this had included qualifying as an accountant. Nicholas was the lucky one. He had been able to indulge his passion for music, lapping up the carefree, hip life of a New York DJ, nightclub manager and professional party host. He had been insulated from so many of the ghosts and nightmares that had haunted other family members in faraway Wimborne St Giles.

As for Anthony, he welcomed a break from what had been a crushing, pressure-cooker atmosphere for so long on the unmanageable estate without the master. For a few days, all the troubles were 3,000 miles away. Nicholas gave the fresh-faced 11th Earl a conducted tour of the throbbing, sleepless Big Apple, showing him the places where he worked and where so much of the action pulsed for respectable, trendy New Yorkers of their own generation; the sophisticated, young professional class with spare dollars to spend and high-flying careers to forge. Anthony talked at length and effusively about his plans. He was determined to restore St Giles House to its former grand, glory days, although that would entail pumping millions of pounds into the project. He was seeking Nicholas's blessing and it was readily forthcoming, which must have made him happy. There was also so much work to be done on the estate itself and all the properties for which they were responsible. Anthony had despaired when he had been unable to drag out decisions from their father, who, for years, had procrastinated over so much.

For a long time the 10th Earl had not been a decision-maker, except when it came to ordering the next round of drinks, getting high on cocaine, making propositions to vivacious French women, mostly prostitutes, proposing marriages and initiating divorces. He had become a master of debauchery and chaos. Yet the sons and even their tortured mother, Christina, who had been so callously discarded for an avaricious harlot, were forgiving and sympathetic towards the murdered Earl. Their humanity went far beyond what could be expected of anyone struggling to survive those chaotic, outrageous circumstances, which would, surely, have tried the forbearance of a saint. These were very special people.

But just as that light at the end of the tunnel was being glimpsed by Anthony, so it was snuffed out. With his brother at his side in New York, he collapsed. By the time the paramedics raced him to hospital, he was dead. Cause of death was a heart attack. Regardless of the medical language, lay folk back home in Dorset put down his death to a broken heart. Everything he had loved so much seemed to have conspired against him. He had been the 11th Earl of Shaftesbury for less than a month.

Not surprisingly, there was speculation within the UK aristocracy and corridors of power of a curse on the Shaftesbury family, comparable to that on the Kennedys and the Guinness clan. Certainly the twists were coming thick and fast. As for Nicholas, Lady Frances and Christina, the Dowager Countess of Shaftesbury, they were too shell-shocked to readily absorb the enormity of the latest blow to their already blitzed lineage. Certainly it would take days for Nicholas to realise that he was now the 12th Earl of Shaftesbury. His chilled, halcyon days in New York, trend-setting in clubland and the music industry, were over. The land of the gentry beckoned.

Nicholas flew to Heathrow, still numb with shock. His brother returned in a casket, met at the airport by black-suited strangers – undertakers. This was not the homecoming that had been planned for either Anthony or Nicholas. Now there were two funerals to prepare for – and a new Earl to get bedded in, from scratch. An Earl, who by self-admission, was a raw recruit, totally untrained and unprepared for the battles ahead.

Anthony Nils Christian Ashley-Cooper, 11th Earl of Shaftesbury, was laid to rest in the family crypt after a private family funeral service, conducted by the Reverend David Paskins, in the peaceful parish church of Wimborne St Giles.

The Shaftesburys had been inflicted with an unfair ratio of catastrophes. Surely now they deserved a fair wind behind them, filling their sails with a degree of atonement and stability, though there could never be full recompense for such an overload of adversity. Fairness is rarely distributed equitably. Tragedies tend to come along like taxis and buses – in clusters. Unknowingly, just as the Shaftesurys were piecing back together their lives in some sort of orderly and dispassionate fashion, misfortune was preparing to strike yet again. The curse showed no mercy.

After the necessary formalities had been completed with the French judiciary, the funeral of the 10th Earl was able to proceed on 30 September 2005. Hundreds of mourners attended the service at the Wimborne St Giles parish church. Many had to stand outside, having the service relayed to them electronically; in this respect, Nicholas's New York musical expertise had come in handy.

Charles Palmer-Tomkinson read from Khalil Gibran's

book *The Prophet*, while Lady Frances delivered a relevant portion of George Santayana's 'For These Once Mine'. The 12th Earl, Nicholas, addressed the congregation with the 'Prayer of St Francis Assisi'. Leading the mourners were Nicholas, Lady Frances and second wife Christina. The service lasted forty-five minutes, after which the 10th Earl was placed in the crypt next to his son, Anthony.

After the dignified ceremony, parish priest the Rev. Paskins said, 'It was a very inspiring occasion. They have had a very difficult time [some understatement!] and have borne it with great dignity and fortitude.'

Unfortunately, the test had only just begun.

Meanwhile, in France, the wheels of justice, if not exactly moving in reverse, were barely progressing.

Jamila's brazenness was untethered. She had made an application, in the name of Sarah, Countess of Shaftesbury, to be allowed to attend the funeral of her husband. She argued that she should lead the mourners, deliver an address during the service, and take charge of a champagne wake in the village in the evening. Champagne would be appropriate, she said, because it was her husband's favourite tipple. 'I'm as devastated as everyone else by his death,' she said. 'I have my human rights. I have the rights of a widow. And I most definitely have special rights as a countess. As in British law, everyone in France is presumed innocent until a trial has established otherwise.'

She had not been tried and therefore she remained innocent. Neither could her status be ignored. She was, she alleged, a lady of considerable substance who was being 'barbarically' detained. She demanded that the prison governor, gaolers, fellow detainees and lawyers address her as 'Countess'. She expected men to bow to her and women – staff and prisoners – to curtsy. Much more than champagne and cocaine had gone to her head!

To everyone within this bizarre circus, it was a great hoot. Prison staff actually looked forward to going to work. Jamila was the cabaret, the light relief to an otherwise gruelling, monotonous day.

Of course the Shaftesburys were revolted by Jamila's effrontery and in the firmest possible language pointed out that her presence would be an affront, not only to the family but all decent-minded people. But Jamila had not finished with her plea. Although not having been granted bail – wrongly, in her estimation – it was not uncommon for even convicted prisoners to be allowed out on day-release when there were compassionate grounds. What could be more compelling than to attend the funeral of one's own husband? She also considered it right to have the opportunity to inspect *her* estate and to establish that everything was in order. On her release, when acquitted, she would be visiting Wimborne St Giles again to ensure that '*that* Christina woman' and Frances (no *Lady* appellation) were 'sent packing'. There would also be some straight talking with that 'rude Nick', who was clearly out of his depth and also needed tuition in 'manners towards women', something he had failed 'miserably' to learn from his father.

Of course the whole charade was a stunt. She was being as mischievous as possible, knowing that her request would have to be processed. As mentioned earlier in the book, France was the world's most bureaucratic nation. Some ninety-eight forms, handled by almost fifty officials, might have been involved in considering this one application. Every document that required her signature was signed, 'Sarah, Countess of Shaftesbury'.

Naturally, the request had been rejected. Firstly, if granted, it would have caused a riot by locals in Wimborne St Giles. Secondly, Nicholas would have ensured she was barred from the estate. And as the church was within the estate boundary, she would have been unable to attend the service and burial, but she could have been a distraction from the periphery, playing to the gallery, namely the press, who would have turned out in force. However, apart from the family objections, there would have been strategic problems for the prison authority, who could not spare the staff needed to escort Jamila by plane from Nice to Heathrow and then westward to Dorset in a hired vehicle. Jamila would have been in handcuffs both ways. Meals and drinks would have to be bought for all three. The expense could have been considerable.

Cheekily, Jamila offered to pay everything, including first-class return flights. 'I am not short of money,' she bragged. 'I never have been. I've never needed a husband for money.' Her offer was curtly declined. Jamila was denied the chance to play the tearful countess in black and matching veil, hijacking the funeral as she posed for cameramen from all over the world.

The French liked to believe that their legal system dated back to 1789 and 'Napoleonic Law'. There is a core of truth in that supposition, but much has changed, certainly in recent years since the EC has imposed codes of judicial conduct on member states. In the past, suspects in France could be held for months or years without any process of law being initiated. Nevertheless, the jury system was abolished in 1941, during the Nazi Occupation, and was replaced by a mixed tribunal of six lay judges and three professionals. A two-thirds majority was sufficient for a conviction. However, in major cases and murder trials, heard in a *Cour d'Assises*, there would be nine ordinary jurors making up a *jury populaire*. The supreme appeal court was the *Cour de Cassation*. The death penalty was not abolished until 1981 and the maximum gaol sentence that could now be imposed was thirty years. Other amendments, including the right to a lawyer within three hours of arrest, were implemented in 1993 and 2000, plus larger juries.

Gigantic strides in human rights (controversially called Man's Rights) in France had been made, as the French penal system was among the most brutal and inhuman in the world. Many people will remember the movie *Papillion* and, of course, the barbaric discipline of the old French Foreign Legion is notorious.

Despite the immeasurable improvements to the French legal system, Jamila and her brother had to wait a year before even the preliminary trial procedures began. In June 2006, pre-trial proceedings started in Grasse, presided over by the investigating magistrate, Catherine Bonnici. This was not the start of the trial. It was merely the beginning of the beginning, the first milestone in a long and sinuous journey, equivalent to a Grand Jury hearing in the US or committal proceedings before magistrates in the UK.

In France, however, the process and preliminaries were much more protracted. The purpose of the hearing in Grasse was for the state prosecutor Jean-Louis Moreau to demonstrate that there was sufficient evidence for both Jamila M'Barek and her brother, Mohammed M'Barek, to be sent for trial on murder charges.

Attorney Franck De Vita represented Jamila. Mohammed's defence counsel was Melanie Juginger. All the lawyers involved were legal heavyweights on the French criminal justice circuit. Everyone recognised that if this went to trial it would be a showpiece, pure theatre, playing to the public's insatiable appetite for scandal, underpinned by sex, aristocratic profligacy, 'Champagne Charlie' boozing, recreational drug abuse on a serial scale, and murder the icing on the cake.

One might have expected a case of this magnitude to have been staged in Nice, the capital of the Côte d'Azur, but Grasse, although a small town with a population of less than 50,000, is of considerable importance to the French economy. The town and its suburbs sprawl over hills and valleys, inland between Cannes and Nice. The ancient city, which was once ringed by ramparts, is a cramped labyrinth of narrow streets. On all sides of this historic town, for as far as the eye can see and the nose can smell, are fields illuminated with lavender, jasmine, cent folia roses, orange blossom and violets. These fields are the giveaway to the area's industrial significance: it is the beating heart of the world's perfume industry. There are dozens of perfumeries in Grasse. Not only are the much sought-after essences sold to the prestigious couture houses for upmarket perfumes, but also to factories to aromatically enhance food and soap. One of the big-name production companies based there is Fragonard Perfumery. The N85 highway, equivalent to US route 66, better known as Napoleon's Road, cuts through the middle of Grasse and is, basically, the town's high street.

As for the court hearing, amid the heady aroma of pollen, the police had known from the initial interviews with Jamila that her defence would be that she had no part in the killing, she was not in the room when the Earl died, she was not voluntarily involved in placing the body in her brother's car, and she had not accompanied Mohammed when he disposed of the Earl. In fact, she had never been near the location where her husband was found: that would be the basic storyline.

This hearing was the chance for her attorney to establish to the magistrate that the case against Jamila, even of conspiracy, let alone murder, was too flimsy, a non-starter in fact, and should be thrown out. To continue would be a waste of public money, with no chance of a conviction, and would bring the justice system into disrepute. Also, keeping Jamila in custody infringed her human rights, especially when the police were speculating over so much of what occurred on that fateful day in Jamila's apartment, the defence argument continued. Even her alleged accomplice, Mohammed, would testify in support of his sister. The prosecution, of course, accused DeVita of grandstanding: all rhetoric and no real rebuttal.

The magistrate was too experienced to be swayed by grandiloquence. Facts and evidence were her king. Everything else was either froth or a smokescreen, maybe both. She decided that a trip was necessary to the location where the remains of the Earl had been recovered. The party included the two prisoners, all the attorneys, court officials, senior police officers, and prison escorts. Mohammed M'Barek was transported in leg chains as well as handcuffs.

The defence attorneys had devised a little experiment. They produced a human dummy that matched the weight (182lb) and height (6ft 1in) of the Earl around the time of his disappearance. The dummy had been made secretly to specification and kept under wraps until produced, like a conjuror pulling a white rabbit from a top hat, at the grisly scene.

The police and the magistrate obviously wanted to know the object of the exercise. DeVita explained that if Mohammed could lift and carry the dummy on his own, then he would not have required assistance to load the Earl into the boot of the car. Neither would he have needed help to remove the body from the car and to hide it in the ravine. This would serve to back up Jamila's version of events, in particular that she had not travelled in the car to the dumping ground and therefore was not lying when she stated that she was unaware of the location where her brother had concealed the corpse.

The magistrate had no objection to allowing the experiment to go ahead. When Mohammed lifted and carried the dummy, De Vita exclaimed that his client was exonerated and had no case to answer. The magistrate, however, decreed that the preliminary hearing would continue in court the following day, with Jamila still very much a subject of investigation.

Next day, Jamila gave evidence before the magistrate. She was adamant that she had nothing to do with the killing, apart from carrying the body with her brother to the car, something she had been compelled to do or suffer violence. There were inconsistencies in her testimony that did not go unnoticed. From the outset of the police investigation, she had changed her statement several times, something that always made juries wary. Her evidence became even more contradictory when she said, 'I did not want him to die. I just wanted my brother to intimidate him so that he would continue to pay me my allowance. But he didn't want to have anything to do with it, so a violent quarrel broke out. I left the room because I could not stand to see what was happening.'

This statement from Jamila, under oath, astonished the prosecution. It contradicted all her previous claims that her brother had arrived unexpectedly at her apartment and that there had been no prior planning between them. Now she was saying that her brother was there for the explicit purpose of intimidating the Earl. She was losing her own plot.

De Vita must have been tearing out his hair in frustration. Skilful liars need good memories. But even bad liars should be able to remember what they said the previous day. For the defendants, the hearing was beginning to go pear-shaped with a giant P.

To be fair, there were two consistencies in Jamila's

testimony so far: 1. That she had not been present when the Earl was killed. 2. She had not been in the BMW when Mohammed drove away with the body.

The forensic medical evidence revealed that the Earl had suffered a double fracture to the larynx, establishing that he had been strangled. An ankle had also been broken. These findings had been made from the skeletal remains. There had been little flesh left.

After hearing concluding arguments from the defence attorneys and the prosecutor, Magistrate Catherine Bonnici decided that both Jamila and her brother should be charged with premeditated murder and tried before a jury with those alleged offences.

Brother and sister had almost a year to wait for their trial. The waiting was no less traumatic for Nicholas, the 12th Earl, and the rest of the family. The evidence against the couple seemed overwhelming, but there is always an element of the lottery about all trials by jury. There could be so many twists and turns before the end of the most straightforward-looking case. As in horseracing, there is no such thing as a certainty when it revolves around a collective judgment that tests impartiality to the limit. Prejudices can surface, and one strong-willed, barrack-room amateur lawyer or armchair sleuth has been known to bully the other jurors into a dubious verdict. There is also the horrifying spectre of a case being lost on a technicality; forensic samples contaminated, evidence lost, paperwork incomplete, or defendants not afforded their legal rights at the appropriate time. Courtrooms could be minefields.

When the trial did commence, on 22 May 2007, it was in

Nice at the imposing Palais de Justice, an edifice in the style of classical French architecture. Journalists spilled over into the seats for the public. This trial was a genuine cause célèbre. Hundreds of would-be spectators were turned away because there was no room for them. Some had even flown down from Paris and Geneva, such as escort agency proprietor Catherine Gurtler. Others had queued all night, as if poised for the New Year sales to kick off. The Shaftesbury family had their interests protected by attorney Philippe Soussi.

The trial, presided over by Judge Nicole Besset, began with controversy. Before the jurors were even sworn in, Mr De Vita requested that his client should be addressed throughout the proceedings as 'Countess' because she feared that her Arab bloodline might 'alienate' the jury, due to the undertones of racism simmering in France.

Mr Soussi objected on behalf of the Shaftesburys, maintaining that it would be an 'insult' to the family of the deceased. Prosecutor Jean-Louis Moreau could see a more devious motive for the request: would a woman of such social standing allow herself to be embroiled in a low-life, cold-hearted murderous plot as alleged? But Mr De Vita stressed that Jamila was an innocent woman until the jury decreed otherwise and it was a matter of indisputable fact that his client was the current Countess of Shaftesbury, like it or not. She was the real deal, a blue-blood from the red-light districts of many a place! The family's feelings in this respect were irrelevant, the contention continued. Jamila was entitled to the court's respect.

The judge used her discretion in Jamila's favour. The

evidence would speak for itself. Such a judgment also ruled out an appeal on the grounds of prejudice and impartiality by the judge. Jamila's request was also double-edged. One side of the sword gave her gravitas, while the other offered the adage, the bigger they come, the harder they fall.

At last, with technicalities dealt with, the trial proper got underway, with the fate of the two defendants resting with seven women and four men.

The prosecutor set the tone by denouncing Jamila in the 'investigative report' as an 'escort girl who loved the high life'. She had chosen 'the life of a kept woman with multiple affairs with men she chose for their bank accounts and assets'. He outlined the downward spiral of the marriage and told how, after 'striking gold' but with divorce impending, she faced 'looming financial disaster' and set out 'consciously and without constraint to accomplish his [the Earl's] assassination'.

Testimony was presented that in October 2002, Jamila M'Barek (not a countess then) had tricked the Earl into believing that she was pregnant with his child. As a result, the Earl had married her, immediately making a new will that left properties to Jamila in France and Ireland. Two years later, 'with no child forthcoming', he began 'looking elsewhere for affection'. When the Earl initiated divorce proceedings, Jamila visualised losing her valuable inheritance and 'began to take steps to secure her financial future'.

Before the couple separated, the Earl was persuaded by his wife to sell the Versailles apartment, Lady Frances testified. 'When my brother said he would divorce her [Jamila], she would not accept it.'

Antique furniture and family artefacts, much of which had belonged to the mother of the Earl and Lady Frances, had mysteriously disappeared – a similar fate awaiting the Earl. 'Jamila and Mohammed arranged to empty the flat,' she said, 'and when my brother [the Earl] asked where his mother's furniture had gone to, she said it was on a boat to Tunisia, where it was going to be sold. My brother was distraught. This was cruel, emotional blackmail. In fact, the furniture was in storage in Cannes, but my brother never knew that. I have just managed to get hold of the key.'

Jamila attempted to discredit the 'investigate report', stating that her marriage to the Earl was a 'curse'. At least this tallied with the consensus of opinion in Dorset. She vilified the Earl as a 'loner without friends', the reason why 'he drank a lot'. The vilification intensified when she alleged that the Earl was a 'violent, sex-crazed alcoholic, hooked on cocaine'.

Now in front of the jury, she repeated the admission that her brother had killed the Earl, but by mistake. It had not been intended. 'There was blood on the floor. I did not know if it was my brother's or husband's blood. My brother could not believe my husband was dead.' This was followed by yet another completely fresh contradiction. 'He forced me to follow him as I thought we were going to hospital. Then he asked me to go away.'

In the witness box, she denied having any financial motive in wishing her husband dead and repeated consistently that she had 'no need of his fortune. I have always been prosperous'.

Naturally, she was asked by the prosecutor to explain

where her money had come from. Her explanation was that the source of her affluence was the 'generosity of wealthy individuals who were prepared to pay me for my company.' She then named George Clooney, Bruce Willis and Bjorn Borg as having been among her generous clients. She also claimed to have been 'extremely close' to Prince Albert II of Monaco. Attempts had been made to subpoena all four of the internationally famous men to attend court as 'character witnesses' for Jamila and to demonstrate the kind of money she commanded.

It had been impossible for these subpoenas to be served and Clooney, Willis, Borg and Prince Albert all stated through their attorneys that they had never been in the company of Jamila (Sarah) M'Barek or a Countess of Shaftesbury and that she was not known to them. Hence, they had no intention of attending a trial as character witnesses for a complete stranger. Neither would the judge countenance trying to put pressure to attend on these men who could add nothing to the issue in front of the jury.

Jamila's response in court was to promise that she would have her revenge on them. She said, 'I am always loyal to the men who were close to me, but they did not want to know me when I was facing the biggest trial of my life. Most were too scared to appear because they are married or have steady girlfriends.' She was still trying to use them as a vehicle for her defence. By dragging their names through the judicial process, she was attempting to superimpose those household names on the psyches of the jurors, elevating herself into the social orbit of the celebrities and VIPs, almost putting herself on the red carpet, a planet away from the grubby narrative unfolding by the prosecution to the jurors.

Under cross-examination, she asserted that her arguments with the Earl were unconnected to money, but arose from his excessive sexual demands, purportedly induced by injections of testosterone.

Throughout the mere four-day trial, Mr De Vita remained bullish, telling reporters daily, 'I am convinced Jamila will walk free.'

Mohammed told the court that he had been drinking heavily and smoking cannabis when confronted by an 'excited and aggressive' 10th Earl of Shaftesbury. There was a fight during which he 'accidentally' strangled his brother-in-law, while attempting to restrain him. 'I don't know how it happened,' he said. 'It happened in a minute.'

Emotionally, he outlined his attempt to revive the Earl, including mouth-to-mouth resuscitation and heart massage. 'It was too late,' he said. 'He had left us.' He then made a direct appeal in broken English to the Shaftesbury family, who sat stony-faced at the rear. 'I am sorry to you. Pardon, please. It was only an accident. He's my brother-in-law. I am sorry for you. I am too sad.'

He voiced anger at the French penal authorities for keeping him in prison 'for two and a half years for nothing'. He expressed his disgust and outrage that the police could consider it a crime to be 'dumping in a ravine an inconveniently dead body'. He had even written to the new President of France, Nicolas Sarkozy, pleading for his intervention in the name of justice.

Mr Sarkozy had not replied.

The third day brought unexpected drama. Mohammed burst into tears, then jumped up and pointed at members of the Shaftesbury family who were there to witness the final stages. 'You're the guilty ones,' he shouted. 'You the rich who want to take his inheritance.' He continued his tirade as police wrestled with him in the dock. The courtroom descended into disarray, despite the repeated rapping of the judge's gavel. Mohammed's own lawyer pleaded with his client to be quiet, but he continued with his rant. The judge issued him with a final warning, which he ignored. Whereupon, the judge ordered Mohammed to be taken to the cells and the trial was temporarily adjourned.

The damning evidence against Jamila was the secretly recorded phone conversation with her sister, Naima, when the £100,000 'blood money' had been discussed. The recording also heard Jamila admitting that she had visited the remote location where her husband's body had been found. Also incriminating was her detailed attempt to make her brother the 'fall guy'.

Jamila had an explanation for the £100,000 she gave her brother the week after the killing: it was to enable him to buy a house for their ailing mother.

And that was it, apart from the nail-biting wait for the jury to ponder and then to pronounce.

The jury took a mere two hours' deliberation before returning guilty verdicts against both defendants. Jamila and her brother stood stoically in the dock as the judge read the verdicts. When both were sentenced to twenty-five years in prison, there was not a twitch of emotion from either of them.

Under French law, they had an automatic right to appeal. Peculiar to France, an appeal amounted to a complete re-trial automatically.

Outside the court, Catherine Gurtler said of Jamila, 'When she wasn't working for agencies, she was working in hostess bars. She just wanted to take advantage of the Earl as much as possible. She's a bitch.'

But Mr de Vita declared the outcome a 'bad day for justice'. On the steps of the courthouse, he pledged that he would be launching an appeal on behalf of his client, Jamila. 'The fight for justice goes on. This is not the end of anything. We are only halfway through. We start right now, this very minute, preparing for the appeal.'

As he left the court, Nicholas, the 12th Earl, said, 'I don't understand how people can place no value on human life.' Rejecting Mohammed's apology, he said, 'I do not forgive him and will never forgive him as long as he does not admit to the murder of my father. I am very relieved this week is finally over and I am looking forward to starting the next chapter of my life. I believe justice was done and we are satisfied with the twenty-five-year sentences given to both defendants.

'During the trial, we heard a lot of excuses and I don't think we saw any remorse or compassion from the accused, but I was expecting that from the kind of people they are.'

Before leaving, Nicholas thanked the police officers, one by one, for their 'unstinting diligence' in really rigorous and testing circumstances.

When he learned of Mr de Vita's statement that there would be an appeal, the Earl was unflinching. 'I'll come back to fight for the memory of my father, despite the ordeal.'

Equated to a football match, it was only half-time, but with the Shaftesburys and the prosecution holding a comfortable lead. Nicholas was not buckling under the continued stress and pressure, although they had been prepared for closure. He was fit. Endurance sports were his speciality. This marathon would not crack him.

In the land of vineyards, 2007 was a good year for justice, according to the palate of the Shaftesbury family. But would the verdicts mature with age into vintage quality or be ruined by the foul taste of successful appeals? Nicholas was warned that it would be a further two years before the re-match was scheduled, casting a shadow for the family over every new dawn, whatever the weather.

Meanwhile, Jamila was showboating with unbelievable chutzpah about the travesty of a countess, a *lady* of the aristocracy, being locked up with all the country's unsavoury riff-raff. This was risible considering that, not too long ago, she would have lost her head, never mind her freedom and social status, just for being an aristo.

Nevertheless, sunshine was slowly returning at last to Nicholas's life. He had met and grown fond of an attractive young German woman, Dinah Streifeneder. The 10th Earl's preference for European women clearly lived on in his younger son and heir. Dinah's father was Dr Fritz Streifeneder, a retired orthopaedic surgeon; her

Argentine-born mother, Renate Leander-Streifeneder, was a physiotherapist.

Born in Munich on 12 September 1980, Dinah was a year younger than Nicholas. The bond between them soon morphed into love. For Nicholas, it had been 'wow!' at their first meeting. Dinah had not been so immediately awe-struck. So very different from grasping Jamila M'Barek, a title, fortune, properties scattered across the globe and land almost too large to measure, meant absolutely nothing to Dinah; in fact, she viewed the package more of a burden than a glittering magnet or prize to go for.

By profession, she was a veterinary surgeon, so from the outset they had much in common – animal welfare and conservation. Charity work was also high among her priorities, especially organisations that helped children with disabilities.

Helping poor and afflicted children had always been a passion of each successive Earl of Shaftesbury. Philanthropy was part of their DNA, as much their heritage as the great estate and all the social reforms that had gilded this dynasty with so much glory and affection over the centuries, which had been sadly tarnished in a few maniacal, unhinged years. Centuries of service to mankind flushed into the sewer by one runaway earl. More destructive than a runaway train.

However, the slide had been halted. The Shaftesburys were back on track. Nicholas was blessed with atavistic grit and integrity. And in Dinah, he had serendipitously stumbled upon a kindred spirit – someone with a similar vision and matching philanthropic outlook.

On balance, the year 2007 was to prove an exceptional year for the Shaftesburys. A significant turning point.

And yet, over the horizon, a new storm was gathering, giving legitimacy to the curse fable.

16

BLOOD
SPORT

Nicholas, the 12th Earl of Shaftesbury, is certainly not your stereotype aristocrat, not of any country, let alone Britain and its chinless toffs. Under his clothes, he proudly sports the colourful zeitgeist testimonials to his previous nocturnal life. The tattoos on his arms and body, for example, are a kind of road map, charting his journey through the music world in his spirited New York days. The fact that he resembles David Beckham when in a T-shirt or should he decide to sunbathe on a public beach does not faze him one bit. He wears his symbolic milestones with humble pride. 'I love them all,' he is on record saying. 'They are all a sign of a moment in time.'

His first tattoo – Eros and Psyche – was etched on his left shoulder when he was twenty-three and had newly arrived in New York. There is immense pathos to this particular painting on his flesh. Its depth of meaning would float over the head of the casual observer, yet it is a monument to a man of history and his noble deeds – the 7th Earl of Shaftesbury, whose social crusades inspired London's Eros statue in the capital's West End, where the lungs of London blow oxygen throughout the city. Eros is a permanent fixture. Nicholas's memorial to the 7th Earl is alive and mobile; wherever he goes, it keeps him company. It is a round-the-clock reminder to him of the torch he carries. People go to Eros. The Eros on Nicholas goes to the people, into the community, and crosses continents, borders and time zones.

'He was a great reformer,' Nicholas said to me of the 7th Earl. 'He is a huge inspiration to me. I am very protective of the family name and heritage. It means so much to me and the history of our country. Although it was the 7th Earl who made most impact, others were remarkable men, especially the 1st and 3rd. Neither should it ever be forgotten that my father did a tremendous amount of good work here on the estate and for charitable causes. But he was an alcoholic and that is a very serious disease. It made it hard for him. But I'm still very proud of his legacy of goodness.'

In view of the fate of the 10th Earl, there was something rather prophetic in this eulogy to Eros by author Peter Ackroyd in his *London: The Biography,* published in 2000 by Chatto & Windus and then in paperback a year later by Vintage:

When the Shaftesbury Memorial Fountain, otherwise known as Eros, was unveiled in 1893 at Piccadilly

Circus, it was only a few yards from the infamous Haymarket where mothers had brought their young daughters for sale. Eros was the first statue ever made of aluminium, and in that conflation of ancient passion and new-minted metal, we have an emblem of desire as old and as new as the city itself. Eros has been drawing people ever since...

Throughout this century [the 20th] Piccadilly Circus has been the site of nightly sexual encounters, and an area where young people drift in search of adventure. It is a place where all the roads seem to meet, in endless disarray, and it exudes an atmosphere both energetic and impersonal. This is perhaps also why it has been for many decades a centre of prostitution and easy pick-ups, both male and female. It has always been the part of London most identified with casual sex...

The statue of Eros has, after all, commanded a strange power. The city itself is a kind of promiscuous desire, with its endless display of other streets and other people affording the opportunity of a thousand encounters and a thousand departures.

The statue's *strange power* certainly had the 10th Earl under its spell; so, too, did its *emblem of desire* and its representation of *promiscuity*. There is a case for saying, emblematically, the 10th Earl was corrupted by this memorial to the rectitude of his famed forefather.

Nicholas's second tattoo is even more poignant: an ant on

his left breast, in memory of brother Anthony. The placing of it, near to the heart, was so emblematic. It depicted love and, alas, the heart that failed Anthony and took him from the family so prematurely. But for that broken heart, Anthony would have been doing what he was groomed for and Nicholas would still have been luxuriating in his love of music promotion across the Atlantic – completely ignorant of what he was missing, unaware of the existence of Dinah Streifeneder. These little quirks of fate were not lost on Nicholas or Dinah. More than most, they appreciated the sinuous, sometimes cruel, road that had set them on a soft-landing collision, a crash course to love.

Nicholas had come through his rollercoaster ride with nerves of steel reinforced and mentally stronger than ever. You had to be tough and streetwise to conquer the Big Apple in your early twenties with your morality intact and your reputation stainless.

The music industry of New York knew nothing of his background. To New Yorkers, he was simply, 'Nick the DJ' or 'Cool Nick' or his professionally stylised name of 'nick ac'. At no time did he trade off his aristocratic credentials. Unlike his father, he had cut the umbilical cord without anguish and womb homesickness. He had grown up fast and Dinah was drawn to his dynamism and youthful maturity.

Few people in the UK, even in the music scene, were aware that in 2004 Nicholas formed the notable collective ROBOTS with several other New York DJs, establishing a weekly event at Club Deville. And in the summer of 2006, he was resident DJ and music promoter at the Privilege club in Ibiza, where young Brits on holiday danced through the night to his pulsating output.

'I was very heavily entrenched in the music world and becoming successful,' he said in 2013 when showing journalists around refurbished St Giles House. 'People just knew me by my stage name. But when Anthony died, I had this sense that my life was about to go through a huge change. I wanted something to anchor myself; a permanent reminder.' The tattooed sleeve down the length of his right arm depicts a mechanical robot, a constant reminder of his hardcore musical past. Those heady days were over and that was something he acknowledged with no lingering regret. He remains philosophical: 'When the call comes, you have to be ready to answer it.'

He will probably not thank me for saying this, as his ancestors were all steeped in Liberal politics, but there is something almost Churchillian about him. To defeat the forces of evil that had murdered his father, he would fight them in the courts, on the beaches…and would never surrender. And that was his attitude over restoring St Giles House, re-branding the Shaftesbury name, caring for his charities and upgrading the estate with state-of-the-art methods of husbandry; it also applied to his endeavour to have Jamila stripped of her countess title, a difficult, if not impossible, exercise, he was to admit.

Having Jamila issuing statements from custody in the name of the Countess of Shaftesbury must have become a tormenting demon for the Shaftesburys. Doubtless she was spurred on by the knowledge of how it would enrage the new Earl, with whom she had previously had a spat in a London restaurant. Going to extremes to taunt was a kind of blood sport Jamila would enjoy.

By February 2008, there was still no news of a date for the re-trial. With so much to be done at Wimborne St Giles, Nicholas had to keep the forthcoming court hearing very much on the backburner, but this was made impossible when the whole saga was aired on TV in an episode of Channel 4's *Cutting Edge*. Suddenly it was all in his face again, and worsened by the fact that it included a clash between two of the women who featured in the court proceedings.

On camera, Jamila's sister Naima claimed that the Earl had written 'lurid love letters' to her just after he wed Jamila.

As for Nadia, she said that, despite the Earl's heavy drinking, she was prepared for a long-term relationship in their love-nest cottage in Vence.

If Naima M'Barek was telling the truth, it added a fresh dimension to the extent of the 10th Earl's rakish lifestyle. It insinuated that he was disloyal to his wife, Jamila, with serious sexual intent, within a few hours of the marriage. Unfortunately, for reasons beyond his control, the 10th Earl was not around to confirm or deny the allegation. Conversely, Nadia, then thirty-six, assessed her life with the Earl, after he had separated from Jamila, as blissful. 'I found him different to most men,' she said softly. 'He was very kind and respectful. He spoke calmly and knew how to treat a lady.' When he discussed his marriage with her, he described it as 'the biggest mistake' of his life. 'Her [Jamila] only goal was to take and take and take from him. She studied his personality and used his weaknesses to get what she wanted.

'During the time I spent with him, I made him very happy. We spent some very simple days together, simple outings, a simple life. He drank less when he was with me. He was a normal man with normal needs. He was affectionate and soft. He had no strange habits, at least not with me.'

She denied 'stealing' Jamila's husband. 'I met him and he did not want to see her any more. She did not love him any more. She did not want him. She just wanted his money.'

It was at this juncture that Jamila's sister, Naima, meta-phorically went for the jugular. 'You will never have any luck in your life because you separated two people who loved each other,' she ambushed Nadia. 'Anthony is not here any more. His bank account is closed.' She disclosed that, after learning of the affair between her husband and Nadia, Jamila 'came to me in such a state that I thought she had Parkinson's disease. You messed her up.'

After berating Nadia for allegedly breaking up a loving marriage, Naima then recounted how the Earl had begun propositioning *her* while still on honeymoon with her sister. The narrative descended into outlandish farce when she said, 'I was always getting messages from him. He kept calling me from the suite.' The honeymoon suite, no less! The theme of the litany of letters was, 'I love you, Naima, you're so beautiful, you are my dream.' Pitiful, maybe, but hardly *lurid*!

Did Jamila's sister reciprocate the Earl's advances? Apparently not. But if she was unmoved and scornful of the letters, why did she horde them? Obviously she had her reasons.

The reality was that it was Nadia who had pressed as much as the Shaftesbury family for police intervention when the Earl went missing. It was she who raised the alarm and was distraught as the days passed without any news of his whereabouts. She really cared for him and grieved over his death with a widow's sorrow. To my mind, among all the Earl's philandering conquests and defeats, Nadia stood head and shoulders above the rest. She might even have saved him if she had gone on holiday with him to Antibes on the day he flew into Nice, having been in Hove for a few days; that is a hypothesis she will carry with her to her own grave. But her infuriation with him that day was understandable. She felt horribly let down and deceived. She really had believed that his alcohol consumption was receding. He had made hand-on-heart pledges. There was a pact between them. And there he was, on the phone, obviously smashed.

Her acerbic explosion had been triggered more by disappointment in him than anything else. Broken promises by alcoholics over kicking the habit are legion, like a skip of empty bottles after a weekend rave. Poor Nadia was probably oblivious to the *sobering* fact that alone she had no chance of significantly reducing his boozing.

However, Nadia should not blame herself in any respect for her lover's death. If it had not happened on 5 November 2004, it would have amounted to nothing more than deferment, a temporary reprieve. The Earl was doomed from the moment he filed for divorce, a ghost waiting for his death.

So much did not add up about the televised clash between these two women. After all, Naima was the sister to whom Jamila had confessed on the phone to having paid Mohammed £100,000 'blood money'.

This feisty television feature about the 10th Earl and the women in his life was an intrusive distraction that Nicholas could have well done without at a time when the future of his dynasty was imperilled and he was walking an economic tightrope.

At last, on 9 February 2009, Jamila's appeal (a full re-trial) began in Aix-en-Provence. By then, Mohammed was in a prison psychiatric unit, 'incoherent and mostly in a delirious state'. As a result, his appeal was formally dropped and the original twenty-five-year sentence stood. Consequently, the court was further informed that Mohammed was unfit to testify on behalf of his sister and would not be called as a witness.

On this occasion, after the prosecution and defence cases were repeated, the jury took four hours deliberating, twice as long as at the original trial, though still very brief when murder was the charge. Despite the harrowing longer wait for the verdict, Nicholas need not have been apprehensive.

Jamila had been as unconvincing and discrepant as before. The guilty verdict was upheld. After all the suspense and tension over so many years, the Shaftesburys could finally relax, although closure for Nicholas was not yet complete. There was still the matter of Jamila clinging on to her countess title and, presumably, preparing to exploit it on her release, to be resolved.

His bitterness still raw, he told reporters outside the court, 'Essentially, she didn't really give much of a shit about my father. From the beginning, she was only out to get whatever she could. And she probably saw that the end was coming, so I don't know, "Get my father down, get rid of him and then I'll get everything in the will." She knew exactly what she could get her hands on.'

As for the re-trial, the only real dissatisfaction for Nicholas was the reduction of Jamila's prison sentence from twenty-five to twenty years. Nevertheless, he was visibly relieved and admitted as much, saying, that with all legal appeals exhausted he could now 'get on with' his life, after a 'very painful chapter'.

How wrong he was!

17

A SCANDAL
FOR ALL SEASONS

The Shaftesburys could be forgiven for believing that the worst was behind them. Two earls had died within six months of one another. Scandal upon scandal had been emblazoned across newspapers throughout Europe, as well as the UK, as much in the sober broadsheets as the shouting tabloids. When an earl went a-whoring, making a countess of a prostitute, squandered a fortune on cocaine and alcohol, allowed his ancestral estate to be reduced to the brink of rack and ruin, and was murdered for an unfair share of his heritage, then that was a story that transcended all social barriers. Sprinkle on that shameful fusion the illustrious and ascetic Shaftesbury name and you had rabid gossip that percolated down from the House of Lords to every spit-and-sawdust pub.

There were even three massage parlours in Brighton, next

to Hove in Sussex, that displayed promotional signs declaring, 'The Earl S had fun here!' This was slightly bawdier than the rather refined restaurant/hotel in another seaside resort on the south coast that was popularised by the titillating feature that the Prince of Wales, Queen Victoria's rascal of a son, regularly dined and slept there in a four-poster with one of his stable of mistresses. The Brighton brothel advertising campaign was a boost for the prostitution cottage industry of Britain's south coast, but distressful for, through the ages, such a principled and incorruptible family as the Shaftesburys.

Escort girls in Paris and the Riviera traded on the truth that they were regularly *dated* by a British aristocrat who mixed with royalty and heads of state. The Shaftesburys had lived with this sewerage for five years. Surely, all that was now dead and buried? Mind you, Jamila was still very much in Nicholas's thoughts, but only in the context of how he could deprive her of the Shaftesbury countess title to which she was clinging, aware that it could be her future financial lifeline. In a way, Jamila was just as bad for the 12th Earl as she had been for his father. Her presence in Nicholas's head was sufficient to raise his blood pressure.

Thankfully, Dinah acted as a counterpoint. She was the steady, calming influence, the salve and love of his life. She had been to Wimborne St Giles numerous times and was immensely popular there, not with just the Shaftesbury family but all the staff on the estate and locals in the village. 'So down to earth' was a comment I heard repeatedly, as well as, 'No airs and graces, a breath of fresh air'.

Surely the storms could not last for ever. With all

the criminal proceedings put to bed, everyone believed optimistically that the sun must shine again soon on the Shaftesburys. Everyone close to Nicholas assumed that he and Dinah would soon marry. But marriage to an earl was not something Dinah intended rushing into: here was a completely different creature to Jamila.

'I was hesitant at the beginning,' she confessed. 'I was worried about the burden and responsibilities.' She also had her veterinary career to consider. But Nicholas would not be taking no for an answer. He was a hardened marathon runner, not a sprinter. He could go the distance and was used to having to prove his stamina. This same true grit would eventually win him his bride, but not before more misery and drama.

The December of 2009 was bitterly cold, but this did not deter Nicholas from his outdoor activities. Building up steam cross-country running or horse-riding into a face-smacking, icy wind was a sure way of clearing his head of all the interwoven cobwebs of distraction. When he was exercising, everything else was put on hold; he became an island, insulated from the pressures that accumulated from a barrage of emails and text messages, and the cacophony from telephones, competing for attention.

There was still frost in the ground when he trotted from the St Giles House stables on his snorting horse together with family members for a morning ride. Both rider and horse were frozen, so Nicholas kicked on. Soon they were galloping over the undulating fields of a neighbouring farm, surrounded by woodland, some of the trees naked skeletons, while the evergreens fully decked in dark green forming a stark contrast.

Hot breath began pluming from the horses' flared nostrils. Nicholas was warming up, too, exhilarated by the pounding thud of hooves on the rock-hard turf and the rush of air stretching the flesh of his cheeks and whistling in his ears. He was buoyed by that *good-to-be-alive* feeling, the perfect start to any day. He was riding high and very soon so too would the estate.

Then, without warning, the curse struck again.

The horse under Nicholas was spooked by a rabbit bobbing in front of him. The horse veered and reared, and Nicholas was hurled out of the 'side door'. Lady Frances, who was living in France, explained later, 'It wasn't a bad fall. He more or less just slipped out of the saddle, but landed awkwardly.'

The Shaftesburys were masters of understatement. The fall was bad enough to break Nicholas's back. He could not move. The pain was excruciating. One side of his body was instantly paralysed. 'Luckily, I was not alone,' Nicholas told me in the conference room of St Giles House. 'If I had been, then I would have been in real trouble. The speed of getting emergency treatment probably made all the difference.'

The despatcher with the emergency services warned that no attempt should be made to move him. Another problem was soon identified. Because of the remote location, it was doubtful that paramedics would be able to reach him by ambulance, so a search-and-rescue helicopter was launched, with a crew of three – an A&E specialist doctor, a nurse and the pilot

During the short flight to the general hospital in Dorchester, Dorset's county town, the Earl was given a shot of morphine to kill the pain. After examining X-rays at the hospital, doctors there decided that the injuries were too serious and life threatening for them to treat. He needed to be in a specialist unit as quickly as possible; the nearest was Southampton General Hospital, some forty miles east along the coast.

The ambulance made the journey at a crawl, with a police escort. The technique was the same as with a patient suffering from severe head injuries: any bump or sudden braking could be fatal or lifelong disabling. Speed was essential, but so was a smooth transfer; it was a kind of catch-22 for the paramedics. Doctors clearly feared that, at the very least, Nicholas would never walk again.

Talking later about his fall, Nicholas said, 'I landed very badly, basically on my coccyx bone, or my seat bone, my middle vertebrae compressed and cracked, and the bone came in and whacked my spinal cord.'

Southampton General was a renowned teaching hospital. Every department had several of the country's leading consultants and professors. For example, it performed heart bypass surgery as routinely as a dentist pulled teeth. An operation to decompress Nicholas's spine was essential, without delay. Within an hour of the decision being made by the specialist medical team, Nicholas was in an operating theatre, where they also inserted a metal plate and screws. The odds were still against him ever walking again, but his life had been saved. Of course the high-powered painkilling shots and the general anaesthetic had made his mental faculties fuzzy. And he cannot remember with any clarity what was going through his mind in the critical moments before surgery. However, it is legitimate to assume that Dinah was central to his thinking and also the future of his sizeable but down at heel empire that was in need of surgery just as much as its master.

Dinah was determined that whatever the outcome of Nicholas's injuries, it would not be allowed to impair their relationship. She had spent much of her early life in Rome, and had first met Nicholas in London, where she was living. There was a natural rapport and affinity between them, easy in each other's company and sharing values. Some people had speculated that it was Nicholas's musical initiatives that had brought them together, but he assured me, 'No, not at all; it was nothing like that. She was not part of my music scene. We came across one another socially in London. You know, the way these things happen. But I'm not one of those people who believe in fate, that something was meant to happen. Similarly, I don't go in for thinking that the family has ever been cursed in any way. Things just occur randomly and you have to get on with it.'

Nicholas was equally steadfast that he would not have a wife whose only future and function was as his personal nurse. Dinah was comfortable with the Shaftesbury flock and Nicholas's friends. The thought of wearing the title "countess" every day of her life became less daunting when she realised that she would be on show only as much as she chose and there was no reason why her privacy should be violated. She could continue with her veterinary career and blend into the country life. Consequently, Dinah was ready to commit herself to marriage, but now it was Nicholas who argued for deferment. He wanted to be certain that he would not be an invalid for life and a burden on anyone. He was a hard taskmaster on himself.

From Southampton, he was transferred to a spinal rehabilitation unit at Salisbury District Hospital. He was in a wheelchair and staff continually preached to him the precept that time and his own positive attitude would dictate the chances and extent of his recovery, also the timescale. His dogged tenacity came by the bucket load, but as Nicholas saw it, time was in short supply. He wanted to walk, not be wheeled. There was so much to be done that he viewed time as another of his enemies. To walk again was not his ambition; he intended to run, and not just jog.

Marathon-running once more was his goal. A marathon runner he had been and a marathon runner he would be again; that was his intransigent mindset.

With his best interests at heart, the staff were a shade patronising. 'Having a target is the right approach, as long as it's a realistic one. There's no magic bullet, only rest and time. One step at a time. It's going to be a long haul.'

Nicholas was not inspired by such a prognosis. He was impatient. For him, progress would have to be at least two steps at a time. As always, he was a man in a hurry; that was his nature. There was so much to be accomplished without delay and here he was, a prisoner in a wheelchair.

Long-distance runners do not cope well with immobility. In his favour was the fact that, as noted earlier, Dinah's father was an orthopaedic surgeon, albeit retired, and her mother was a physiotherapist. Dinah was continually the harbinger of sound, helpful and encouraging advice from her parents.

Despite his frustration, Nicholas finally had to admit to himself that his fate and future would rest with Old Father Time. Reflecting some while later, he said, 'I have been an endurance runner. I went from the best shape in my life to taking one step a day and then back to bed, exhausted. I could have given up in despair, but I'm just really stubborn. I came to accept that at a certain point you have to wait for the nerves to regrow. And nothing much was going to do that other than time.

'I was very close to being paralysed from the waist down. I really should have been confined to a wheelchair for life. Luck was on my side. My family are applying pressure that I pick up a new hobby, but it's really just this sort of buzz to see if you can do it. You set yourself impossible tasks and see if you are capable.'

One step a day became two, then three, four, five…until he could manage fifteen minutes at a shuffle, sweating as if he had just completed a full marathon, to the applause of the physiotherapists. This breath-taking optimism and willpower was a seam that ran deep through the family. For example, a few weeks after his operation, Lady Frances was predicting that Nicholas would 'be back as good as new in a few months'. Meanwhile, the specialists were still far from certain that he would ever walk independently and properly again. But there was no chance of Lady Frances's faith being fragmented. 'He's very athletic and muscular. He'll pull through. He always does.' And the Lady, not for turning, was right.

With the aid of a stick, Nicholas was, indeed, soon walking again, although with a distinctive stoop and a limping gait. And the icing on the cake was the wedding of Nicholas and Dinah in Dorset on 11 September 2010, the day before the bride's thirtieth birthday, making for a double celebration. Hobbling and still held together by a metal plate and screws, Nicholas walked stiffly but proudly into matrimony. With marriage came three titles for Dinah: the Countess of Shaftesbury, Baroness Ashley and Baroness Cooper.

Additional pleasure for the Earl was the knowledge that from that day, Jamila M'Barek, the bane of his life, was no longer the Countess of Shaftesbury. However, even as a convicted murderer, she was legally entitled to call herself the Dowager Countess of Shaftesbury, an issue that remained high on Nicholas's agenda of things to be sorted. He was still very much a man on a mission for retribution and unqualified justice.

Despite all that he had been through, and the many setbacks that would have sucked every drop of spirit from many men, Nicholas said to me, intensely, grim with sincerity, 'I am a very lucky man. Just look at what I've been through in my life and compare it to the eternal suffering of so many people in the world and you realise that I have no right to complain or feel in the least unlucky. Quite the reverse: I have been blessed.'

18

REBEL WITH
A CAUSE

Despite regaining much of his mobility, Nicholas remained a registered paraplegic, which to him was just another title and not an obstacle. Simply a new challenge, like transmuting from one of the key figures on the US electronic music scene to a British lord of the manor, to which he was not born, a monster albatross that had surely contributed to the death of his elder brother within six months of its inheritance.

In the year following their wedding, on 24 January 2011, an heir was born – Anthony Francis Wolfgang Ashley-Cooper. Although the couple stuck to the Shaftesbury practice of naming the firstborn son Anthony, the new Earl and his cultured wife were not stodgy traditionalists in their outlook. They would soon be making their own significant statements, changes that bore their signatures. Without any tub-thumping, mutinous announcements, Nicholas would diplomatically demonstrate that he was slightly more rebel than traditionalist, leaning more towards Robin Hood than to the Sheriff of Nottingham. They were existential, freethinkers and would do things their way. They would not be slaves to Shaftesbury lore, though everything good about it would be preserved.

In 2012, a daughter was born, becoming Lady Viva Constance Lillemor. A son and daughter, born within a year of one another, made the family replete.

One of Nicholas's first initiatives on taking over from his brother was to invest £10 million of his own money in the refurbishment of St Giles House to awaken this mouldering, 'sleeping giant'. Through his own entre-preneurial endeavours, he was high on the young millionaires' rich list, equal with pop star Charlotte Church and classical soprano Katherine Jenkins.

The first restoration phase was to make the roof watertight, allowing the couple and their youngsters to take up residence in one of the reborn wings. Nicholas was proud to be in six decades or more the first earl to properly live in the great house, which he opened to the public through a series of special themed events.

Before *absconding,* the 10th Earl had had the north wing and tower demolished and the bay windows of the nineteenth-century library removed, home to books unequalled in any other private collection in the entire nation. Rather than denigrating his father, Nicholas was fiercely defensive of him. 'The fact that he left St Giles behind must have been an enormous decision. There obviously was a tipping point, where he just couldn't take any more. But he then had to live with that decision. And I don't think he could cope. I think this was just a denial, you know; bury it with everything else.'

As for having to succeed his brother and leave his beloved New York and the buzzing, high-octane music scene, he said, 'The new role didn't feel like me for a long time. I felt like I was a substitute, filling in for a bit until the real person came along. Maybe you can't ever be Lord Shaftesbury until you've got a stick, grey hair and a beard and can't hear anything. I'm the new Lord Shaftesbury and I'm still trying to figure out who that person is. A lot of people say that I must have regretted leaving New York, but I totally don't.

'This is way more important than anything I was doing before. I just feel this enormous need to actually take responsibility and just get things back on track and not only for the family. *We* want to bring back everything that's been good about this family and everything that we stood for.'

Of the bold gamble with his own £10 million, he said, 'I just saw that it was worth taking all the risk, gambling everything to make this happen and to keep it the family home, because it's been with you for generations, has so much history and it is really the heart of where your family has been. I'll be willing to put everything into trying to keep it that way and trying to preserve it. I've always said you're never going to get anywhere unless you're willing to take some risks at some point, and this was so worth taking a risk for.'

Nicholas has never been one for standing on ceremony, even though his godfather is Simon Elliot, the Duchess of

Cornwall's brother-in-law. He really means it when he says he 'could not care less' what people call him. As soon as he makes a new acquaintance, he casually invites that person to call him Nick. 'But I have respect for the title,' he has impressed upon interviewers. 'I don't want to downgrade it, but I don't expect people to put me on a pedestal. I don't feel that I need to be elevated in any way.'

Of the house he said, 'This house was always shuttered up, semi-derelict. Because my dad had such a difficult relationship with the place, he didn't encourage us to go there. We lived in the dowager's house on the other side of the village. It was pretty grim.

'But one of the things that is often skated over is how much respect and loyalty the people in the estate had for my father. There was a huge fondness for him. Until the drink started to take over and dominate his personality and life, he was a very charming man and spent many years doing amazing things with the estate and running this place very well. Sadly, his ultimate demise cast a shadow over everything else. But still there isn't a single person around here who would have a bad word for my father. He was loved and respected by everyone – and still is. You have only to mention his name and you'll see it in their eyes and faces.

'My father had tried to downsize and then ran out of steam. Various Victorian wings were removed and it left lots of holes. The house has always been the big issue, the unresolved matter. It is the heart of the estate and family, but in this era we no longer need such a massive house and must regard it more as a venue.'

By 2011, many of the most urgent repairs had been completed and the first public event was staged in the grounds in June that year – 'The Great Shaftesbury Run', a 10km race and a half-marathon, raising money for a school for children with learning difficulties, a sports college for the disabled and the spinal injuries charity, Wings for Life – a sponsorship package very personal to both Nicholas and Dinah.

'There is a change of mindset about how we run these places,' the Earl elaborated. 'Really creative people are doing interesting things with their historic homes.' His long-term strategy is to generate an 'income-stream' to make life easier when his son inherits.

News of the 12th Earl's resolution to strip Jamila M'Barek of her 'undeserved' title, restore the historic Grade I-listed stately home and reinvent its purpose provoked a tidal wave reaction on the Internet. Here is a varied selection:

'Anyone who poses looking like that [Jamila] with boobs heaving out of her jacket and no top, doesn't deserve a cent' – Dry Heat, USA

'Good luck to you [Nicholas], she looks sick and it would be terrible for the likes of her to get her hands on family heirlooms' – petulapeel, Royston

'It must be a lot of hard work and responsibility, but well done that man for restoring his family home and his family dignity' - P3 frx, Sunderland, UK.3

'Wow! This will make a great movie' – scalovi, Brookhaven, New York

'There are infinitely many more aristocratic families

with huge, historic properties that have not a penny...all due to the greedy, hedonistic lifestyle led by aristocrats in the sixties and seventies. Most family trusts were meant to keep the properties and their history intact for centuries, with the family more as a caretaker, not for them to steal the money for their own greedy, high-life stupidity. The fact that the second son, now Lord, has spent £10 million of his OWN hard-gained money to restore a historical place shows a recent trend, with many more of the newer generation doing the same to restore estates that their greedy predecessors squandered. We are coming around again full circle to having a bit of pride in our history, our Britishness and our culture. It's not about titles meaning "rich" any more, it's about them wanting a British culture protected, and it should be.' – Beth, Royal Tunbridge Wells, UK.

'Only twenty years in jail for premeditatedly murdering someone for money? Really? – Saganite, London

'Good luck with all your efforts and I hope common sense prevails with the title' – Ican, London

'Men need to wise up about women' – Visceral Rage, London

'I wonder how many aristocrats today are the result of bedroom antics of so-called nobles from past decades, and what makes a person an aristocrat? Someone who has pillaged other countries in the name of the Crown? Just asking' – Stuart, Bradford, UK

The 10th Earl lost his seat in the House of Lords when hereditary peerages were pruned. On the death of the 4th Viscount Colville of Culross in April 2010, Nicholas challenged for the vacancy as a cross-bencher. Considering the political giants among his illustrious precursors and the resonance of the Shaftesbury name through the corridors of power in Westminster, one might have foreseen a landslide victory for young Nicholas, despite his disgraced father. But it was not to be: in the election that June, Nicholas lost the vote to the 9th Earl of Clancarty. Several times since, Nicholas has stood in House of Lords by-elections, but, so far, has never been successful. I am not in the least surprised.

In New York, he was a cult figure, a legend, no less, in what his disciple-like followers hailed as the underground, alternative-society music experience. Nicholas was the leader, the trailblazer. In threadbare jeans, with long, unkempt black hair, a rash of garish tattoos decorating his body, and a face almost Goth with its pallid, brooding appearance, you could not possibly imagine a more anti-Establishment social mutineer. See him today in Savile Row suit, silk blue socks, black polished shoes, tiepin, white handkerchief squared in his breast pocket and hair swept back tidily, and he is unrecognisable as the 'creator of the infamous ROBOTS parties' in New York. Old buffers of the Palace of Westminster who clicked on to the nick ac promotional website must have thought they were seeing a foreign language. Here is a taste:

Originally hailing from the UK, he was heavily influenced by London's club scene during the early nineties…Afterwards, he helped inject life into a floundering US electronic music scene and the city's outlook on electronic music. He was instrumental in sustaining a vibrant underground music scene in New York, bringing over and exposing numerous artists and musicians, as well as imprinting his own unique sound on the city.

Drawing from a rich diversity of influences for over a decade in the industry, Nick developed a unique style that relied on sophisticated, cutting-edge sounds…His keen ear, knowledge of what worked on the dancefloor and appreciation for varying styles of music enabled him to stand out from his peers and become a big influence on others.

'It was also a combination of sounds – the futuristic, electronic and emotive that were really appealing to me.' [Quoted by Nick on the site]

Inspired by the freshness and innovativeness of the music, he became eager to get involved. In 1996, at the age of sixteen, he purchased his first set of turntables and has since never looked back.

In 1998, he moved to Manchester and secured his first break with a job at Sankey's Soap, the home of Tribal Gathering and Tribal Sessions – one of the UK's most notorious club nights [certainly not conventional peerage electioneering material for a robed place in the stuffy House of Lords, you may think, but certainly different and a catalyst for a shake-up, yes?]

Overseeing promotion for the club, Nick was quick

to establish contacts and friends amongst many major players in the international music industry. He also found time to set up and promote the successful dub party 'Luvclub' at the unique Mancunian venue, 'Band on the Wall'. During his time in Manchester, Nick completely submersed himself in the club scene and could be found in venues all across the city, either promoting or spinning tunes.

In 2001, Nick met Mike Bindra (previously of Twilo, New York) and accepted the opportunity to work with him in New York on the legendary club Space at 6, Hubert Street: Vinyl became the landmark club. From the start, the emphasis was firmly on the music and Nick hosted the internationally celebrated Friday night party 'Be Yourself' with Danny Tenaglia. His passion for DJing and keeping the scene pushing forwards led to Nick setting up ROBOTS in 2004 [the year his father was murdered], exposing underground talent to new fans and veterans alike.

'The idea was about pushing a variety of artists from electro to minimal house, to techno, that did not previously have much of a platform in the US.'

In a little over a year, ROBOTS gained worldwide recognition and has become one of New York's most acclaimed parties. Nick has seen his reputation and fan-base grow considerably. In 2005, Nick teamed up with Chris Liebing for a bi-monthly residency at Avalon, New York. He held down a packed party at Miami's Winter Music Conference with Sven Vath (a feat which he repeated the following year) and completed the ROBOTS one-year anniversary with legendary DJ and producer Francoise K. He also set up and ran a weekly radio show, RobotRadio out of the East Village in New York, which he operated with fellow residents Bill Patrick and Dennis Rodgers.

Showcasing upcoming artists and featuring guest interviews and new releases, the show acted as another tool Nick used to push the electronic music scene to the masses.

In 2006, Nick made a move back to the studio to start work on producing for a forthcoming Robots label, 'We are Robots'. The same year also saw the launch of the first Robots compilation CD and a focus on Europe, taking his music back home! He scored major club gigs in Germany at Fusion in Munster and Studio 632 in Cologne, home of Kompakt. During the summer, he 'kicked-off' a residency in Ibiza with friend and fellow DJ Chris Liebing at Spinclub and Privilege on Sundays.

Of the residency in Ibiza, Nick described it as 'a dream come true' and a chance to really showcase the music and vibe he had been creating in New York. 'There were so many cool things going on in electronic music it's nice to embrace as much of it as you can.'

Although becoming the 12th Earl of Shaftesbury dragged him away from his beloved New York, Nicholas's onerous duties at Wimborne St Giles did not completely separate him from his music adventures. In 2010, he became the chief operating officer with GoMix, an interactive music software platform company, which launched a widget designed specifically for use on social-networking sites. He was noted for his solid grounding in business management and for his work as a consultant in 'strategic design'. Prior to being headhunted by GoMix, he served as a member of a team that raised more than $5 million for Saatchi Online, a forum and art gallery showcasing the work of more than 100,000 artists and receiving an estimated 73 million hits per day. Before teaming-up with Saatchi, he worked in digital strategy and business development with Terra Firma Capital Partners, following its acquisition of British music company EMI Group Limited. Terra Firma was best known for its widely publicised investments in EMI.

The Earl's earlier work involved providing strategic analysis at Discovery Networks International who offered a portfolio of channels, led by Discovery and Animal Planet, which were distributed in virtually every pay-TV market in the world. He was a core member of the strategy team for Europe, the Middle East and Asia.

Obviously the 12th Earl is a natural born entrepreneur. And probably a natural-born peer, too, given the chance. It's hard to see how people could not have been impressed by the way he slipped seamlessly from his life in the sub-culture of New York to lord of the manor, a nobleman at the helm of a rural dynasty in deepest Dorset.

Should the wind of *real* change blow through the corridors of power in the Palace of Westminster, Nicholas is likely to be embraced as a fugleman.

Of the Earl and Dinah, one commentator wrote, 'You cannot help but root for such a couple: a wife who described her husband as easy to live with and a husband who exclaims "Wow!" whenever his wife walks into the room.'

Quite an acclamation, though I am not sure that *wow* would be considered acceptable speak in the Palace of Westminster!

To be physically and mentally indomitable is a formidable combination. Nicholas seems to have been blessed with this flinty combination. Not from birth, though. As already chronicled in an earlier chapter, at the age of sixteen he could have been heading the way of his father.

At that critical crossroad, with his future education in the balance, he could so easily have made a ruinous choice of direction. Instead, he performed a U-turn. No more drugs. No more unacceptable carousing. No anti-social stupidity. He consciously took control of his life and future, pulling out of a nosedive before it was too late.

Nicholas had witnessed what alcohol abuse was doing to his father. If he had not applied the brakes and had forged ahead regardless, taking the low road instead of the high ground, people long before now would have been speculating about drugs and booze being in the blood of the latest crop of Shaftesburys, almost as if these negatives had infused their DNA and defined the male side of the family.

Nicholas had seen the way the demons worked and how his father was taken over by devils that devoured him, so relevant to fully understanding the remarkable achievements of the 12th Earl of Shaftesbury in the face of obstacles that would have daunted and overpowered most people.

For a start, Nicholas knew no fear. His starting point with everything was that there was no challenge that he could not overcome. He had vision and a life plan. There were no grey areas. He saw the landscape in front of him in black and white. He was scarily decisive and incisive. With everything, there was a right and a wrong way. At any given moment, he knew exactly where he was going – and how. Enemies were there to be defeated, not to be compromised with. There were to be no pragmatic deals.

His whole modus operandi in the music industry was geared to pushing back frontiers. He conquered New York, surely the toughest market in the world to master, and was beginning to taste the fruits of an international reputation. And at a stroke, he boarded a plane at JFK and flew away from it all; no tears, no sadness, no regrets, no posturing or vacillating; he did what he knew was right. Duty called, a duty for which he was never groomed. He just went with the jet stream and the transformation was made as effortlessly as changing clothes – from T-shirt and jeans into the uniform of the Establishment. He has a knack of being able to wear both with distinction.

Even when he lay on the frozen ground, partially paralyzed with a broken back, the notion that his goals might be thwarted never crossed his mind and being registered a paraplegic was simply another confrontation with a demon that had to be conquered.

For me, the tawdriest moment of the murder trial of

Jamila and Mohammed M'Barek came outside the court-room when a female controller of escorts presented Nicholas with a bill. This woman claimed that the 10th Earl had been provided with sexual services which had not yet been paid for. 'I want this debt honoured,' she said. This was obviously a cheap and sordid publicity stunt. It was no accident that press photographers were lined up like a firing squad, ready to shoot the moment the bill was handed over.

Anyone with a cursory knowledge of the flesh market would know that every prostitute, whether a streetwalker, a brothel inmate or on the books of an escort agency, demanded payment upfront before taking off even an overcoat. There was no such thing as running up a tab and settling the account at the end of the month.

Nicholas was unfazed. If the media had been hoping for a theatrical showdown, they were disappointed. Without histrionics or the slightest manifestation of emotion, he coolly tore up the bill, allowing the torn pieces to flutter down like confetti around the woman's feet. 'I shall not be paying this,' he said peremptorily, his expression disdainful, before turning away and walking off unhurriedly, as if untouched by the shabby episode, then using his mobile to discuss a completely different matter. Everything of the previous five minutes had been wiped from the slate in his head. Nothing would be allowed to encroach on his long-term game plan. He had turned tunnel vision into an art form, yet he also had the ability to juggle tasks without dropping any, a unique skill.

19

A SHOT IN
THE FOOT

Although this book is primarily about the tragic downfall of the 10th Earl of Shaftesbury, the cloud of disgrace it cast over his revered family name and how his successor, against all odds and adversities, turned around the fortunes of the dynasty, it seemed necessary to explore in some depth the credibility of Lucille, for example, hopefully without digressing too much from the essence of the saga.

During the murder trial, Jamila M'Barek testified that arguments with her husband, the 10th Earl, 'had nothing to do with money', but were a result of his 'excessive sexual demands', triggered by his 'seemingly endless injections of testosterone'. Although she did not expand on this, the insinuation was that the 10th Earl was into kinky sex, obsessed with squalid fetish, or maybe something even more deviant.

This undertone upset Nadia Orch, who was adamant that he had 'no strange bedroom habits.'

The prostitute Lucille, so often a companion of the 10th Earl in France, was adamant, too, on another issue: 'I can tell you with absolute certainty: the idea of him attacking Jamila's brother, starting a fight, is absurd. If you knew him as well as I did, then you'd know that such a story was pure fiction. A pack of lies from beginning to end. And that's what the court decided. The judge hinted at it, too. Tony used words to make his point, not fists.'

Nadia, who came on the scene later than Lucille, was more concerned about the Earl's drinking, but that was due to their emotional involvement. Nadia was living with him, on and off. She was preparing to be his wife, as soon as possible after he had divorced Jamila. So she was tormented by health issues and how his drinking, if it continued at the same strident tempo – or even at an increased level – would impact on their future. Lucille did not have the same considerations.

Lucille had never met Jamila, so there was no personal animosity there. A noteworthy factor in her favour is that so much of her story complemented what was already known in the UK about the Earl's foibles, whereas Jamila's account, for example, was at odds with everyone else's evaluation of the tormented man.

Why had Lucille become a prostitute in the first place, when she had an abundance of qualifications for many highly paid careers? This was something that had intrigued the 10th Earl, too. When I put the question to her, the answer was an unabashed and honest, 'Quick money. As much as possible as fast as possible, for my education. Then I stockpiled it. That was my game plan, to make a pile and then parachute out. I was honest with myself. I didn't bury my head in the sand and try to justify myself morally. I went into it with my eyes wide open: be wicked for a few years, then remove the camouflage and be myself again. Lots of girls go into it with that plan, but very few manage to escape; that's because they're not qualified for anything else. They're faced with the choice of going on for as long as possible or working on the checkout of a supermarket.'

As she went on to say, the money is hard to give up. 'Once you've earned £1,000 an hour, tax-free, you have either to be a saint or a fool to give it up for a pittance that demands you work eight hours a day, five days a week. The decision wasn't so hard for me because I wasn't going on to earn a pittance salary. That said, there were many nights when I was escorting that I thought working at the pit-face of a coalmine would be easier.

'I'm not judgmental of others, so why should I be of myself? Prostitution served a purpose. It was a positive career move. I was then able to look for a respectable job without having to worry about the rental cost of a decent apartment and having to be careful about how much money I spent on food. I can still afford to be extravagant.

'There was no inconvenient gap in my CV. For the years that I was escorting, I put down travelling and freelance interpreting. Neither was a lie, though not the whole truth, of course.'

Jamila and others on the French side of the action, apart from Nadia and Lucille, of course, mostly relied on labels to impugn the Earl: sexaholic, alcoholic, cocaine addict, roué, playboy pensioner, out of control, self-destructing. All the people muck-raking had self-seeking reasons to distort their portrayal of the Earl. Lucille replaced the labels with anecdotes that give breath and definition to the Earl's mental state and behaviour patterns, introducing clarity where there was bafflement. The only editing I have done to her earlier and quite elaborate account is to omit repetition, comments on unconnected matters, and exclamations made as she grappled for the appropriate expression in English, which was not often. As you would expect from a professional translator and someone proficient in six languages, she was extremely articulate and precise. All dialogue between her and the Earl is as she recalled it. If not exact, as it could not possibly be, it is a faithful attempt at reconstruction and no meaning has been altered.

During his time with Lucille, the 10th Earl took Viagra regularly. 'Not owing to a lack of sexual desire but because the alcohol kept his manhood limp. Viagra overcame that,' Lucille explained, matter-of-fact. 'He didn't have a psychological problem but a physical dysfunction, caused by too much alcohol.

'The only sex-obsession I witnessed with Tony was that he wanted it every day, like clockwork, and it had to be performed as a one-act play. Always the same play, the same script and the same props.' Probably tedious for someone like Jamila, but if you were going to be mercenary and cynical about it, you would have to conclude it was easy money.

Searching for objectivity and impartiality in this imbroglio would have been impossible without someone like Lucille, who really was the proverbial needle in a haystack. Everyone else had an angle; as partisan as football followers, they were either an inveterate fan of the Earl or a staunch supporter of Jamila. Nothing exemplifies this more than an article in the *Guardian* newspaper in 2006, written by Alex Duval Smith, in which several sources were quoted. One of them was Fatima, the youngest daughter in the M'Barek family, who worked as a translator (obviously a popular job and the only thing she had in common with Lucille) with the French embassy in Tunis. Her depiction of sister Jamila could not possibly have been more disparate than the one presented by the prosecution and accepted as the truth in the two trials:

'Jamila is a trained beautician and she worked in hairdressing in Paris. She had a job in gourmet cuisine, with the chef Alain Ducasse, in Monaco. Since her marriage to the Dutchman, the father of her two children, she has not needed to work. She did not need money.'

Fatima was in denial about Jamila ever having worked as a hostess in the sleazy pick-up bars of Cannes or as an escort. To be fair, Fatima's *truth* probably came from Jamila. After all, Fatima was rooted in Tunis, while Jamila was more nomadic: Paris, Nice, Cannes, Monte Carlo, wherever she was needed. Jamila would have drip-fed her *success story* to her relatives in Tunisia.

And of the 10th Earl, Fatima was reported declaring, 'He

was very moody. You never knew where you were with him. He was sickly and had incontinence trouble. My sister had to change the sheets all the time. She had to look after him like a baby. He was an alcoholic and he was always taking Viagra. He was unfaithful from the start. He made my sister very miserable. When we had the wedding party in Holland, he walked naked into the room of my sister, Wassilia, and got into her bed. When he visited us in Tunisia once, he tried to fondle my breasts.'

Of the divorce, she said, 'Jamila could not bear the lord any longer. She loved him, but he was so unfaithful all the time. Mohammed tried unsuccessfully to reconcile them.'

Fatima's quotes are full of intimate details that could only have originated from Jamila: *sickly and incontinent,* for example. There had been no other reference to incontinence; certainly there had been no evidence of it when he was with Lucille and Nadia. It must be remembered that Jamila eagerly pursued the marriage. She was claiming to be pregnant and bearing the Earl's child, so they had been sharing a bed long enough for her to be familiar with all his habits and foibles, and yet she was the one pressing for marriage and countess status. He could not possibly have been making Jamila *miserable* then.

As for the comment that Jamila had to look after the Earl 'like a baby', there may be some truth in that, but only in relation to his sexual propensity, and it further strengthens the authenticity of Lucille's reminiscences. However, compare the statements of Fatima with the comments much earlier to the British press of Lady Frances, the Earl's sister: 'My brother suffered a great deal from being uprooted, first by the war, then by his father's death. He needed to be prepared to become the next Earl of Shaftesbury, yet it was difficult for our French stepfather to have authority over him. Our grandfather, the 9th Earl of Shaftesbury, was very kind, very English, but he was already an old man.'

Regarding her brother's initial attachment to Jamila, Lady Frances said, 'He was desperate for company. She impressed him as a wealthy divorcee at a time when he was very needy. She was feminine, attractive and attentive. She cooked nice meals for him. She was experienced with men and made him feel important. She was obsessed with money, possessive. Once they got together, I did not see much of him. She was the wrong person for him. When my brother said he would divorce her, she would not accept. I never believed money makes you happy and now, more than ever, I am certain of it. He loved birds and wildlife. He was funny, generous, very English in that way.'

Lady Frances believed that Jamila had caught him during a deep depression in his life, when he was very vulnerable.

Another perspective came from Anis Selah, who had been a friend of Mohammed since childhood in Nabeul, rating him as 'gentle, kind and totally unmaterialistic'. She further said, 'He was a sporty type, very good at football. He was even invited for trials at Espérance Sportive [a top Tunisian club]. The women he married – first a German he met in Tunisia, then another German who is the mother of his three children – were very possessive of him.'

Fatima also defended her brother as vehemently as she

did Jamila. 'He is God-fearing and generous. When he did military service in 1986, they put him in the first-aid corps because he was a caring person. He would never allow anyone to pay for him in a restaurant. He arranged for our mother to go on the pilgrimage to Mecca.'

Yet this was the same man Jamila labelled a psychopath, capable of any violence and of whom she lived in fear, especially after he had milked £100,000 from her as 'blood money' and a bribe to silence him.

For every strong view and conviction there was an equally powerful contradiction. Nothing was squared. As for the contention that the Earl made Jamila 'miserable', it is abundantly evident that very soon into their marriage they made each other depressed. And when it came to infidelity, they were both as culpable: one was doing it for money, while the other was at the mercy of his warped chemistry.

When Mohammed was in the remand centre in Grasse, before the trial, his only visitor was his lawyer, Melanie Junginger, except on one occasion when Fatima turned up unexpectedly. Ms Junginger presented yet another side to the man who was eventually convicted, with Jamila, of violent, premeditated murder. 'He is extremely popular at the prison, a devout man who is calm and says he deserves ill because he has done ill. He speaks well of Jamila and claims he should have controlled himself. Jamila, on the other hand, says he is a violent man and frequently asked her for money.'

There was certainly much bullish optimism in Jamila's legal camp. Her lawyer, Franck de Vita, even prophesied that Jamila would be released before standing trial. 'She tried to stop the fight [she said she hid in the bedroom]. If she had anything to gain from the lord's killing, she would have skipped the country [unless, of course, she was confident that the body would never be found and, if it was, she had a patsy in Mohammed]. She had ample time to do so between November 2004 and her arrest in February [2005]. She was receiving 10,000 euros a month and she was looking forward to getting 400,000 euros out of the divorce.'

Highlighting the financial implications was a shot in the foot, of course, because the Earl was worth far more to Jamila dead than alive.

20

JAMILA'S
TRASH

The 3rd Earl of Shaftesbury was an eminent philosopher. The 10th Earl was well read and philosophy was something else that had probably attached itself to the Shaftesbury DNA through the generations. Therefore, it is highly likely that the 10th Earl was familiar with the work of Sigmund Freud and, in particular, his controversial theory of the Oedipus complex, discussed earlier in this book. If so, it would explain why he deemed 'normal' his physical passion for his mother, though this is only an assumption because I have no evidence of his having discussed it with any of the women in his life. There is a phrase relating to a lifespan that we use today: 'from womb to tomb'. Freud coined this phrase but applied it to young boys who were attracted to their mothers and aroused by them. However, growing pains – or yearning pangs – do not always disappear with maturity. Many 'pet' fantasies are for life, certainly not just for Christmas and puberty. Freud had devout disciples and detractors in roughly equal numbers within his profession.

The 10th Earl was a freethinker. He would have researched and rationalised his sexual fetish, and doubtlessly concluded that it was within the framework of normality and not degenerate, yet his outlet for this fantasy was confined to prostitutes. Perhaps Jamila was alluding to the Earl's mother infatuation or Oedipus complex when protesting about his sexual demands.

The Earl must have gravitated towards prostitutes because he could be forthcoming and honest with them, free from repression. The demi-monde were a sub-culture to themselves, offering their own brand of alternative society in which nonconformity was the mantra and no fixation was classified abnormal; maybe strange and different, but not taboo, and a price list would distinguish the rare from the common. Obviously, as shown by his drastic response the 10th Earl had felt trapped in a straightjacket, from which he had to burst loose. Unable to confide in his wife and wider family, perhaps fearing disbelief and renunciation from them, he fled into the embrace of whores, his pain numbed by champagne and his depression lifted by cocaine. He paid a high price for his freedom, though: it was a case of escape to captivity. The final price, of course, was his life.

In the words of Peter Ackroyd, the Eros statue has always *commanded a strange power*. Now a miniature Eros has been erected by Nicholas, the 12th Earl, in the grounds of St

Giles House in Wimborne St Giles. That *strange power* is the welcome to visitors as they approach the house.

Although the feedback from the public was scant during the five-month search for the Earl, there were a couple of reported sightings of him in Ajaccio, Corsica. What is not known, of course, is to how many people the Earl divulged his curiosity for France's Napoleonic tradition and the allure for him of Corsica. It is unlikely Lucille was the only person with whom he shared his sentiments on this subject. These tip-offs could easily have been malicious, misinformation calls, designed to misdirect the police, not that there was anything resembling a trail at that time. But quite a few days of police time were wasted. They could not dismiss the possibility of the sightings being kosher, so airline passenger lists and those of ferry operators had to be checked. However, because Corsica was a part of France, all flights there from the mainland were classified as domestic, so there were no customs or immigration formalities to navigate. If the Earl paid in cash, he could have travelled incognito, using any name at random. The same applied to hotels, so the police had to circulate photographs. Considerable plodding, leg work was involved, with officers calling on hotels, car-hire companies and airline check-in staff with photos of the Earl. Cabin crews of airlines were also questioned.

Antibes was another focus for the police, during the frustrating period when they were still hopeful of finding the Earl alive. Because of his tendency to take off on a whim and be out of touch for weeks at a time, it was difficult for the police, at the beginning, to gauge whether the Earl was missing or simply being missed by people such as Nadia. He had an affection for the place, though it had nothing to do with it being an A-list celebrity hotspot.

Most tourists are drawn to Antibes by its material, glitzy attractions. The Hotel du Cap-Eden-Roc, if not the world's most expensive hotel was certainly in the A list. Its swimming-pool had been dynamited out of the Cap d'Antibes in 1914. Nearby, Roman Abramovich's chateau overlooks the diminutive yet exclusive beach, Plage des Galets. The sumptuous Villa Eilenroc struts its stuff across eleven hectares of coastal wilderness, where in 2015 real estate prices were £25,000 per square hectare. Also close to the hotel, is the masion Aujourd'hui, where Charlie Chaplin and Ava Gardner shacked up peacefully, long before the paparazzi was spawned. And privacy was purged.

Antibes trades on its reputation for high-society decadence, but as we have heard from Lucille, the attraction for the Earl was the town's links with Napoleon Bonaparte. Daily, tourists are steered by guides to the Villa Eilenroc, once owned by American billionaire Louis Dudley Beaumont, and where maharajahs and Russian princes danced throughout the night in a spacious and ornate ballroom, Napoleonic in regal concept. The guides make the abstract connection between the palatial villa and Napoleon's epic bedroom one-liner, 'Not tonight, Josephine,' which is a corruption of what he actually said. For accuracy, his words were, 'Patience, my darling. We will have time to make love when the war is won.' His libido was low because all he could think of was beating-up the Brits. What the guides do *not* talk about, of course, is the abstruse link between Napoleon and the 10th Earl of Shaftesbury. 'Boney's' wife, Josephine, was six years older than her husband and, when they married, she already had two children. Napoleon, just like the Earl, was bewitched by his mother. Josephine looked and behaved far older than her years, and therefore her vicarious role as mother to Napoleon, as well as wife, must have been instinctual. The 10th Earl doubtlessly saw his alter ego in Napoleon, hence his obsessive affinity with the ex-emperor. Perhaps the pull of gravity was the architect of the Earl's final years?

The professional guides regularly relate to their enraptured audiences the yarn of F Scott Fitzgerald partying in the art deco orangery, a scene he re-created in his sex-fuelled novel, *Tender is the Night*. The guides point to a first edition of the novel, presented to Louis Dudley Beaumont, which has pride of place on a bookshelf. The Eilenroc mansion is now publicly-owned — by an organisation similar to the UK's National Trust — including its 500m driveway, set amid a carpeting of wild cyclamen, sentinel Aleppo pines, several fragrant footpaths, flowering aloe and pistachio mastic trees.

The Plage des Ondes was Madonna's favourite beach at one time; tourists gag on this revelation before aiming cameras and videorecorders, and shooting rapid-fire. Pergolas and tennis courts in the secluded gardens of villas are as common as mosquitoes at sunset. The nouveau riche residents are sniffy about the noise from the open-top tour buses, cabriolet charabancs that belt out fumes and, over the loudspeaker systems, the titillating VIP history of the Cap d'Antibes, from Pablo Picasso to Edith Piaf.

Poor old Boney does not warrant a postscript from the guides, yet he was the only enticement for the Earl, who was accepted by the old brigade of Antibes as an adopted local dignitary. He paid with old-made money, which made him worth far more than the possibly wealthier parvenus. He was welcome as a French grandee rather than a brash foreigner trying to buy his way into the planet's priciest peninsula. The flashy cars, movie stars, pop singers, showy boats and modern mansions were the ugly and unacceptable face of Antibes for the Earl, his scar on the landscape. He would go there only because of its past perfect, not its grotesque present – in his eyes – and almost certain inglorious future. Boney's life there was the attraction for him. He told one of his soulmates that Antibes was another of Napoleon's conquests (a peaceful one) that had finally been lost to the philistines.

So Antibes became yet another false trail for the police to follow until the search for the Earl changed suddenly into a body hunt. For me, although the search for his body is long over, the quest for his soul is not.

One of the saddest and tackiest sights was witnessing spiv hustlers in Cannes taking tourists on guided tours of the grotty patch where the 'chewed-up body of the murdered British lord was found'. The equivalent of £30 per person was charged, more than any other day-excursion on land in the region. Roll up! Roll up! It was like a fairground attraction. Mini-buses took the ghouls into the hills to the Vallon de la Rague, about six miles west of the town's scented centre.

A stream, appearing clean enough to drink from, trickled through a gully in the red rock to the Mediterranean. But the idyllic scenery was an illusion, not a trick of nature but the desecration of man. On closer inspection, it was evident that this whole area had become a paradise, not for nature lovers but for fly tippers. Beneath the ragged ivy and other knotted undergrowth was a graveyard for every conceivable item people wanted to be rid of – even a human being. The Earl had been discarded under a laurel tree, surrounded by household debris.

An aristocrat thrown away with household rubbish. A makeshift graveyard for anything disposable and unwanted. Jamila's trash…

20

SPURRED BY
ADVENTURE

To say that the house-restoration challenge confronting the 12th Earl was formidable would be to minimise it to mockery. There was so much to be tackled simultaneously, and on so many different fronts and levels.

Put bluntly, St Giles House was a shipwreck, a grand old stately liner that had run aground and been left to corrode and come apart at the joints. The task had already broken one man – Nicholas's father. No one will ever know for certain, but the burden of responsibility may well have also contributed to the premature death of Anthony, the 11th Earl. So what chance Nicholas, thrown in at the deep end, from the highly specialised and individualistic music industry of cut-throat New York to being the saviour of a multifarious rural enterprise? Reducing the challenge to a basic betting analogy, bookmakers would probably have offered odds of 1,000-1.

As Nicholas freely admitted, he really did not know where or how to begin. As for St Giles House, first and foremost the rot had to be halted before any programme of restoration could be contemplated; this was easier said than done. Yet in some ways the reconstruction of the stately home was the easiest project to embrace. Nicholas could sit down with architects, surveyors, designers, builders and professional restorers and hammer out a constructive action plan. As for expenditure, Nicholas wanted reality and accuracy, rather than creative accounting and fingers-crossed conjecture. The pressures on him were too enormous for any onlooker to fully assimilate. Not only had one of the most *impossible* missions been thrust upon him, he was still grieving the loss of his father and brother, plus dealing with the distasteful legal fallout in France and the spurious rumours percolating through the aristocratic ranks in Britain.

Paradoxically, perhaps youthfulness worked in his favour. Whereas an older person might have been daunted, Nicholas was spurred by the spirit of adventure, in the image of those *boy* Battle of Britain pilots who believed they were immortal and could win the war on their own. Although his knowledge for running a diversified, bucolic empire was virtually non-existent, he was a fast learner. He surrounded himself with trusty experts. If he did not know what should be done, he knew a man/woman who did. Another thing in his favour was that marathon runners do not quit when mountains, to be climbed or circumnavigated, come into view.

However, the invisible test for him was by far the stiffest – how to re-establish the Shaftesbury brand as one of the most revered and respected in the land. During the previous decades, the family name had taken a bigger hammering than the house. By comparison, repairing the house was simple. But there was no quick fix to restoring a reputation. The only way back from perdition for the once-lustrous name was through personal example. It was to be a long, circuitous road, but one Nicholas immediately tackled with gusto and also humility. Not once did he blame his father for the mess he had inherited, but neither has he attempted to underrate the long-term ruination which came about as a result of the 10th Earl's abandonment of his obligations and his very public profligacy. Any defence has been in the form of mitigation, an appeal for understanding rather than for clemency, for a basically good man who was blown off course by ill winds that became cyclonic, causing him to lose his grip on the tiller. Implicit in Nicholas's appeal for tolerance has been the age-old balm: 'there but for the grace of God...'

Every day, whatever the weather, Nicholas could be seen running for miles around the estate, not jogging but pounding, building up a full head of steam as he crossed meadows and threaded his way through forests, jumping streams and ditches, and leapfrogging gates and ranch-style fencing. This immense, sprawling acreage was all *his*. There was a sense that he could run for ever and always be on Shaftesbury soil, a sort of fiefdom or principality within an island, where there was home rule and the Earl was the benign dictator, yet moored to democratic principles; he was a man of his people, yet also a lord among them, which was a testing balancing act, very heady but at the same time very sobering.

Running was more than physical exercise for Nicholas. It cleared his head and gave him space for thinking and planning, free from domestic and commercial diversions. There was a rhythm to rural life that helped to energise a long-distance runner: the birds' morning chorus, the mooing and stamping of cattle, the frisky gambolling of horses making the most of their freedom in fields, wild deer gracefully gliding into camouflage, disturbed rabbits bobbing along unable to make up their minds whether to hop to the left or right, grey squirrels zipping up trees in vertical take-offs, and, in summer, the soft, soothing hum of bees. Nature's symphony. Everything coming together as if composed and orchestrated.

For Nicholas, his daily runs were invigorating. They were not just a means of keeping fit but also exercised and flexed his brain. With every stride, more oxygen was pumped into his head and ideas flowed with the motion of his limbs.

While at school, athletics had been a permanent feature of his everyday life. But in New York, his fitness had suffered. Night owls were not noted for hitting the ground running with the milkman at the crack of dawn; 'the early bird catches the worm' was most certainly not their mantra. Yet Nicholas took this life change in his long, loping stride, as if with the flick of a switch he became a day person, perfectly content not to be working vampire hours. But he had a lot of catching up to do before he would be back in acceptable physical shape, acceptable to him, that is; he was a hard taskmaster when it came to driving himself onwards.

By the beginning of 2008, his ambitious target was to compete in the London Marathon that year. In everything he did, he had a goal. Never, since the age of sixteen, had he ever been a drifter. There had to be an aim for each day and he would never rest until it was achieved. He applied this credo to every aspect of his life, from sport to business. It was the format for progress. And his horrendous accident, incidentally, was not to change his philosophy and ambitions one iota. If anything, it toughened him and made him even harder on himself. Despite all that he and his family had endured, and his domain continuing to be in dire straits, his motivation for competing in the London Marathon was to promote the centuries-old virtues of the Shaftesbury creed and in no way to boost the coffers of his estate, even indirectly.

His running partner was close friend Rob Jenkins. From January 2008, every workout was a torturous sweat against the clock. Being blessed with tunnel vision was a great asset. The morning training sessions gave him a physical focus, which, although strenuous and temporarily energy-sapping, were a useful counterpoint to the mental stresses of the remainder of the day. The charity he chose to run for was Phab, which had been established to encourage and help disabled people to live and work in an integrated and welcoming society. However, the charity reaches out to all people, not just the disabled, who might feel excluded by society and a hostile environment.

Nicholas imposed on himself a four-hour deadline in

which to complete the course of 26.219 miles, quite a challenge for his first marathon. If he didn't break the four-hour barrier, he would consider it a failure. The race would be fun, but very *serious* fun. Passing the self-imposed test was almost as important to him as raising a substantial amount of money. He was endowed with the psyche of a born winner. Failure was not an option. Although winning was not everything to him, losing was!

Anyone of a superstitious disposition might have had misgivings about the date of the London Marathon that year – 13 April, but not Nicholas: 'I'm not one for that superstitious stuff.' In strategic military fashion, he had worked out at what time he should pass certain landmarks in order to be on schedule. As it transpired, at every point he was well ahead of his target and crossed the finishing line in three hours and twenty minutes: aching, sore, tormented by cramp, but with forty minutes to spare. More pertinent was the fact that he had raised a creditable £8,657 for his charity of choice. It would have taken a truly special soothsayer to have foreseen that by the following year he would be the type of victim for whom he had just pounded the streets of London.

Marathon running was now in his blood, perhaps almost verging on an obsession. Maybe addiction was a recurring component of the Shaftesbury DNA? For the males through the generations, it had been addiction to good deeds, except for the one notorious exception.

With the London Marathon over, the stakes had to be raised in order for Nicholas to obtain a similar buzz.

Trawling the Internet for that elusive new inspiration, he came across the 4 Deserts Race Series, one of the world's genuine 'killer' endurance events, too gruelling even for most of the hardened professional military elite, such as those from parachute regiments, the SAS, Royal Marines and US Navy Seals. The event comprised a series of four six-day races, each over 160 miles of some of the most inhospitable, scorched-earth regions of the world. Each competitor was expected to be self-sufficient, running without a support team and carrying all provisions, in particular drink because dehydration and sunstroke were the main hazards. While the days were furnace-hot, the nights could be bone-chillingly cold. The deserts in the series were China's Gobi, Chile's Atacama, the Sahara in Egypt, and Antarctica. The final race of the four was known as 'The Last Desert', which was Antarctica, the frozen wasteland, with frostbite replacing excoriation from heat. To qualify for this final test, the runners must have successfully completed at least two of the other races. On 26 October 2008, the same year that Nicholas had taken part in the London Marathon, he embarked on the six-day hike across the Sahara, having spent all summer preparing, while not neglecting for one moment his onerous duties at St Giles House.

The Sahara is the hottest and largest desert in the world. The heat is relentless until the sun finally dips. But there is no dusk, no lingering exchange interval when the moon is slipped the baton discreetly by the sun. The descent of darkness is as sudden as a train thundering into a tunnel, when the temperature plunges; for the competitors it is equivalent to stepping from an oven into a freezer. For thousands of miles, whichever way they looked, there was nothing but soft sand. It is hard to visualise such a seemingly endless expanse of dazzling, golden desert, occupying 9 million square kilometres of North Africa, extending all the way from the Atlantic Ocean to the Red Sea.

The softness of the sand was a hindrance rather than a help. With every stride Nicholas took, his legs sank almost up to his knees in the blistering sand. It was tantamount to wading through a boiling swamp. The dunes, like massive camels' humps, drained all his strength. Nicholas staggered and stumbled, rolled down dunes and picked himself up for the next hurdle. Then came the sandstorms, blinding in their whirlwind ferocity and capable of puncturing flesh. During these storms, it felt like running into a hail of shotgun pellets. Despite the vortex that whipped up the sand into a swirling rage, the sun continued to burn down with an intensity that had killed many a man.

In some areas, rock and gravel lurked just beneath a thin suffusion of sand and was hard and rugged enough to break bones should anyone fall. Oases, apart from mirages – a part of desert magic and myth and all too frequent – were far and few between. Despite the uncompromising barrenness, however, the Sahara is rich in minerals, including oil, gas, phosphates, manganese, zinc, iron ore and salt. All the oases were farmed, while other traditional inhabitants herded goats, camels and sheep. Little of this was seen, however, along the remotest of routes selected for the contestants.

During the day, Nicholas sweated away pounds of weight,

while at night he shivered, with every joint, muscle and limb as painful as acute toothache. Sleep was another mirage. Dreaming of it was the closest he came to it, and even counting camels instead of sheep failed to work. This was an endurance test of the spirit as well as of the body, a Foreign Legion-type initiation. Numerous soldiers have died during endurance exercises in heat and terrain far less hostile than this Sahara run, which highlights the level of the ordeal.

With every punishing step, there was the temptation to give up. There is an old movie, *Ice Cold in Alex* (1958), starring John Mills, Sylvia Syms and Anthony Quayle, in which a group of stranded World War II men – and a woman – have to make it on foot through the Sahara to Alexandria in order to survive. They make a pact that, if successful, they will rendezvous in 'Alex' and celebrate with ice-cold lager, which they did.

Raising cash for AbleChildAfrica was the incentive that kept Nicholas's mind and body sufficiently lubricated to hang in and conquer everything nature hurled at him during those seven days. Dead beat but undaunted and raring for more, he crossed the finish in thirty-first place and earned £4,000.90 – his ice-cool lager in Alex! – for his nominated charity, having achieved it in Herculean fashion.

A mere eight months later, he was embarking on his second desert race, this time in Namibia, in an ultramarathon named, 'Racing the Planet'. Once again it was a seven-day event over 160 miles, with similar rules to the previous. The course carved its way through towering sand dunes, deep canyons and mountain ranges, before zig-zagging along the Skeleton

Coast, so named because anyone shipwrecked along that arid region in the past was doomed to die of thirst. Skeletons are still found and human bones removed from the route by organisers before the start of the run.

Once again Nicholas was undefeated and unscathed by the elements. This time his finishing place was twenty-fourth, and the £6,282.69 he garnered for his extraordinary effort directly contributed to the college fees and vital, basic education of poor and orphaned children in South India through the charity Child-Link. Surely he was now entitled to a lengthy rest in order to recharge?

Maybe a respite was merited, but it was not going to happen; Nicholas was too restless and driven for that. He now had his sights set on the 'Ultra-Trail du Mont-Blanc', for good reason known as the most difficult foot race in Europe. The course took runners over the Alps, across France, Italy and Switzerland. As if that was not arduous enough, it was scheduled to begin on 29 August, a mere three months after the Namibia slog. At the highest point in the event, they had a 6,700-metre climb, where the air was thin and hearts and lungs beat like the speeded-up windscreen wipers on a car. Many were beaten by this mountain marathon, but not Nicholas. He forged his way to the finish, crossing the line in twenty-ninth place, triumphant and exhausted but also exhilarated.

Back home, Nicholas was starting to get on top of the restoration programme, to which there were three stages. Initially, the decline had to be halted. It is not being over-dramatic to liken St Giles House and the estate, at the point Nicholas took over, to patients on their deathbeds.

Continuing with the metaphor, the end of the first phase saw the house taken off the life-support machine. It was not on the mend yet, but neither was it deteriorating further. Next came the shoring-up of the most vulnerable and damaging points of the house and land. Only when those two stages were complete could the mammoth restoration project begin, not just with Grade I-listed St Giles House, but on every acre of the estate. And at last the future could begin to look bright instead of blighted.

Nicholas had slipped comfortably into his aristocratic role. He had been a fast learner in husbandry and management. His personality elicited the best from people who worked for him. He had inherited his father's natural charm, so there was nothing artificial or patronising about his chummy rapport with those who depended on him for a living. Not having been specifically groomed for the job was now probably proving to be an asset. Instead of having been cocooned in the rarefied air of life among the cosseted landed gentry, he had blazed a trail in the *real* world.   B u t just four months after Nicholas had conquered Mont-Blanc, running, the 'curse' was waiting to trip his horse on that fateful December morning, just as he was preparing for his next desert race. Meanwhile, big plans for stage three of the Shaftesbury renovation and revival were on the launch pad, ready for Nicholas to press the button to generate lift-off. Then calamity.

So many other people in Nicholas's position would have considered themselves or their family jinxed, but for him it was just another mountain or desert to be run up or crossed, nothing more than a banana skin. 'People bandy the word *curse* around, but I never think in those term,' he said. 'I don't believe anything like that is ordained. You know, there isn't a script. But I do believe I'm incredibly lucky to be walking pretty normally to meet you. Though I may need a walking stick by the time I'm fifty.'

Despite his injuries, life was not put on hold. The wedding went ahead, he forced himself to learn to walk again, and work on the estate continued at breakneck speed. If anything had changed, it was that Nicholas had become more impatient. He did not have the temperament to settle for being a long-term invalid. Paraplegic was a label he intended to quickly lose. It was with disbelief for so many in Wimborne St Giles that, just over a year after being thrown from a horse, snapping his spine and being confined to a wheelchair, he was announcing that he intended taking part in the Atacama Desert race in north-west Chile in March 2011. Of course, the people emotionally close to him were fearful. The weakness in the spine could easily cause it to fracture again under the intense strain and he could be left permanently disabled – or even lose his life. But they all accepted ruefully that there was no mileage in trying to dissuade him. Stubbornness was the steel rod in his backbone.

The Atacama Desert is the driest place on the Earth; parts of it are never touched by rain. Armed with strict medical instructions of many dos and don'ts, Nicholas flew to Chile in 2011, ready for the beginning of the race on 3 March. There was as much trepidation among the organisers as in the Earl's family.

'Of course we were worried,' said an official of the organisers for the 4 Desert and Racing the Planet. 'We had to insist that the Earl would accept personal responsibility should it go horribly wrong for him. We did have our reservations, but we respected his determination and confidence. He is no fool and these endurance races are all about overcoming every kind of obstacle. To succeed, you have to be someone very special; one of a very few elite endurance people in the world.'

When Nicholas completed the 160-mile course unharmed on the seventh day, he was presented with a special 'Spirit' award. A spokesperson for the event said, 'We have just witnessed a young man make obsolete the word *impossible*. Anyone who completes the course in one of these desert endurance races is a winner. The placings are immaterial. Finishing is everything.'

Next stop – the last stop – was Antarctica in November 2012. But in the meantime, there was much to be done on the home front.

Just weeks after the accident, and long before any significant recovery, Nicholas and Dinah had collaborated over the launch of a new national charitable event to be known as the 'Grand Shaftesbury Run', which would be staged on the estate. Three months after Atacama, the inaugural 'Grand Shaftesbury Run' took place on 12 June 2011. There were two courses, one 6.2 miles and the other a half-marathon (13.1 miles), collectively in support of three charities, Wings for Life (funding research into treatment for spinal injuries), the Philip Green Memorial School (providing medical and general welfare support for sick and disabled children) and the Sparkle Appeal (helping children and young adults with disabilities and development difficulties).

By late April 2014, the 12th Earl was announcing proudly, 'It's been quite a journey.' The refurbishment of St Giles House was almost complete. Nicholas said that when he inherited from his father, he had not dwelled for a single second on the option of walking away from his dilapidated inheritance: 'When you come from a family like mine, with all of these amazing ancestors, I couldn't get rid of the house and the heart of the family. The whole thing has completely snowballed. We've been surprised and happy at the progress we've managed to make in a relatively short period. It [St Giles House] has to pay for itself and it gives it a reason to exist. These are incredible buildings that were built in a time that has long gone. The land and the house are such a beautiful combination, which are nice to share with people.'

The sharing is realised through the hosting of weddings and corporate events. There is also Allenbrook Trout Farm, St Giles Stud, commercial shoots and fly-fishing along the River Allen. Commercial properties and fifty houses and cottages bring in rent. In addition, there are archaeological sites to be explored and 'The Friends of St Giles', a sort of supporters' club founded by Nicholas, grows by the day, boosting funds. Then there are the community activities, such as food festivals and, of course, the charity runs.

However, at this time, there were still rooms in the great old house without floorboards and walls. In some of the rooms, experts were diligently restoring wallpaper that was more than a hundred years old. Scaffolding covered the once-imposing main entrance like a spider's web of iron rods. The grand entrance was being reconstructed with bricks and even mortar to match its original appearance.

Unique techniques were devised to bring back the glory days. For example, original tapestries were rejuvenated by steaming them in a gigantic and specially designed Jacuzzi in Belgium. Oil paintings depicting the long lineage of earls survived undamaged. In the celebrated library, leather-bound tomes, introduced by the 3rd Earl, the intense philosopher, rest uncomfortably alongside brash, modern novels, such as those of Jeffrey Archer. Nicholas's imprint on the stately library is a biography on Guns N' Roses guitarist Slash. Many of the walls are now hung with damask silk fabric. Ceilings are lofty and extravagantly decorated. A decade after the tragedy in France, and despite still needing some cosmetic surgery, St Giles House was looking new, as if returned by a time-machine to the 1650s, when it had been originally built during the stewardship of the 1st Earl.

'A lot of things got sold in the 1980s, but some of the really key things we've been able to keep hold of,' Nicholas explained. 'So the rooms have not lost their feel. We really wanted to create a feeling at St Giles that you've come somewhere special. That takes time to develop. It was painstaking getting the right bricks and mortar. But all things matter so much that you can't really rush it. There are certain elements we wanted to keep, so we looked at the age and feel. The temptation was to go in and rip everything out and put in everything new. You become more sensitive to the character of the building as you go through. The statue in Piccadilly Circus, commemorating the 7th Earl's philanthropic work, is a huge symbol for the family and something we're incredibly proud of.'

Hence the replica Eros statue, one of only ten made from the same mould as the original, set in a pivotal position among the network of broad, interlaced shingle paths in the manicured grounds. 'It felt so sad to see the history of the house not being cared for properly, but it also looks magnificent now,' he added. It did, too. His commercial was not in the least embellished.

'The house has always been the big issue, the unresolved matter. It is the heart of the estate and the family, but in this era we no longer need a massive house and must regard it more as a venue. There is a change of mindset about how we run these places. Really creative people are doing interesting things with their historic houses.'

No one could question the fat that the Shaftesbury motto – *Love, Serve* – lived on. The 10th Earl did more than enough loving for all twelve earls. And Nicholas, the 12th Earl, is passionately obligated to the second half of the family motto. To *serve* is his watchword.

A note of caution, however: the 10th Earl was younger than Nicholas when succeeding his grandfather to the title and was bristling with high-minded principles and an indefatigable sense of duty, all of which were not enough. Like the chalky white cliffs of Dover, he could withstand only so much buffeting before succumbing to erosion. Father, unlike son, never got on top of the deeply rooted problems besetting St Giles House. Nicholas, however, went for the jugular from day one and there is no reason to suppose that his resolve will be eroded. He withstood everything 'killer' deserts could throw at him. He taught himself to walk again after being paralysed, discarding his wheelchair in disgust. Considering his track record, sickly, withering St Giles House, which had been a liability for so long, did not stand a chance of getting the better of him.

By 2015, St Giles House was off the sick list after sixty years and was back at work, earning its keep in lordly fashion.

But for the marathon man, there was still a long way to go.

21

DAY OF
JUDGMENT

Public personas usually produce distorted portraits, and good works can be confused with good people when so often the two are unrelated.

The 7th Earl of Shaftesbury is a case in point. He is popularly remembered as a champion of the downtrodden, as already discussed, but there was also a dark side to him. Just like the murdered 10th Earl, his psyche was a jungle of contradictions that caused him immense anguish. His belligerent, vehement rhetoric over the treatment of the mentally ill provoked Florence Nightingale to declare that *he* would have been incarcerated in a 'lunatic asylum' had he not devoted so much of his life to reforming them. Sir Edwin Chadwick, a Royal Commissioner on the Poor Law Enquiry, wrote of the 7th Earl, 'Age did not ossify his mind, for it was ossified before he was old'.

Because a Shaftesbury (the 1st Earl) founded the Whig (Liberal) Party, it was taken for granted that the family had always been in the vanguard movement of democratic expansion. Another myth. In the *Who's Who in Victorian Britain*, author Roger Ellis described the 7th Earl thus, 'As a landed aristocrat, he held fast to the traditional values of a hierarchic country society [...] This devotion to tradition made him suspicious of Parliamentary reform and hostile to democracy.' And yet no one exploited Parliament or the democratic system of government for his own ends more vigorously than the 7th Earl of Shaftesbury. In essence, he was a tub-thumping evangelist, 'hard and narrow', intransigent over his beliefs and never willing to concede an inch. His emotions – frequently barbed rants – were always near to blowing a fuse. He hated his parents as uncompromisingly as he reviled cruelty and the wretchedness of the poor. His parents even evicted him from St Giles House as an unworthy heir to such a noble title. He had been deliberately kept short of money for years, so, although on a completely different scale, he was acquainted with proportionate financial hardship and its impact.

He had also been deprived of love as a child and was desperate for it as an adult, and was fortunate to find it in abundance in marriage. His wife, Minny (née Cowper), was the daughter of the 2nd Viscount Melbourne's sister. Melbourne, a member of the Whig cabal and therefore having a natural affinity with the Shaftesburys, was Queen Victoria's first prime minister.

Minny gave birth to ten children and her husband vowed

to give each one the love of which he had been denied as a child. Echoes of this sentiment were to chime like distant church bells through the lives of future Shaftesburys as a too often recurring melancholy theme.

Despite the wealth in the family, few of the earls were competent managers. The 7th Earl inherited a financial mess and his stewardship was little better than his father's — yet more echoes through the generations! Contrary to the popular image of the 7th Earl, he was much more fanatical evangelist than inspired politician. In fact, all his inspirations came from the Bible, in which he believed there to be absolute truth in every word, from beginning to end.

He was not really interested in saving society, per se. His one and only mission was to save souls. In this respect, he was a fervent millennialist, convinced of the Second Coming, when Christ's kingdom would reign for a thousand years before the Day of Judgment, when the wicked would be exiled to Hell while the good souls would be exalted in Heaven. This underscored one of the many complexities in his character: he believed penury bred depravity. So his crusade was to rescue the deprived and oppressed from sin, rather than focused on fairness and a decent standard of living as a stepping stone towards an earthly utopia, which was not a concept of his.

As a cheerleader of the Victorian Sabbath, he was opposed to any form of entertainment and work on Sundays. Allied with Whig Prime Minister Palmerston, who had begun his Parliamentary career as a Tory, he did everything to thwart the Tractarians, supporters of the High Church seeking to restore the teaching of the Catholic church. This holy war of his meant just as much to him as all his social reforms and illustrated his complex character.

A century or so later, the brooding depressions of the ill-fated 10th Earl mirrored those of his more famous ancestor in the latter years of his life, a similarity that has tended to cast clouds over St Giles House.

Most of the 10th Earl's life was shrouded in mystery, especially relating to his sudden and frequent disappearances, followed by his equally abrupt returns days or even weeks later, resuming from where he had left off, as if he had just been napping. Nobody in his family seemed to explore those curious interludes, which were simply dismissed as 'Tony's very personal way of coping', his little vagaries. Many of these mysteries have been resolved to my satisfaction through my meetings with Jacques Reichert and Lucille. So much of the 10th Earl's outré lifestyle was encapsulated in the four prevailing loves of his life: his mother, Paris, the Riviera, and sophisticated European women.

During my research, I was originally steered to Jacques Reichert by a French narcotics counsellor. Jacques was born to a French mother and an Egyptian father. He is as pivotal as the 10th Earl to the anecdotal narrative – the provenance of which is critical – that lies ahead. Jacques grew up in Nice. His father was a swashbuckling property speculator. Jacques, an only child, was educated in the UK at a boarding school in Bedford. His father died relatively young in Cairo of a heart attack while on a business trip. Jacques benefited financially:

the will provided for all assets to be divided equally between widow and son. And Jacques's father had been a rich man.

Jacques's mother, who had been lonely for much of her marriage because her husband travelled so frequently, had turned elsewhere for *companionship*. Within weeks of becoming a widow, she was being entertained by suitors. Before Jacques's father had been dead a year, his mother ventured into her second marriage with a man not to Jacques's liking. 'After that, I went my own way,' said Jacques, who, by the time I encountered him, must have been around sixty years of age: short, corpulent, semi-bald, remnants of black hair combed straight down the sides of his head, leaving a shiny dome, crowned teeth and lugubrious features. In white shirt and black trousers, he could have been mistaken for a café waiter.

Our initial meeting took place in Le Barracuda bar in Cannes. This bar, of course, was a regular haunt of the Earl and Jamila, as previously outlined. Reichert had been acquainted with the Earl for as long as forty years and described his occupation as 'bringing happiness to the lives of bored people with too much spare time on their hands'. He treated me to a sneaky, *knowing* smile. I had already been tipped-off that he was a 'high-class dealer', which translated into selling pure or crack cocaine to users who had more money than brains. He preferred to call his buyers 'socialites with serious leisure pursuits'.

Whenever in town, 'Tony [the 10th Earl] was a heavy user,' he said. 'He bought from me regularly because he knew I dealt only in high quality. I buy from the best suppliers in

North Africa. Tony was always very frank about his intentions and what he was up to. He never exaggerated. Everything was low-key and matter-of-fact with him. He thought all women were fair game. If he liked, he would go after her.'

As previously highlighted, the Earl had a long obsession with Grace Kelly and Reichert expanded on this when he told me, 'She was as iconic to him as his mother – well, nearly. And, my, did he go on about his dear old mamma! Anyone would have thought his mamma had been sanctified. Grace was the only reason he ever went to Monaco. Looking up Rainier to exchange pleasantries was just an excuse.'

Grace's own story of how she lost her virginity was a lascivious inspiration to the Earl, according to Reichert, which ties in and runs parallel with so much else that is known. The fact that she was the opposite of her public persona increased her desirability in the Earl's eyes, apparently; and it was consistent with all his seedy attachments in the final years of his degenerate life.

'He'd never be discourteous and boast that he was fucking someone's wife, not like some men. In many ways, he was a gentleman to the end. He was also a disgrace to his class, a real Jekyll and Hyde, if ever there was one, but there wasn't a spark of malice in him. He was an old-fashioned English gentleman lecher. You couldn't help but enjoy his company, as long as you weren't his wife and had to live with him, I guess.

'He once said to me that if he wasn't drunk by noon, then he was having a bad day. I suppose he was a completely different man when he was sober, but I never got to see that man. He could be a real rogue, but I've no complaints: he always paid top price for my stuff and never haggled. He had more than his fair share of money and he liked to help the world keep on spinning. I miss him. I suppose what I really mean is that I miss his money. Same as a lot of other people around here!'

Reichert remembered vividly the day the Earl wagged a finger at him, warning, 'Never let anything or anyone own you. It's a mistake I made, but not of my own making. I had no say in the matter. I'm stuck with it.'

Reichert didn't understand what the hell he was talking about and told him so. It turned out that he was talking about his estate and large country house in England. 'What he was saying,' he continued, 'was that the land and buildings owned him, not the other way round. He was a tied man and felt as if he was being crushed by it all and he couldn't get out from underneath it. I actually felt sorry for him, despite the fact that he was loaded and could do whatever he liked and go wherever he wanted. He didn't have to save for anything.'

What he was telling me, Reichert said, didn't come from one conversation. He'd seen the Earl change over that period. When they first met, he was a pharmacist, professionally trained and with a degree and a wife.

'People have been misled into believing that Tony got into drugs only after he flipped and deserted his family,' he told me. 'That's not true. Way back, when we were both relatively young men, he was sniffing. You know, cocaine and smoking the occasional joint, just social, recreational stuff, not hurting anyone else. The rich have always messed with coke. I was getting a lot if it from where I worked and through my professional connections. It was, you know, a bonus, a perk, yes? I had easy access to all kinds of drugs, including morphine, but Tony didn't go down that spiral. He never injected himself, as far as I'm aware and I'm sure I would have known. If he'd got into heroin that would have killed him before *that* woman and her crap-head brother did.'

Tony liked his drink, too, he explained. 'He'd happily get drunk on champagne any time of day. I really mean *happily*. It brought him out of his shell, the same way the coke did. None of it ever made him aggressive. See where I'm going with this? He told me that the first thing he did in the morning, as soon as he woke up, was to light a cigarette and pour himself a glass of champagne. He'd never get out of bed until he'd emptied his glass and finished his cigarette. And when he did get up, it was only to pour himself another glass of champagne and light up again.

'The cigarettes and early drink blunted his appetite so he didn't feel hungry till at least noon, which fitted his lifestyle nicely.'

Of course, as we've already seen, he also liked the women, but that was something else that didn't happen suddenly. 'He'd pay for it mostly because he wanted emotion kept out of sex. He hated being tied, but he didn't go for what I think you call a *quickie*. Even with a bar girl he needed a semi-relationship. By that, I mean he'd want to wake up with her still beside him. They had to have a late breakfast together and talk about news in the *International Tribune,* which he always read with his coffee and croissants.

'The women had to have personality, strong views, and be reasonably intelligent. Yes, he definitely went for strong women He said his mother was a very strong woman. From the way he talked, I think that's the woman he would have married, if she hadn't been his mother.'

He added, 'The Earl would blow in and out of the Riviera like a mistral, maybe not seen for six months, only to reappear suddenly in and around Cannes or Nice for several weeks. What brought him here, though, were the women, much more so than the climate.'

Reichert was sacked and blacklisted when he was caught stealing drugs, and that is when he turned to trading on the black market. 'I knew the sources and those people in the legit trade who could be bribed, especially in North Africa. There's always been a *healthy* demand for cocaine among the wealthy. Used responsibly, it's harmless; that's my opinion and it was Tony's too. He was very liberal, liberated – liberty, fraternity…you know, very French – and hated laws that tried to treat adults as children. Before he went home, he'd always stock up so he had enough to keep him going until he visited again. Mind you, I'm sure – I *know* – I wasn't his only supplier. I don't suppose the British customs officials ever bothered to check the baggage of one of their aristocrats, yet, in the past, they were always the biggest users.'

Other stories involving Grace Kelly that Reichert recalled the Earl having regaled him with included the one about Alfred Hitchcock's perverse love for his favourite leading lady. He did not want to kiss, make love to her or even touch her. His sexual pleasure was voyeuristic. When Grace was living in

Los Angeles, Hitchcock had a house about a mile away along Laurel Canyon. She leaked the fact to *Hollywood Confidential* that Hitchcock asked her to undress slowly in front of her bedroom window, without curtains obscuring the view, as she prepared for bed. She did this willingly, knowing full well that Hitchcock owned a high-powered telescope that he kept positioned in his bedroom for snooping on women. Hitchcock fans will recall this voyeurism was reproduced as a pivotal element of the plot in his movie, *Rear Window*, in which James Stewart starred.

Another story involved Bing Crosby: 'Who'd have thought that frosty Princess Grace had been bedding dear old crooner Bing Crosby, while his wife was dying of cancer, yet there it was in Tony's folder, in print, and written by Grace's own mother,' said Reichert. 'Is nothing sacred!'

He continued, 'Tony reckoned it proved his theory that most of the beautiful and intelligent women in the world were attracted to older men, drawn to their maturity, experience in life, and finances. However, he didn't like Crosby and called him a cad because he used the pool house of his next-door neighbour for fucking sessions with Grace. The neighbour happened to be actor Alan Ladd, another movie star, who was a close friend of Dixie, Crosby's wife. What upset Tony so much was that Crosby, with all his millions, was too mean to pay for a room at a decent hotel. His actual words were that what Crosby did was no different from "shitting on his own doorstep". Tony would talk that way when it was man to man.'

In many ways, it seems that the 10th Earl was as voyeuristic as Hitchcock. When he focused on a woman, he was eager to be conversant with her extended sexual CV. The more lurid it was, the greater the allure. Women saddled with notoriety appealed; in today's idiom, they were a *must-have*.

In some ways, though, this does not square with his reputedly discarding Nathalie Lions when he learned that she had been a Penthouse Pet. After all, he went on to marry Jamila M'Barek, who had posed naked for *Playboy* magazine. What was the difference? In my estimation, the Penthouse Pet angle was a contrived excuse for the break-up, or a case of media misreporting. There had to be something more to it. Maybe Nathalie was unnerved by the prospect of having to role-play his mother for the rest of their sexual lives? So perhaps *she* ditched *him* and the *Penthouse* charade was a cover story for his benefit; though, by then, he did not appear the least concerned with damage limitation, in respect of whatever remained of his decimated reputation. He was a lost cause by then. Lost to his family, his heritage and to himself. He was almost playing out the agonising role of Faust, having sold – not pawned – his soul to Mephistopheles and thinking he might as well milk it to the full to the pitiable end.

The Earl's purported fixation with Grace Kelly is particularly fascinating because it helps to tie loose ends relating to the deaths of them both: two high-profile deaths that spawned conspiracy theories. The Earl had a dossier documenting all Grace's acknowledged affairs, which she mistakenly believed her husband, Prince Rainier, was blind to. It was a major error to underestimate a man who had Mafia figures from the US Cosa Nostra as invisible partners in his casino, which had started to lose its glitter and was no longer the cash cow it had once been. Who else, other than Frank Sinatra, would be the go-between, bringing together US Mafia gunslingers with a patriarchal monarch of the European old school? Much of this is conjecture, but it has to be remembered that Sinatra brokered a working, symbiotic relationship between the Cosa Nostra and President Kennedy. And a moll of one of the most notorious US mobster's became one of Kennedy's many mistresses, all of which was authenticated long ago. According to Reichert, rumour was rife about an affair between Grace and Sinatra, who, for a time, was a constant visitor to Monte Carlo. The Earl knew the story, along with Grace's catalogued affairs with the Shah of Iran, Aly Khan, Gary Cooper, Clark Gable, Cary Grant and British actor David Niven.

Grace was made internationally famous by the iconic Western, *High Noon*. The Earl delighted in recounting to his Riviera bar cronies, such as Reichert and some of his risqué women, how Grace's affair with Gary Cooper began: Cooper had just two words to say in a wedding scene, 'I do.' Cooper, a doyen of Hollywood and renowned for the ease with which he memorised scripts, deliberately fluffed his two-word line fifty times, which meant he had to embrace and kiss Grace again and again with each re-take on set. 'Truthfully, Tony literally wet himself once while telling that story and two of the bar girls had to help clean him up,' said Reichert.

Princess Grace died on 13 September 1982, when she crashed her car at high-speed on a hairpin bend along the notorious Moyenne Corniche in France. She was fifty-two.

The Earl was distraught by her death. She crashed and died on the same stretch of road along which she drove at breakneck speed with Cary Grant, her one-time lover, in the movie *To Catch a Thief.* 'Tony had it all figured,' said Reichert. 'She repeated that crazy drive over and over. It revived memories of her movie days, her romancing with Grant, and it was literally orgasmic for her.' How did the Earl know? 'Because he had been with her on many of those nostalgic drives.

'Racing like the wind on that twisting, rollercoaster road gave Grace more sexual satisfaction than she ever achieved with Rainier, Tony reckoned. Rainier just used her as an accessory, an advertising logo for Monaco; she was nothing more to him than human bling. This wasn't Tony just guessing; he'd had long pillow talks with Grace. He'd driven that death-road with her so many times, he knew what it meant to her. It was a drive back to her movie days, her first love.'

The timeline here is very interesting indeed. The Earl would have been seeing Grace during his first marriage to the Italian Bianca Maria de Paolis. She divorced him for adultery with an unnamed woman. It had been assumed that the *unnamed woman* was Christina Eva Montan, whom he married soon after his first marriage was dissolved. But could that mystery woman have been Princess Grace and not Christina? The dates are right for that to be the case and Rainier would have offered almost any-sized carrot to keep a scandal of that magnitude under wraps.

In the last two years of Grace Kelly's life she had become embroiled with a number of shady characters, ranging from fringe criminals to outright gangsters. Her husband was away from Monaco so frequently, often out of the country, that he was ignorant of the danger she was in. Maybe he did not care too much; for a long time their marriage had been put on ice, though by nature the Prince remained very much a control-freak.

Unknown to Grace, many of the men with whom she mixed socially had been responsible for murders, kidnappings, and other serious crimes, such as money-laundering and fraud on an international scale. The 10th Earl of Shaftesbury, according to Reichert, knew of her involvements with very dangerous people and feared for her safety and permanent damage to her international reputation. Despite her Hollywood past and the fact that she was a seasoned mother, Grace was still universally glorified as the 'Virgin Princess'.

The Earl was anxious to protect Grace from charlatans – and worse – who were after her money. His intervention would certainly have put himself at considerably risk. Perhaps the drink and drugs had hoodwinked him into a false sense of security, deluded into believing in his own immortality.

Certainly for much of his life it seemed that he had a fairy godmother looking after him, but that was his mother, of course, and as soon as she was gone, so he became easy fodder for the hungry wolves.

Although the 10th Earl was an outrageous womaniser, he never ceased to be a patriarchal gentleman. He really did care for each woman he seduced or by whom he was seduced, and felt a duty towards them. Duty was in his blood and explains his protective instincts towards Grace Kelly, the Princess of Hollywood.

The 10th Earl doubtlessly talked to his wife, Jamila, about his friendship with Prince Rainier and Princess Grace; certainly before the marriage turned sour, maybe even before they married. Prior to her trial, and through her lawyer, she tried every ruse imaginable to inveigle Rainier's son, Albert II, and head of the principality following his father's death in 2005, to give character testimonial evidence on her behalf.

The 10th Earl's double life had spanned several decades, although it appears that his drug and alcohol addictions did not manifest until after his mother's death, whereas debauchery was in his DNA. Before Gurtler's reign, many women had been procured for him by Fernande Grudet. Legend has it that she had been a ruthless fighter in the French Resistance and turned to prostitution in Paris after World War II.

It was soon evident to her, however, that she was better equipped for the management side of the game than as a frontline action girl, doing battle in the bedroom, so she decided to sell others rather than herself, for 30 per cent of the spoils. To this end, in 1961, she made her headquarters, a brothel-cum-escort-emporium, on the Quai des Orfèvres.

From the outset, her ethos was to recruit women who were gifted conversationalists and blessed with beauty, charm, intelligence, liberal sexual experience and, most importantly of all, discretion. She somehow managed to hire legitimate fashion models from the prestigious Paris catwalks, universities and exclusive colleges for the elite. She even despatched her stable of thoroughbred fillies to private tutors for lessons in art and philosophy. Furthermore, she funded trips overseas for her girls to broaden their outlook, to learn foreign languages and become au fait with a variety of diverse cultures.

By the time the 10th Earl drifted on to her radar, she was trading in the name of Madame Claude. Already some of her girls would not climb into bed with a client for less than $10,000 a night. 'Expensive but worth it' was a quote of hers which, years later, was to be tweaked into a famous advertising slogan.

William Stadiem, who wrote an unpublished biography of Madame C, claimed that her clients had included Colonel Gaddafi, Marlon Brando and half the French Cabinet. The Shah of Iran had a standing order for girls to be flown to Tehran from Paris every Friday, while the boss of an international motor company enjoyed an orgy with Madame C's protégés before escorting them all to Mass.

The 10th Earl was steered to Madame C during the early days of his first marriage. Because of her reputation for absolute discretion and her enforcement of it on her workers, the Earl was not at all worried about revealing his true identity, something of which he was proud. Although she would never discuss the proclivities of her clients while they were alive, she was not averse to telling tales after their death. In that respect, she disclosed that President Kennedy wanted girls who were lookalikes of his wife, Jackie, but 'hot' rather than 'morgue specimens'. Greek shipping magnate Aristotle Onassis, Jackie Kennedy's second husband, was 'depraved' and would visit the brothel with his mistress, opera singer

Maria Callas, to discuss outré sexual services that could be provided for him.

Very shortly after starting her lucrative business in the 1950s, she began accepting bookings by phone and from this innovation the term 'call-girl' was coined, she boasted. 'Perhaps something for my epitaph,' she joked with friends, of which there were few.

In an interview with a French magazine, she told the journalist, 'It makes me laugh when I see the photographs of the ladies and countesses featured in the social pages of *Tatler, Harper's* and *Vogue*, and count which ones started off working for me.'

The 10th Earl's initial meeting with her came about because he had been invited to a masked ball and was without a mistress, so needed a partner, quickly, for the one night; preferably French, definitely attractive and essentially sagacious, without rounded shoulders and no inclination to gargle with pink champagne. Consequently, one of his louche chums pointed him in the direction of Madame C and it was lust at first sight. 'I was a bit sceptical,' he was to relate years later to his old reprobate drinking and drug-dealing pal Reichert, 'but she came up trumps. I went to the ball with the queen of hearts; an absolute stunner. Very, very expensive, but value for money.' He recalled that they talked about everything from politics to opera and dialectic materialism, Marx and Buddhism. 'She was far more knowledgeable than me on every subject,' he said. Rocking with laughter, he had added, 'And as far as sex was concerned, I really was the new kid on the block. She opened my eyes to wonders of the bedroom that I had no idea existed.' The Earl had one complaint only to make about Mme Claude's first offering to him: she did not resemble his mother sufficiently.

Mme Claude kept large ledgers documenting all her clients and their sexual predilections. The 10th Earl was later to be known by this legendary queen of upper-class vice as 'Lord Mummy's Boy'. This is a perfect match with the assessment of the Earl by Gurtler and so many of the prostitutes with whom he had long-running relationships.

As for Mme Claude's background, there are several versions; although very different, there is some cross-pollination. Not surprisingly, the most colourful and creative is her own account: the daughter of a politician from a French aristocratic family, educated by nuns, captured by the Nazis for her heroism with the Resistance, saved the life of President de Gaulle's niece in a concentration camp, and survived in the pitiful aftermath of war by selling Bibles. Her enemies, of which there were many, said her father ran a snack-bar at Angers railway station and she learned her trade on the street-corners of Paris's red-light districts. As one would expect with such a divisive character, there is no definitive version, but one ineluctable fact is that a concentration camp number had been tattooed on her wrist.

Despite the *grande-dame* image she liked to cultivate of herself, she was unpopular with her girls and not just because she deducted almost a third of their earnings. The actress Francoise Fabian, who portrayed Mme Claude in a 1977 French movie, famously described her as '*une femme terrible*' for whom 'men were wallets and women were holes'. The 10th

Earl disliked her because she was 'so hard and humourless'. She hated sex and advocated it being banned for anyone aged over forty because of its 'anti-social vulgarity'; very tongue in cheek because, if enacted, she would have instantly castrated her supply of customers.

Although she retired to Nice, which seemed to have morphed into God's waiting-room in France, the 10th Earl had no inclination to socialise with her. 'She gives me the creeps,' he told Reichert. 'The blood in her veins is metallic and her heart is stone – an uncut diamond.' In the 1980s, he frequently said inscrutably to one of his friends among the landowning gentry, 'I won't be around for a few days. I have to see Claude in Paris.' It was assumed that Claude was a business associate of the Earl's and contributed in some way towards the running of the estate in Dorset.

Mme Claude died friendless in Nice on 19 December 2015. She was ninety-two.

There will be many men – and women – of elevated social status who will be fearful of whose hands Mme Claude's business records end up in.

Reichert had one last piece of information touching on the murder. During the Earl's marriage to Jamila, rumours were doing the rounds that Mohammed, the Countess's deranged brother, was a hired 'strong-arm', among other nefarious activities, for a group that beefed-up their funds from prostitution – 'flighty fishing' – and drug-dealing.

'That made me mad because it meant Mohammed and his lunatics were cutting into my profits,' complained Reichert, who died in a light aircraft crash on the Skeleton Coast in Africa in 2013. (My interviews with him took place in 2011/12.)

'I think Mohammed did a runner to Germany because he was in danger of having his throat cut if he stayed around here much longer. Tony banned him from the Cannes flat, but he'd given it to Jamila, so she could have who the hell she pleased in there. The brother and his disruptive ways, plus the bad company he kept, was a major cause of the marriage breakdown, in addition to their chaotic lives. Let's face it, Jamila was no wife and Tony was no husband to her. They had no family life. They were untameable. But no way would Tony have gone to that apartment on the day he was murdered if he had suspected Mohammed would be on the premises.'

By the summer of 2015, the 12th Earl was beginning to come to terms with the exasperating reality that it might be impossible to officially strip Jamila of her title. For many years he had vowed there could not be closure to his father's death until he had achieved his avowed goal of disconnecting Jamila M'Barek from the Shaftesbury name irrevocably. Expunged! But Nicholas is a pragmatist. Having explored all legal channels, he had been advised that it would take an Act of Parliament to reduce Jamila to the ranks of an untitled citizen and there was little prospect of that happening. An Act of Parliament would be necessary because there was no precedence.

'I've now put all that to the back of my mind,' he said

philosophically. 'There are much more important things to be getting on with. Success here, on the estate, is more important to me now than anything else.'

In addition to being a pragmatist, the 12th Earl is also very perceptive. A legal battle, necessitating elongated debates in both the House of Commons and the House of Lords would thrust Jamila into the limelight and give her free rein to run a prolonged publicity offensive in the media spotlight. For Jamila, it would be her curtain call for the performance of a lifetime, a palace-sized window of opportunity for retribution. The Earl might win, but at what cost? A high price would be paid in that it would be an impediment to the long-term recovery programme. More mud-slinging would certainly be a very unwelcome diversion.

Even without an attempt to sever Jamila's connection with the Shaftesbury dynasty through Parliament, there is another danger from which there is no plausible escape. When Ms M'Barek is paroled, she will emerge into the public arena as Jamila, the Dowager Countess of Shaftesbury, something she must have given much thought to during her years behind bars. What plans might she have? One can only surmise at the Machiavellian mischief she might be plotting, especially if sponsored by one of the more lurid French magazines. The current generation of Shaftesburys might yet have to face the prospect of the murderer of the much-loved 10th Earl shamelessly disgracing their doorstep.

'It is not something I think about,' said Nicholas, not looking me in the eye.

Even if the 12th Earl should ever be successful in having

Jamila divested of her title, there is a corner of England – namely in and around Wimborne St Giles, the heartbeat of the Shaftesbury *imperium* – where, to locals for miles around, Jamila will be forever the countess, not even reduced to Dowager. For in their own Dorset dialect, they spell and pronounce it a little differently: omitting the first vowel in countess…and would not have it any other way.

In fact, they would willingly fight to the death to ensure Jamila retained *that* title!